Corporate Governance and IFRS in the Middle East

The rapid globalization of capital markets has increased attention toward examining the quality of the disclosure practices implemented by companies, as internationalization and globalization are the most important motives of the harmonization of financial statements preparation and presentation. Given the expansion of trade and the openness to foreign capital markets, investment decisions became not limited only for local users, but also international users may need to access the financial information. The issuance of International Financial Reporting Standards (IFRS) to be used throughout the world aims to improve the comparability and understandability of financial statements, and hence, to enhance investment decisions through helping investors across the borders to invest in multinational companies. Although fluid and under-developed institutional arrangements remain central features of emerging markets, ensuring effective corporate governance mechanisms would indeed support companies in complying with IFRS – the latter imposes a challenge for companies operating in emerging markets.

This book evaluates the differences in the level of compliance with IFRS across the GCC states, exploring the impact of corporate governance on the level of compliance with IFRS and presenting an empirical analysis of companies across the GCC. It makes an important contribution by providing a detailed empirical analysis of the interplay between corporate governance and IFRS in emerging market setting and highlights the way for future research. It will provide international business, management, and accounting and finance students and senior practitioners with a completely new and updated guide to the work in the field of corporate governance and IFRS compliance in emerging markets.

Muath Abdelqader is an Assistant Professor at the Australian University, Kuwait and research fellow at University of Gloucestershire, United Kingdom.

Tamer K. Darwish, PhD, is a Reader in Human Resource Management (HRM), and the Head of HRM Research Centre in the Business School, University of Gloucestershire, United Kingdom.

Khalil Nimer is an Assistant Professor of accounting and finance at Gulf University for Science and Technology (GUST), Kuwait and Doctorate supervisor at University of Gloucestershire, United Kingdom.

Routledge Studies in Corporate Governance

Enhancing Board Effectiveness
Institutional, Regulatory and Functional Perspectives for Developing and Emerging Markets
Edited by Franklin N. Ngwu, Onyeka Osuji, Chris Ogbechie, and David Williamson

Corporate Governance and Effectiveness
Why Companies Win or Lose
Dipak R. Basu and Victoria Miroshnik

Corporate Governance in India
Arindam Das

Corporate Governance and Whistleblowing
Corporate Culture and Employee Behaviour
Moeen Umar Cheema, Rahat Munir and Sophia Su

Corporate Governance, Ownership Structure and Firm Performance
Mediation Models and Dynamic Approaches
Hoang N. Phan and Sardar M. N. Islam

Corporate Social Responsibility and Governance
Stakeholders, Management and Organizational Performance in the European Union
Panagiotis Dimitropoulos and Efthalia Chatzigianni

Supply Chain Management and Corporate Governance
Artificial intelligence, game theory and robust optimization
Catherine Xiaocui Lou, Sardar M. N. Islam and Nicholas Billington

Corporate Governance and IFRS in the Middle East
Compliance with International Financial Reporting Standards
Muath Abdelqader, Tamer K. Darwish, and Khalil Nimer

For more information about this series, please visit www.routledge.com/Routledge-Studies-in-Corporate-Governance/book-series/RSCG

Corporate Governance and IFRS in the Middle East

Compliance with International Financial Reporting Standards

Muath Abdelqader,
Tamer K. Darwish, and
Khalil Nimer

Routledge
Taylor & Francis Group
NEW YORK AND LONDON

First published 2023
by Routledge
605 Third Avenue, New York, NY 10158

and by Routledge
4 Park Square, Milton Park, Abingdon, Oxon, OX14 4RN

Routledge is an imprint of the Taylor & Francis Group, an informa business

ISBN: 978-1-032-07791-8 (hbk)
ISBN: 978-1-032-07793-2 (pbk)
ISBN: 978-1-003-21155-6 (ebk)

DOI: 10.4324/9781003211556

Typeset in Bembo
by MPS Limited, Dehradun

To our families and friends

Contents

Figure and Tables

Figure

Tables

1 Introduction

Overview

The level of International Financial Reporting Standards (IFRS) compliance and companies' disclosure practices are governed by the accounting standards that these companies use as guidelines in preparing their financial statements. As a result of globalization, the expansion of trade, and the openness to foreign capital markets, investment decisions became not limited only for local users but also international users may need to access the financial information, which confirms the need of having a unified set of international accounting standards (e.g. Pricope, 2016; Diep, 2021).

The rapid globalization of capital markets has increased researchers' attention toward examining the quality of the disclosure practices implemented by companies. The internationalization and globalization are the most important motives of the harmonization of financial statements preparation and presentation (Isabel and Mariela, 2009; Pichler et al., 2018). Accounting harmonization is defined as the practice of improving the comparability of the accounting procedures through deterring the variations in such procedures (Mbir et al., 2020, Ezejiofor, 2022), which could be achieved by adopting a single set of accounting standards worldwide (Joshi et al., 2008; Lin et al., 2019).

The International Accounting Standards Board (IASB) has made huge efforts to produce a high-quality set of International Financial Reporting Standards (IFRS) aiming to unify the accounting procedures around the world. A single and widely accepted set of accounting standards improves the reliability, comparability, and understandability of financial statements, which consequently enhances the efficiency of capital markets through attracting more investors across the borders (Chen et al., 2019; Lin et al., 2019).

Given the importance of the information included in the financial statements, companies' disclosure behaviors became an area of interest for several scholars. The interests in measuring companies' level of disclosure started in 1960s by Cerf (1961). Thereafter, several studies were conducted aiming to develop a theoretical framework that provides a basis for explaining the disclosure practices applied by companies (see, for

DOI: 10.4324/9781003211556-1

example, McNally et al., 1982; Cooke, 1989). Recently, the spread of the international accounting standards among countries and the increase in the number of companies implementing these standards have motivated researchers to examine the level compliance with IFRS disclosure requirements.

Besides examining the level of compliance with IFRS, scholars are now also interested in examining the factors that affect such a compliance. This was motivated by aiming to reduce the level of information asymmetry between managers and investors as disclosing more information mitigates this asymmetry, ensures that investors are given an equal access to their needed information, and enhances the value relevance of the information provided to investors (Morris, 1987; Abad et al., 2018; Imhanzenobe, 2022). Scholars reported that country-level variables and firm-level variables affect the level of the adoption of IFRS (Morris and Gray, 2007). The country-level variables are related to the environmental influences in shaping the company's accounting practices, such as economy, capital markets, accounting and regulatory framework, enforcement mechanisms, and culture (Boshnak, 2017; Ab Abonwara et al., 2021).

Regarding the firm-level variables, firm characteristics and corporate governance were reported to have effects on the level of compliance with IFRS. Accordingly, corporate governance was one of the main areas that attracted scholars' attention to examine, building on the ground that the quality of financial reporting is the heart of corporate governance (Mallin, 2002). Thus, several scholars attempted to examine the effect of corporate governance on the level of compliance with IFRS standing on the fact that the former is essential in improving the company's transparency and accountability (Nel et al., 2022), which helps in improving managers' confidence of the users of financial statements (Albassam, 2014). Additionally, improving corporate governance helps in improving the effectiveness of controlling and monitoring managers' performance, which leads to enhance the efficiency of the company's disclosure practices (Macdonald and Beattie, 1993; Firth et al., 2007; Petra, 2007).

The focus of this book is on the Middle East region, particularly the Gulf Cooperation Council (GCC) member states, which was established in 1981, including six Arab Gulf countries, namely: Kuwait, Saudi Arabia, United Arab Emirates (UAE), Qatar, Bahrain, and Oman; the establishment of GCC aimed to encourage the integration between these countries regarding their national security, foreign policy, and economic and financial affairs (Al-Shammari, 2005; Haak-Saheem et al., 2017). The GCC countries are considered as early adopters of IFRS, they have made IFRS mandatory since 1986, which provides a useful setting of examining the level of compliance with IFRS within these countries.

Existing Gaps

The issuance of IFRS to be used throughout the world was aiming to improve the comparability and understandability of financial statements

(Pichler et al., 2018; Mbir et al., 2020), and hence, to enhance the investment decisions through helping investors across the borders to invest in the multinational companies (Tyrrall et al., 2007; Kieso et al., 2010; Nurunnabi et al., 2020). However, mandating the application of IFRS in developing countries does not ensure that they are fully complying with the disclosure requirements of these standards as it was expected by standards' setter organizations (Hassaan, 2012). This is due to the differences in the cultural contexts between developed and developing nations, as well as, to the variations in the effectiveness of the regulatory agencies and professional bodies among these countries (see, for example, Ahmed and Nicholls, 1994; Chamisa, 2000; Ball et al., 2003; Dahawy and Conover, 2007).

In addition, IFRS were created by high-income countries and common law legal systems, which makes the application of these standards in different countries with different cultures and regulations questionable (Pricope, 2016). The lack of the relevance of IFRS in some economic situations is related to the high cost of adopting these standards (Irvine and Lucas, 2006). Scholars have argued that the World Bank and the International Monetary Fund have driven developing countries to implement IFRS or to develop their own national standards in accordance with IFRS (Perera and Baydoun 2007; Hassan, 2008; Al-Omari, 2010). Mandating the implementation of IFRS in the Middle East and North Africa (MENA) region without considering the necessity of sufficiently enhancing the awareness of the importance and benefits of implementing these standards among different parties has led to some barriers that delayed the achievement of a complete compliance with the disclosure requirements of these standards (Hassaan, 2012). This implies that the level of compliance with IFRS disclosure requirements, in developing countries, still needs to be improved in order to experience the desired benefits from issuing a unified set of international accounting standards in these countries. As argued by Samaha et al. (2012), while developing countries share similar characteristics, they are not homogenous regarding their economic, accounting, and professional development. The same applies to GCC countries in terms of their economies and their enforcement procedures toward the adoption of IFRS. This confirms that comparing the level of compliance among these countries will help in detecting the differences, if any, in their disclosure behaviors.

The failure of financial reporting has alerted the interests of researchers toward examining the role of corporate governance in enhancing companies' disclosure practices (Haniffa, 1999; Juhmani, 2017; Sellami and Fendri, 2017). For the majority of institutions, the level of disclosure is the main concern of corporate governance; this is due to the need of the shareholders to a sufficient level of information about the performance of the company (see Haniffa, 1999; Samaha and Dahawy, 2010). However, the desired improvements in the level of compliance with IFRS, that corporate governance is expected to achieve, are conditioned with the adoption of corporate governance best practices in the cultural values of these countries (Hermanson, 2003; Hassaan, 2012). Hassaan (2012) argued that corporate governance best practices may dispute with the cultural values in the MENA society, which may limit the former impact on the level of compliance with IFRS.

Therefore, this book aims to strengthen the theoretical and practical understanding of the underlying relationships aligned with their practices. Accordingly, we intend to undertake the development and measurement of a conceptual framework within the GCC context. This book attempts to answer the two main questions, which are: "what is the extent of the compliance with IFRS disclosure requirements of the listed companies in GCC member states and do corporate governance and firm characteristics play a significant role in determining the level of compliance with IFRS?"

Statement of Significance

The number of countries that mandating their listed companies to apply IFRS in preparing their financial statements is increasing, scholars suggested that countries decided to implement IFRS due to their perceived economic benefits (Pricope, 2016). Researchers have reported that having a unified set of accounting standards best serves the needs of public users of financial statements through decreasing the variations in the national accounting practices that were resulted from the differences in the institutional and cultural dimensions among countries (Armstrong et al., 2010; Herath and Alsulmi, 2017). One of the important concerns of IFRS is the development of the efficiency of capital markets (Chen et al., 2001; Chen et al., 2019); this is due to the desired benefits of IFRS in improving the transparency and understandability of financial statements, which enhances the investment decisions and allows investors to expand their investments across countries (Morris, 1987; Pichler et al., 2018; Nel et al., 2022). In other words, the presence of global stock markets and the increase in the cross countries trading have raised the need to examine the quality of the disclosed information in the financial statements (Dahawy and Conover, 2007). Hence, it is expected that all companies will adopt IFRS in preparing and presenting their financial statements (Edogbanya and Kamardin, 2014).

However, implementing IFRS in developing countries does not guarantee that these countries will experience the benefits of these standards, and it cannot be generalized that adopting these standards would have a significant impact in these countries (Al-Shiab, 2003; Omar and Simon, 2011). This is due to the fact that the benefits of adopting IFRS are associated with the full compliance with IFRS but not with the partial compliance (Queku, 2016). This has shifted the attention of scholars toward examining the level of compliance with the disclosure requirements of IFRS and toward exploring the factors that control the extent of compliance with these standards. Examining the determinants of the level of the adoption of IFRS helps in deciding which factors are having significant roles in controlling the degree of the adoption of IFRS and highlighting the weaknesses in the enforcement procedures in order to overcome such weaknesses. Hence, this book is important as it intends to extend the existing literature in relation to companies' financial disclosure; this will further help in expanding our knowledge about the extent of the compliance with IFRS disclosure requirements in GCC countries, and in particular to explore the factors that control such a compliance. Additionally, it aims to investigate the variations in the level of compliance across GCC countries' listed firms in a greater depth. Such work would have relevance not only within the GCC region, but also beyond the region, given the relative similarity of national institutional features and realities across many emerging economies.

Corporate governance was one of the factors that reported by scholars to have an impact on the level of compliance with IFRS (Firth et al., 2007; Petra, 2007). However, the results of the prior work regarding the effect of corporate governance on the level of compliance with IFRS are mixed, and the majority of it was conducted in developed nations. Therefore, given that the focus of this work being on developing countries, this book adds to existing knowledge in relation to the factors influencing the extent of IFRS compliance. The GCC countries have introduced their corporate governance codes, which were based on Organization for Economic Co-operation and Development (OECD) principles, intending to enhance the disclosure and transparency of financial statements and to empower managers to effectively carry out their monitoring and controlling role.

Likewise, the significance of the current book appears at the theoretical level; it attempts to provide a recent evidence in the theoretical foundation of the financial disclosure practices in GCC countries. This would have important implications for the role of institutional theory in explaining the differences in the level of compliance across countries and explaining the relationship between corporate governance and the level of the adoption of IFRS disclosure requirements in the GCC region. In addition, this book attempts to provide an overview about the awareness of the different parties who are involved in the financial reporting process and explore the barriers of the full compliance with IFRS in these countries. As well as, to examine the effect of corporate governance on the disclosure behaviors of their listed companies. This will help all the parties who are involved in issuing financial reporting regulations in evaluating and improving the current situation of the disclosure practices implemented in their capital markets. This work will help the current and the potential investors in making better investment decisions.

Finally, due to the lack of the number of studies that examined the level of compliance with IFRS of the listed companies in the MENA region, and due to the changes that were made to some standards and the issuance of new standards, this book is important as it provides a recent evidence about the level of compliance with IFRS disclosure requirements. Moreover, some standards were ignored by most of the previous studies based on the idea that they are not applicable for their research contexts. However, the extensive review of these standards has concluded that they are not applicable in some of the MENA region contexts, but meanwhile, they are applicable to others, particularly GCC countries, and thus, we include them.

Rationale

Annual reports issued by companies are considered the main communication channel between the company and the users of financial statements (Kieso et al., 2010). Globalization and trade expansion had led to the openness of capital markets, which made the investment decisions not limited only for local users (Pricope, 2016). This raises the need to ensure the transparency and the comparability of financial statements and to improve the quality of accounting data, which could be achieved by improving the disclosure practices implemented by companies (Barth et al., 2008; Kieso et al., 2010). Hence, the cross countries trading and the existence of global stock markets have led to the increase in the interests of examining the extent of the disclosed information in the financial statements (Dahawy and Conover, 2007).

Accounting standards are considered an important standing ground in improving the efficiency of capital markets (Chen et al., 2001; Chu et al., 2019). As discussed previously, one of the main goals of issuing IFRS is to ensure accounting harmonization through decreasing the variations and the differences in companies' accounting procedures (Nobes and Parker, 2008). Hence, the extent of the adoption of IFRS has attracted researchers' attention, specifically after the spread of the idea that the globalization of these standards is debatable, particularly in developing countries (Pricope, 2016). In addition, the impact of implementing IFRS and their financial consequences in developed countries had grown the need of examining the level of compliance with IFRS in developing countries; this is due to the idea that knowing the status of the financial disclosure helps in identifying whether implementing these standards in developing countries is succeeding or not (Al-Shiab, 2003). Researchers stated that the adoption of IFRS in developing countries may not be beneficial in increasing the effectiveness of the quality of financial reporting as it is in the developed countries (Kapaya, 2000; Irvine and Lucas, 2006). The latter may be explained by the fact that in order to experience the desired benefits of implementing IFRS, the full compliance with all of the disclosure requirements of these standards must be achieved (Queku, 2016). The shortened capabilities of applying IFRS in these countries may lead to the possibility that they will not experience the desired economic benefits and outcomes of implementing these standards (Dahawy and Conover, 2007). This emphasizes the need to investigate the level of compliance with IFRS in developing countries.

The inclusion of GCC countries is justified based on the fact that they are early adopters of IFRS, which implies that companies listed in these countries have a reasonable level of experience in implementing the disclosure requirements of IFRS. In addition, examining the level of compliance with IFRS among the six GCC countries helps in detecting the differences in the adoption of the mandatory disclosure requirements across these countries, and in figuring out the factors that explain these differences. However, there is a lack in the number of studies that comprehensively examined the level of compliance with IFRS in developing countries in general, and in GCC countries in particular; there is also a shortage in the number of studies that compared the level of compliance of more than one developing country.

Additionally, the environment of IFRS is dynamic and changeable, and hence, IASB keeps amending the existing standards or issuing new standards according to the new accounting issues that may appear. Consequently, a continuous examination of the level of compliance with IFRS using a contemporary data is essential. The current study aims to provide a recent evidence about the level of compliance with IFRS disclosure requirements in GCC countries as the most recent study that examined such a compliance is Boshnak (2017), who examined the level of compliance with the international accounting standards that were issued up until the end of 2013. Nevertheless, since that date, some standards were amended and new standards were issued, therefore, the examination of these new standards is needed. Moreover, he used a modest sample size, which has limited the ability of detecting the country effect on the level of compliance with IFRS. Therefore, this book takes a further step by including all the listed companies in GCC countries.

Notably, after the numerous financial and economic crises and the failure of financial reporting in serving the needs of the users of financial statements, scholars became interested in examining the role of corporate governance in determining the disclosure practices of companies (Haniffa, 1999; Juhmani, 2017; Katmon and Al Farooque, 2017). These collapses have stressed the significance of improving corporate governance to promote the financial reporting quality (Pergola, 2005); this stands on the idea that implementing corporate governance codes is expected to improve companies' transparency and accountability and enhance the level of confidence in their managers' performance (Albassam, 2014). As stated by Verriest et al. (2013), the stronger the corporate governance, the more transparent the IFRS restatements, which implies a high level of disclosure. However, although there has been a widespread recognition of the important role of corporate governance practices in determining the level of compliance with IFRS, most of the studies implemented were in the developed countries and their results were mixed. Therefore, the need of a recent evaluation of the impact of corporate governance on the level of compliance with IFRS is needed, particularly within the context of developing countries.

Moreover, this book will be of interest to all the parties that are keen to know the strengths and weaknesses of the compliance with IFRS in the MENA region capital markets, including both national and international institutions. Policy makers and regulators need an evaluation about the current status of the disclosure practices in their capital markets' listed companies. This will help such institutions in making decisions and developing new approaches to overcome the weaknesses in the disclosure practices of these companies. Additionally, the enforcement bodies in GCC countries will be interested in examining the variations in the level of compliance with IFRS by their companies and determining the reasons that are responsible for such a level of compliance. This helps these bodies in evaluating their current enforcement mechanisms in order to decide if these mechanisms should be improved or not, aiming to develop their companies' disclosure practices. Furthermore, this book provides a recent evidence for the accounting regulatory agencies, such as IASB about the level of compliance with IFRS in a particular region and the factors that are associated with the differences in such a compliance within countries. As well, it gives an insight to OECD regarding the extent of the application of the corporate governance best practices in GCC countries, and the role of corporate governance codes in enhancing the level of compliance with IFRS in these countries.

Structure of the Book

After this introduction, the book is structured as follows:

> Chapter 2 presents the main aspects of financial reporting frameworks in the GCC member states through discussing the rules and regulations which listed companies must comply with, and the mechanisms implemented by these companies to demonstrate their compliance. This chapter highlights the main areas of each country's legislation regarding financial reporting and accounting standards that companies should adhere to, the enforcement procedures, and the responsible agencies of monitoring the disclosure practices of listed companies. Moreover, it outlines the development of corporate governance codes issued in the GCC member states, aligned with a comparison between these codes to express the similarities and differences between some corporate governance mechanisms.

Chapter 3 presents a discussion of the definition of IFRS and tracks the history of forming these standards. It also discusses the main theoretical strands, which support the compliance with IFRS, and sheds light on the motivations of the convergence toward IFRS. The chapter ends with a comprehensive review of prior empirical work that have examined the level of compliance with the international accounting standards' disclosure requirements in both developed and developing countries, including a discussion of the main determinants of the level of compliance with IFRS that have been introduced by scholars focusing on the context of the Middle East.

Chapter 4 discusses the concept of corporate governance and its main mechanisms. It further highlights the main corporate governance principles issued by Organization for Economic Co-operation and Development (OECD). The chapter also explores the level of implementation of corporate governance codes in both developed and developing countries, with a particular focus on the Middle East and GCC contexts.

Chapter 5 enhances our overall understanding of the relationship between corporate governance and IFRS compliance. It starts with the presentation of the key theoretical strands linking corporate governance and financial disclosure that were implemented by previous studies. The chapter also presents a thorough review of prior empirical work that examined the relationship between corporate governance and financial disclosure in developed and developing countries, with a particular focus on the Middle East and GCC contexts.

Chapter 6 aims to discuss the central propositions and establish a theoretical framework in relation to corporate governance and IFRS. The theoretical framework plays an important role in guiding the entire research process. This chapter discusses the level of compliance with IFRS disclosure requirements through presenting key factors that play major roles in creating variations in the level of compliance with IFRS among countries. The chapter also presents a theoretical model, which encompasses the interplay between firm attributes, corporate governance mechanisms, and the level of compliance with IFRS disclosure requirements.

Chapter 7 demonstrates the measurements of the corporate governance mechanisms and firm characteristics that were included in examining their relationship with the level of compliance with IFRS. Additionally, it presents the procedures and criteria implemented in selecting the standards and building the disclosure index used in measuring each company's level of compliance with IFRS. Thereafter, it describes the number of companies included in the analysis.

Chapter 8 aims to present the procedures that were implemented in analyzing the data and the statistical techniques employed in testing our propositions. This chapter starts with a presentation of the descriptive analysis of the level of compliance with IFRS disclosure requirements for all of the GCC countries together and for each country, aligned with a presentation of the descriptive analysis of the level of compliance with each standard of IFRS. It then highlights the descriptive statistics of the independent variables among all GCC countries. Thereafter, the chapter demonstrates the results of the multiple regression analysis.

Based on a comprehensive empirical exercise of the theoretical model presented in chapter 6, chapter 9 aims to discuss key findings of the central proportions in relation to corporate governance and IFRS. A thorough discussion of each proposition is presented in light of the relevant theoretical strands and related empirical work from the existing literature. This chapter locates the practice of corporate governance and IFRS in the GCC region within the wider institutional context, and further discusses similarities with and differences from other emerging markets.

Chapter 10 aims to present the main conclusions and contributions to the accounting and management literature, which resulted from the empirical work presented earlier in this book. It also aims to draw out the wider implications for theory, practice, and methodology. The chapter also offers a number of potential areas for future directions in relation to corporate governance mechanisms and IFRS in emerging markets and beyond.

References

Ab Abonwara, K.M., Ahmad, N.L.B., & Halim, H.B.A. (2021). Determinants and consequence of adopting International Financial Reporting Standards (IFRS): A systematic literature review. *International Journal of Contemporary Management and Information Technology*, *1*(3), 39–48.

Abad, D., Cutillas-Gomariz, M.F., Sánchez-Ballesta, J.P., & Yagüe, J. (2018). Does IFRS mandatory adoption affect information asymmetry in the stock market? *Australian Accounting Review*, *28*(1), 61–78.

Ahmed, K., & Nicholls, D. (1994). The impact of non-financial company characteristics on mandatory disclosure compliance in developing countries: The case of Bangladesh. *The International Journal of Accounting*, *29*(1), 62–77.

Albassam, W. (2014). *Corporate governance, voluntary disclosure and financial performance: Ban empirical analysis of Saudi listed firms using a mixed-methods research design* (Doctoral dissertation, University of Glasgow).

Al-Omari, A.M. (2010). The institutional framework of financial reporting in Jordan. *European Journal of Economics, Finance and Administrative Sciences*, *22*(1), 32–50.

Al-Shammari, B.A. (2005). *Compliance with international accounting standards by listed companies in the Gulf Co-operation Council member states: An empirical study* (Doctoral dissertation, University of Western Australia).

Al-Shiab, M. (2003). *Financial consequences of IAS adoption: The case of Jordan* (Doctoral dissertation, Newcastle University).

Armstrong, C.S., Barth, M.E., Jagolinzer, A.D., & Riedl, E.J. (2010). Market reaction to the adoption of IFRS in Europe. *The Accounting Review*, *85*(1), 31–61.

Ball, R., Robin, A., & Wu, J.S. (2003). Incentives versus standards: Properties of accounting income in four East Asian countries. *Journal of Accounting and Economics*, *36*(1), 235–270.

Barth, M.E., Landsman, W.R., & Lang, M.H. (2008). International accounting standards and accounting quality. *Journal of Accounting Research*, *46*(3), 467–498.

Boshnak, H. (2017). *Mandatory and voluntary disclosures in GCC listed firms* (Doctoral dissertation, University of the West of England).

Cerf, A.R. (1961). *Corporate reporting and investment decisions*. Public Accounting Research Program, Institute of Business and Economic Research, University of California.

Chamisa, E.E. (2000). The relevance and observance of the IASC standards in developing countries and the particular case of Zimbabwe. *The International Journal of Accounting*, *35*(2), 267–286.

Chen, C., Lee, E., Lobo, G.J., & Zhu, J. (2019). Who benefits from IFRS convergence in China? *Journal of Accounting, Auditing & Finance, 34*(1), 99–124.

Chen, C.J., Chen, S., & Su, X. (2001). Is accounting information value-relevant in the emerging Chinese stock market? *Journal of International Accounting, Auditing and Taxation, 10*(1), 1–22.

Chu, J., Heo, K., & Pae, J. (2019). Does a Firmas Corporate Governance Enhance the Beneficial Effect ofIFRS Adoption? Sustainability, 11(3), 885.

Cooke, T.E. (1989). Disclosure in the corporate annual reports of Swedish companies. *Accounting and Business Research, 19*(74), 113–124.

Dahawy, K., & Conover, T. (2007). Accounting disclosure in companies listed on the Egyptian stock exchange. *Middle Eastern Finance and Economics, 1*(1), 5–20.

Diep, N.T.N. (2021). Applicability of IFRS in Vietnam stock exchange listed companies: Perspective from theory of planned behavior. *Ho Chi Minh City Open University Journal of Science-Economics and Business Administration, 11*(1), 109–121.

Edogbanya, A., & Kamardin, H. (2014). Adoption of international financial reporting standards in nigeria: Concepts and Issues. *Journal of Advanced Management Science, 2*(1), 72–75.

Ezejiofor, R.A. (2022). Effect of IFRS implementation on the financial report quality of Nigerian banks. *Research Journal of Management Practice, 2*, 38–50, ISSN 2782, 7674.

Firth, M., Fung, P.M., & Rui, O.M. (2007). Ownership, two-tier board structure, and the informativeness of earnings – Evidence from China. *Journal of Accounting and Public Policy, 26*(4), 463–496.

Haak-Saheem, W., Festing, M., & Darwish, T.K. (2017). International human resource management in the Arab Gulf States – an institutional perspective. *The International Journal of Human Resource Management, 28*(18), 2684–2712.

Haniffa, R.M. (1999). *Culture, corporate governance and disclosure in Malaysian corporations* (Doctoral dissertation, University of Exeter).

Hassaan, M. (2012). *Corporate governance and compliance with International Financial Reporting Standards (IFRSs): Evidence from two MENA stock exchanges* (Doctoral dissertation, Aston University).

Hassan, M. (2008). The development of accounting regulations in Egypt: Legitimating the international accounting standards. *Managerial Auditing Journal, 23*(5), 467–484.

Herath, S.K., & Alsulmi, F.H. (2017). International financial reporting standards (IFRS): The benefits, obstacles, and opportunities for implementation in Saudi Arabia. *International Journal of Social Science and Business, 2*(1), 1–18.

Hermanson, D.R. (2003). Does corporate governance really matter? What the research tells us. *Internal Auditing, 18*(2), 44–45.

Imhanzenobe, J. (2022). Value relevance and changes in accounting standards: A review of the IFRS adoption literature. *Cogent Business & Management, 9*(1), 2039057.

Irvine, H., & Lucas, N. (2006). The rationale and impact of the adoption of International Financial Reporting Standards: The case of the United Arab Emirates. In *Proceedings of the 18th Asian-Pacific Conference on International Accounting Issues* (pp. 1–22). California State University, The Sid Craig School of Business.

Isabel, S., & Mariela, I. (2009). Implementation of IFRS for non-financial companies and its impact on financial stability and monitoring at the Central Bank of Chile. *Central Bank of Chile, SDFP*, 1–26.

Joshi, P.L., Bremser, W.G., & Al-Ajmi, J. (2008). Perceptions of accounting professionals in the adoption and implementation of a single set of global accounting standards: Evidence from Bahrain. *Advances in Accounting, 24*(1), 41–48.

Juhmani, O. (2017). Corporate governance and the level of Bahraini corporate compliance with IFRS disclosure. *Journal of Applied Accounting Research, 18*(1), 22–41.
Kapaya, G. (2000). 'International Accounting Standards and Accounting in Developing/ Emerging Nations-How About Fresh Start?'. *Discussion Paper Series: Accounting and Finance*. No. 9. September. Middlesex University Business School.
Katmon, N., & Al Farooque, O. (2017). Exploring the impact of internal corporate governance on the relation between disclosure quality and earnings management in the UK listed companies. *Journal of Business Ethics, 142*(2), 345–367.
Kieso, D.E., Weygandt, J.J., & Warfield, T.D. (2010). *Intermediate accounting: IFRS edition* (Vol. 2). John Wiley & Sons.
Lin, S., Riccardi, W.N., Wang, C., Hopkins, P.E., & Kabureck, G. (2019). Relative effects of IFRS adoption and IFRS convergence on financial statement comparability. *Contemporary Accounting Research, 36*(2), 588–628.
Macdonald, N., & Beattie, A. (1993). The corporate governance jigsaw. *Accounting and Business Research, 23*(1), 304–310.
Mallin, C. (2002). The relationship between corporate governance, transparency and financial disclosure. *Corporate Governance: An International Review, 10*(4), 253–255.
Mbir, D.E.G., Agyemang, O.S., Tackie, G., & Abeka, M.J. (2020). IFRS compliance, corporate governance and financial reporting quality of GSE-listed non-financial firms. *Cogent Business & Management*, 7(1), 1759856.
McNally, G.M., Eng, L.H., & Hasseldine, C.R. (1982). Corporate financial reporting in New Zealand: An analysis of user preferences, corporate characteristics and disclosure practices for discretionary information. *Accounting and Business Research, 13*(49), 11–20.
Morris, R.D. (1987). Signalling, agency theory and accounting policy choice. *Accounting and Business Research, 18*(69), 47–56.
Morris, R.D., & Gray, S.J. (2007). Corporate transparency differences in the Asian region: The feasibility of global standardization in practice. In *AFAANZ Conference, Gold Coast, July*.
Nel, G., Scholtz, H., & Engelbrecht, W. (2022). Relationship between online corporate governance and transparency disclosures and board composition: Evidence from JSE listed companies. *Journal of African Business, 23*(2), 304–325.
Nobes, C., & Parker, R.H. (2008). *Comparative international accounting*. Pearson Education.
Nurunnabi, M., Jermakowicz, E.K., & Donker, H. (2020). Implementing IFRS in Saudi Arabia: Evidence from publicly traded companies. *International Journal of Accounting and Information Management, 28*(2), 243–273.
Omar, B., & Simon, J. (2011). Corporate aggregate disclosure practices in Jordan. *Advances in Accounting, 27*(1), 166–186.
Perera, H., & Baydoun, N. (2007). Convergence with international financial reporting standards: The case of Indonesia. *Advances in International Accounting, 20*, 201–224.
Pergola, T.M. (2005). Management entrenchment: Can it negate the effectiveness of recently legislated governance reform. *Journal of American Academy of Business, 6*(2), 177–183.
Petra, S.T. (2007). The effects of corporate governance on the informativeness of earnings. *Economics of Governance, 8*(2), 129–152.
Pichler, S., Cordazzo, M., & Rossi, P. (2018). An analysis of the firms-specific determinants influencing the voluntary IFRS adoption: Evidence from Italian private firms. *International Journal of Accounting, Auditing and Performance Evaluation, 14*(1), 85–104.

Pricope, C.F. (2016). The role of institutional pressures in developing countries. Implications for IFRS. *Theoretical and Applied Economics*, *22*(2), 27–40.

Queku, I. (2016) Review of compliance measure in empirical accounting literature: Perspective of international financial reporting standards. *Research Journal of Finance and Accounting*, 7(14), 59–66.

Samaha, K., & Dahawy, K. (2010). An empirical analysis of corporate governance structures and voluntary corporate disclosure in volatile capital markets: The Egyptian experience. *International Journal of Accounting, Auditing and Performance Evaluation*, 7(1–2), 61–93.

Samaha, K., Dahawy, K., Hussainey, K., & Stapleton, P. (2012). The extent of corporate governance disclosure and its determinants in a developing market: The case of Egypt. *Advances in Accounting*, *28*(1), 168–178.

Sellami, Y.M., & Fendri, H.B. (2017). The effect of audit committee characteristics on compliance with IFRS for related party disclosures: Evidence from South Africa. *Managerial Auditing Journal*, *32*(6), 603–626.

Tyrrall, D., Woodward, D., & Rakhimbekova, A. (2007). The relevance of international financial reporting standards to a developing country: Evidence from Kazakhstan. *The International Journal of Accounting*, *42*(1), 82–110.

Verriest, A., Gaeremynck, A., & Thornton, D.B. (2013). The impact of corporate governance on IFRS adoption choices. *European Accounting Review*, *22*(1), 39–77.

2 The GCC Context

Introduction

The Gulf Cooperation Council (GCC) was created in 1981 in order to reach for a cooperative framework between six countries, namely, Kuwait, Bahrain, United Arab Emirates (UAE), Saudi Arabia, Qatar, and Oman (Haak-Saheem et al., 2017). The GCC aims to achieve cooperation and integration among its members in order to improve all fields, such as economic, education, culture, and social (Shehata, 2013). The environment of the country shapes its accounting and financial reporting practices (Cooke and Wallace, 1990; Herath and Alsulmi, 2017). In other words, the degree of economic development, legal rules, availability of information, general level of education, and culture are the main elements of the country's environment that affect the disclosure practices implemented by its listed companies (Cooke and Wallace, 1990).

Economy

Kuwait is a small rich country that has more than 6% of the world's oil reserve (Al-Shammari and Al-Sultan, 2010; Hassan et al., 2017). Kuwait's main source of revenue is oil, which shapes 90% of the export revenue and 80% of the government income (Al-Shammari and Al-Sultan, 2010). The oil output represents more than 50% of its Gross Domestic Product (GDP) (Boshnak, 2017). In order to attract foreign investments, the foreign ownership has been permitted to reach 49% (Al-Shammari and Al-Sultan, 2010). The location of Kuwait presents several advantages in trading and manufacturing, and in order to improve the economy, the Kuwaiti government has promoted privatization through two investment agencies, these are Boubyan Petrochemicals and Qurain Petrochemicals Industries Company (QPIC), which is expected to enhance its competitiveness and profitability in the future (Hassan et al., 2017).

Qatar is the smallest country in GCC in respect to its geographical area and population; it has the second largest gas stocks in the world with 5% of the worlds' total gas reserves (Hossain and Hammami, 2009). The oil output

DOI: 10.4324/9781003211556-2

represents 23% of its GDP (Boshnak, 2017). Several polices were adopted by Qatari government to develop its economic infrastructure and to diversify its income sources, which has led to an increase in investment opportunities, especially in oil and gas exploration projects (Hossain and Hammami, 2009). In 2005, the Qatari government has created Qatar Financial Center (QFC) aiming to attract foreign investments in different sectors, such as finance, health, education, transportation, tourism, and energy (Shehata, 2013).

Saudi Arabia is the largest GCC country regarding its geographical area and population; it has approximately 25% of the world's total oil reserve (Shehata, 2013). Oil export represents almost 85% of total export and 75% of the government revenues (Hussainey and Al-Nodel, 2008). Saudi Arabia is considered the largest exporter of petroleum; additionally, in order to diversify its economy, the Saudi government has started the privatization of the state owned companies since 1990 (Basher and Sadorsky, 2006). In year 2000, foreign investors were allowed to invest in Saudi Arabia, which has attracted several investments to the country (Naser and Nuseibeh, 2003). Recently, the Saudi government encouraged investors to expand the role of the private sectors in health care, education, and tourism industries (The World Factbook, 2017).

The UAE is the second largest GCC country regarding the population; it was established in 1971, including seven emirates (Dubai, Abu Dhabi, Sharjah, Ras Al-Khaimah, Ajman, Fujairah, and Umm Al-Qaiwain). It has almost 10% of world's oil reserve, which shapes around 23% from its total GDP (Boshnak, 2017). The investment environment in the UAE has attracted companies that wishing to invest in a growing market in the Middle East and North Africa (MENA) region (Aljifri, 2008). The UAE has adopted an investment strategy that depends on attracting private investments, which resulted in improving the structure of its national economic and achieving high standards in the services sector (Al-Zarouni, 2009).

In Bahrain, petroleum processing and refining is considered the major industry (Joshi and Wakil, 2004). The oil output shapes almost 19% of the total GDP (Boshnak, 2017). The oil revenue shapes almost 86% of the budget revenue (The World Factbook, 2017). Bahrain is considered one of the earliest GCC countries that opened up its market when it has allowed foreign investors to own up to 49%, which made it the fastest growing center in the Middle East (Joshi et al., 2008; Shehata, 2013). Additionally, in Bahrain, the second major economic activity is the production of aluminum, which is considered the second biggest export after oil. The government has encouraged domestic and foreign investments in the areas of real estate and tourism (The World Factbook, 2017).

In Oman, the oil output shapes 90% of the government revenues and more than 50% of its GDP. However, Oman does not have the same level of oil reserve as other GCC member states, and their oil level is expected to deplete in 2020 (Shehata, 2013). Therefore, the government has managed the transition of its economy toward diversification through taking a number of steps regarding efficient economic planning and development initiatives that have contributed to improvements in the Omani economy. Additionally, the Omani government, in order to improve its economy, has increased its governmental spending on key sectors, such as tourism, agriculture, and manufacturing (Strolla and Peri, 2016).

Capital Markets

The type, nature, availability of information required by investors, and the disclosure practices implemented by companies are affected by the existence of capital markets (Doupnik and Salter, 1995). Among GCC member states, Kuwait has the oldest stock exchange (Shehata, 2013). The Kuwait Stock Exchange (KSE) was established in 1983 and formally opened in the same year (Alfaraih, 2009). The Kuwait Capital Market Authority (CMA) was established in 2010 in order to improve the transparency and to monitor the activities of the KSE (Shehata, 2013). However, in 2014, the Kuwait Bourse was established as a private company that aims to take over and manage KSE and gradually transition its operations. In 2016, it was officially licensed to replace the KSE aiming to upgrade the KSE's infrastructure and business environment concerning to meet the international standards (Boursa Kuwait, 2017).

In Qatar, the Qatar Stock Exchange (QSE) was established in 1995 as Doha Stock Exchange (DSE), and in 2009, it was renamed as Qatar Stock Exchange (QSE, 2017). The efforts aimed to develop the QSE were started in 1995, while it began operating in 1997. It was intended to have major roles in providing fair, efficient, and facilitated trading to protect the rights of investors (Shehata, 2013). Additionally, it aimed to manage the public information access by encouraging timely disclosure of major information, and by enforcing the securities' laws (Hossain and Hammami, 2009). In 2005, the Qatar Financial Markets Authority (QFMA) was established to operate as an independent regulatory authority of the securities market in Qatar. The QFMA is responsible for regulating the QSE and monitoring the Securities Market in order to ensure that it is fair and participants informed (Shehata, 2013). The QFMA was amended in 2009 as an independent regulatory supervision authority over financial markets in Qatar (QFMA, 2017).

In Oman, the Muscat Securities Market (MSM) was established in 1988, aiming to regulate, control, and improve the infrastructure of the Omani's financial sector (MSM, 2017). The establishment of MSM allowed Omani government to have a successful economic environment and to stay aligned with the international developments (Mohamed et al., 2009; Shehata, 2013). Ten years later, the restructuring of the market and the issuance of the new capital law had led to split the regulations and market activities functions, and to separate the responsibilities among three main entities, which are Omani Capital Market Authority (CMA), MSM, and Muscat Clearing and Depository Company (MCD). The Omani CMA was established in 1998 to represent the regulatory government authority that is responsible for supervising and legislating parts, and to organize the issuance and the trading of securities (Mohamed et al., 2009). The MSM concerns with stock exchange, specifically, it is responsible for listing and trading securities, but it is subject to the CMA supervision. The MCD Company was established in 1999, and it is responsible for the transformation of securities' ownership and saving documents (MCD, 2017).

Saudi Arabia has the largest equity market in the GCC region, the Saudi stock market was established in 1985, and it has regulated by the Saudi Arabian Monetary Agency (SAMA), which monitors and issues rules and regulations to control the stock market trading (Albassam, 2014). In 2003, the Saudi Capital Market Authority (CMA) was established, where it became in charge of controlling the Saudi Stock Exchange instead of SAMA (Hussainey and Al-Nodel, 2008). The efforts of Saudi CMA in developing the stock exchange market has led to the formation of the Saudi Stock Exchange (Tadawul) in 2007; Tadawul is a regulatory body that is authorized to organize the financial market in terms of listing and trading securities and all matters of the ownership registration of the traded securities. It is managed by a board of directors appointed by the Council of Ministers comprising representatives of legislators and licensed Saudi stock brokerage firms (Albassam, 2014; Tadawul, 2017).

In the UAE, the Ministry of Economy is responsible for organizing and overseeing the economy of the whole country; before the establishment of Abu Dhabi Securities Market (ADSM) and Dubai Financial Market (DFM) in the year 2000, the securities markets were operated in an unorganized matter (Al-Zarouni, 2009). The ADSM was established as a legal entity that is independent in its finance and management, and it has the authority to establish centers and branches outside the Emirate of Abu Dhabi (ADX, 2017). Moreover, the DFM was established as a public independent entity, and in 2005, it was transformed to a public shareholding company (DFM, 2017). The two stock markets aimed to facilitate fair, efficient, and transparent trading of securities for public listed companies (Aljifri and Khasharmeh, 2006). Additionally, in the year 2000, the Emirates Securities and Commodities Authority (ESCA) was established as the highest level of authority to organize and control the securities markets in the UAE, which is managed by a board of directors chaired by the Minister of Economy (Al-Zarouni, 2009).

Bahrain has an old stock exchange market, specifically, the Bahrain Stock Exchange (BSE) was established in 1987. It aimed to enhance and develop the country's economy through developing the securities market to oversee and regulate securities trading. The BSE was supervised by an independent board of directors chaired by the governor of the Central Bank of Bahrain (CBB) (Al-Ajmi, 2009). In 2010, the Bahrain Bourse was established as a shareholding company to replace the BSE, as a self-regulated institution, under the supervision of the CBB. The Bahrain Bourse aims to facilitate investors', issuers', and intermediaries' exchange-related transactions, to provide them with the best investing and trading solutions, and to offer them valuable resources that help them in meeting their expectations (Bahrain Bourse, 2017).

Legislation

Financial reporting procedures in GCC countries are governed by companies' law and securities market law (Al-Shammari, 2005; Boshnak, 2017). The establishment, the operations, and the dissolution of companies in GCC member states are governed by companies' law. These laws include guidance of various aspects of firms' operations, such as the incorporation of the firm, corporate governance structures, rights and obligations of shareholders, capital raising methods, and firms' dissolution and liquidation (Al-Shammari, 2005). Moreover, these companies' laws, in all GCC countries, include general guidelines about the financial reporting practices, however, they do not determine the format or the content of the financial statements other than requiring a balance sheet and a profit or loss statement to be issued in the company's annual report (Al-Shammari, 2005).

For securities market laws, each GCC country has created a stock exchange as an independent government entity which issues market laws. These laws aim to protect the rights of investors, to monitor the issuing of new securities, to specify directors' rights and obligations, and to develop and promote capital markets (Al-Shammari, 2005). Additionally, these market laws require the board of directors, of each listed company in GCC countries, to submit audited annual financial statements to the stock exchange within a specific period of time after the financial year's end (Al-Shammari, 2005). The period that companies allowed to submit their financial statements varies among GCC countries, more specifically, in Saudi Arabia, companies should submit their financial statements within two months following the financial year's end. In Kuwait, UAE, and Bahrain, companies have to submit their financial statements within three months after the financial year's end. In Oman, the allowed period is four months after the financial year's end. While in Qatar, it is six months after the financial year's end (Boshnak, 2017). Additionally, these laws require all listed companies to comply with the accounting regulations issued by the Ministry of Commerce. Each stock exchange, in the GCC countries, is governed by a board of directors chaired by the Minster of Commerce. This board of directors is responsible for setting general regulations of exchange, setting regulation related to issuing and trading securities, and approving applications from brokers and market makers trade (Al-Shammari, 2005; Boshnak, 2017). Table 2.1 shows the companies' laws and securities laws among GCC member states.

Table 2.1 Legislation in the GCC member states

Country	*Company Law*	*Securities and Exchange Law*	*Company Registrar*
Bahrain	Company Law No. 28 of 1975, replaced by Law No. 21 of 2001	Bahrain Securities and Stock Exchange Law No. 4 of 1987	Ministry of Commerce and Industry
Kuwait	Company Law No. 15 of 1960	Kuwait Stock Exchange Law of 13/8/1983	Ministry of Commerce and Industry
Oman	Company Law No. 4 of 1974	Muscat Securities Market Law No. 53 of 1988 replaced by Capital Market Law No. 80 of 1998	Ministry of Commerce
Qatar	Company Law No. 11 of 1981	Doha Securities Market Law No. 14 of 1995	Ministry of Economy and Commerce
Saudi Arabia	Company Law No. 6 of 1965	Saudi Share Registration Company (SSRC) Law No. 8/1230 of 1984	Ministry of Commerce
UAE	Company Law No. 8 of 1984	UAE Securities Market Law No. 4 of 2000	Ministry of Economy and Commerce

Source: Adapted from Al-Shammari (2005) and Boshnak (2017).

Accounting Standards

In broad terms, among GCC countries, government is responsible for formulating financial reporting regulations, and it is responsible for controlling and managing accounting and auditing professions (Al-Shammari, 2005; Boshnak, 2017). However, four of the GCC countries have created professional accounting bodies, which are Bahrain, Kuwait, UAE, and Saudi Arabia. These professional bodies are The Bahrain Society of Accountants and Auditors (BSAA), The Kuwait Accounting and Auditing Association (KAAA), The United Arab Emirates Accountants and Auditors Association (UAEAAA), and the Saudi Organization for Certified Public Accountants (SOCPA). However, among these professional bodies, only SOCPA was authorized by Saudi Arabia Ministry of Commerce to issue accounting and auditing standards and to certify public accountants (Al-Shammari, 2005; Boshnak, 2017). While in the other three countries, these bodies were not authorized to issue accounting and auditing standards or to license accountants and auditors (Al-Shammari, 2005; Boshnak, 2017).

Regarding setting the national standards, only Kuwait and Saudi Arabia have built their own accounting standards (Boshnak, 2017). In Kuwait, the awareness of the importance of financial reporting had begun in 1960s, when the Ministry of Commerce and Industry (MCI) had issued a resolution in 1960 in order to organize the formation and the administration of accounting profession, these rules were updated in 1965, and later in 1981 (Al Mutawaa and Hewaidy, 2010). In 1986, the Permanent Technical Committee (PTC) was established by MCI to create a set of accounting standards to be implemented by all listed companies. Furthermore, in 1987, the committee has released its recommendations that resulted in obligating all listed companies to comply with three national standards in the preparation of their financial statements (Al Mutawaa and Hewaidy, 2010). The three standards are the following: standard 1, which was related to the information that should be disclosed in the financial statements; standard 2 was related to accounting for investments; and standard 3 was related for real state (Alfaraih, 2009). These standards were faced by some criticisms regarding their ambiguity and insufficiency (Alfaraih, 2009). In 1990, the MCI issued a resolution that obligates all listed companies to comply with international financial reporting standards (IFRS) and it has been effective in 1991 (Al Mutawaa and Hewaidy, 2010). In Saudi Arabia, in 1968, the Ministry of Commerce had issued regulations to govern the auditing profession in Saudi Arabia, later in 1974, a resolution of Certified Public Accountant (CPA) regulations was issued, which is considered the building block in managing and monitoring accounting and auditing profession in Saudi Arabia (Albassam, 2014; SOCPA, 2017). Moreover, in 1992, the SOCPA was established to promote the accounting and auditing profession and all matters that might lead to development of the profession.

The next section presents the adoption of IFRS in GCC countries and the enforcement mechanisms implemented to ensure their listed companies' compliance with IFRS disclosure requirements and companies' laws requirements.

IFRS Adoption in GCC Member States

The financial reporting practices of listed companies in GCC countries are governed by both companies' laws and market securities laws (Al-Shammari, 2005). The adoption of IFRS in GCC countries started in 1986, some of these countries required all listed companies to adopt IFRS, while other countries required listed companies in specific industries to adopt IFRS (Al-Mannai and Hindi, 2015). The rapid growth of the GCC capital markets and the increase in the number of multinational firms have led GCC member states to force companies to adopt IFRS in order to help them meeting the needs of both local and international investors of more detailed information, and to ease the comparability among companies (Al-Shammari, 2005).

The adoption of IFRS in GCC countries has occurred during the period of 1986–1999. More specifically, in Oman, Kuwait, and Bahrain, all listed companies were required to comply with IAS in 1986, 1991, and 1996, respectively. In Saudi Arabia, Qatar, and the UAE, the Central Banks in these countries instructed banks, investment, and financial companies to comply with the International Accounting Standards (IAS) in 1992, 1999, and 1999, respectively (Boshnak, 2017). Table 2.2 shows the regulatory body and the law requires firms to comply with IFRS in GCC member states.

Enforcement

To ensure that companies are implementing the requirements of the both the states' laws and IFRS disclosure requirements, each GCC country has created government enforcement bodies. According to Al-Shammari (2005) and Boshnak (2017), the enforcement process involves three main steps, which are as follows: first, the companies' laws have determined where the audited financial statements should be lodged; in Bahrain, Oman, and Kuwait, all listed firms are required to submit their financial statements to the firm registrar. In Qatar, Saudi Arabia, and the UAE, all listed firms should submit their financial statements to the Central Banks. Second, the enforcement body will check if the audited annual financial statements had been lodged within the appropriate authority. Third, the enforcement body will check the financial statements for examining the compliance with IFRS. Following is a presentation of the enforcement bodies and procedures in each GCC country.

Table 2.2 The adoption of IFRS in GCC member states

Country	*Authorized Body Requiring Adoption of IFRSs*	*Law and Its Date of Issuance*	*Effective Date*	*Application*
Bahrain	Ministry of Commerce	External Auditing Law No. 26 of 1996 issued on February 24, 1996	1996	All listed firms
Kuwait	Ministry of Commerce	Ministerial Resolution No. 18 of 1990 issued on April 17, 1990	1991	All listed firms
Oman	Ministry of Commerce	Professional Accounting and Auditing Law No. 77 of 1986 issued on October 18, 1986	1986	All listed firms
Qatar	Qatar Central Bank	The Central Bank of Qatar Circular No. 27 of 1999 issued on February 19, 1999	1999	Banks, finance and investment firms
Saudi Arabia	Saudi Arabia Monetary Agency (SAMA)	The Saudi Arabia Monetary Agency Circular No. 11/2 of 1992 issued on July 23, 1992	1992	Banks, finance and investment firms
UAE	UAE Central Bank	The Central Bank of UAE Circular No. 20 of 1999 issued on January 25, 1999	1999	Banks, finance and investment firms

Source: Adapted from Al-Shammari (2005) and Boshnak (2017).

The Enforcement Process in Kuwait

In 1960, the Ministry of Commerce and Industry (MCI) has issued the law of commercial companies No. 15/1960 to organize the establishment of new companies and to regulate the management of the existing firms (Alfaraih, 2009). Over the last 40 years, this law lied under several amendments, and despite the existence of several laws in Kuwait, that govern accounting and auditing profession, the commercial law issued is considered the primary law governing firms' accounting and auditing procedures (Al-Qahtani, 2005; Boshnak, 2017). In 1990, the MCI issued a resolution that obligates all listed companies to comply with IFRS and it has been effective in 1991 (Al Mutawaa and Hewaidy, 2010). The law of commercial companies requires all listed companies to submit their annual financial statements to the MCI registrar and distribute them to shareholders within 90 days of the financial year's end (Alfaraih, 2009). Additionally, the commercial companies' law requires all financial statements to be fully audited from at least two external auditors from separate firms (Boshnak, 2017).

In Kuwait, both the Surveillance Department of the MCI and Kuwait Stock Exchange (KSE) are responsible for monitoring listed firms' compliance with both companies' laws and IFRS disclosure requirements. More specifically, the Surveillance Department of the MCI checks if the company implements the requirements of the companies' law including the audited financial statements using a checklist, prepared by the department's staff, before distributing them to shareholders, as well, relying on the external auditor's report for indicating the compliance with IFRS (Boshnak, 2017). The role of KSE is to conduct more detailed monitoring procedures to check the compliance with companies' law requirements; in 1999, before foreign investors were first allowed to trade in Kuwait Boursa, KSE became legally involved in monitoring the compliance with IFRS of all listed firms (Al-Shammari, 2005). This is also done by creating a checklist, prepared by a qualified staff, to check the compliance with IFRS disclosure requirements.

In case if any possible non-compliance with any of the IFRS disclosure requirements was detected through reviewing the annual report and the external auditor did not state this violation in the report, the Surveillance Department can communicate with the company's management and with its external auditor to investigate the case. If the investigation has led to evidence that the company has violated IFRS disclosure requirements, the department can report the case to the Minister of Commerce for assessment and decision. After that, the Minster of Commerce may set up a meeting with shareholders, who have the right to take actions, and if they decided to pursue a legal action the Minister of Commerce may refer the case to court. Additionally, the Minister of Commerce and the Market Director of KSE had the authority to refer the case to the KSE's Disciplinary Committee, which may enact a penalty of the violation, such as warnings, a supervision of dealing in firm's securities, or dis-listing (Boshnak, 2017). If the external auditor issued a qualified report, a representative from the Ministry of Commerce may attend the annual general meeting of the firm and raise the matter to the shareholders' attention where they have the right to take action, such as dismissing management, dismissing members of the board of directors, or dismissing the external auditor (Boshnak, 2017).

The Enforcement Process in Bahrain

All listed firms in Bahrain Stock Exchange, banks, and financial institutions, licensed by Bahrain Monetary Agency (BMA) and the Central Bank of Bahrain (CBB), are required to prepare their financial statements according to IFRS disclosure requirements (Boshnak, 2017). According to the commercial companies' law in Bahrain, all listed firms are required to submit a balance sheet, an income statement, a statement of changes in equity, notes of financial statements, and a managers' report for every financial year within three months following the end of the financial year (Khasharmeh and Aljifri, 2010). Additionally, it requires companies to appoint an external auditor to audit their financial statements.

In Bahrain, both the Surveillance Department of the Ministry of Commerce and Bahrain Stock Exchange (BSE) rely on the external auditor's report in monitoring the compliance with IFRS disclosure requirements. The surveillance department of the Ministry of Commerce checks the compliance with companies' law, including the lodgment of the financial statements within the desired period. In case of the existence of a qualified auditor report states that there is a non-compliance with IFRS, the department will contact the company's management and the external auditor to discuss the non-compliance issue and to advise management of any action that could be taken to correct the case. If management refused to take action, the ministry's staff may raise the case to the shareholders in the annual general meeting where they can take any action available to them, such as dismissing the management, dismissing members of the board of directors, or dismissing the external auditor (Boshnak, 2017).

The Enforcement Process in Oman

In 1986, all listed companies were obligated to comply with IFRS in preparing their financial statements (Al-Shammari, 2005). Before the establishment of Omani Capital Market Authority (CMA) in 1998, the Ministry of Commerce relied only on the report of the external auditor to express the level of compliance with accounting standards due to the idea that auditors are required to express an opinion toward the level of compliance with IFRS. After forming CMA, the Surveillance Committee was created including representatives from the Ministry of Commerce and representatives from Muscat Securities Market (MSM) to monitor the compliance with IFRS and other regulations (Al-Shammari, 2005).

Both the Surveillance Department of the Ministry of Commerce and the stock market in Oman are responsible for monitoring the compliance with IFRS disclosure requirements of all listed firms. The Surveillance Department uses a confidential checklist, created by the department's staff, to conduct the monitoring process. In case if a non-compliance evidence was detected through the review and the external auditor did not report such non-compliance, the department may contact the company's management and the external auditor to discuss the issue. After the discussion and depending on its result, the department may ask the company's manager to amend the financial statements, and if the manager refused to implement the change, the department may report the case to the Minister of Commerce for assessment and decision through the Surveillance Committee (Boshnak, 2017). The committee has the authority to refer the case to the Disciplinary Committee for further actions, where the latter can enact penalty including warnings, suspension of dealing in the firm's securities, or dis-listing (Boshnak, 2017). In case the external auditor's report was qualified because of a non-compliance issue, a representative from the Ministry of Commerce may attend the annual general meeting and raise the case to shareholders' attention to give them the chance to take further actions, such as dismissing the management, dismissing members of the board of directors, or dismissing the external auditor (Boshnak, 2017).

The Enforcement Process in Qatar

In 1999, IFRS were adopted for all banks and financial institutions structured by Qatar Central Bank (Al-Mannai and Hindi, 2015). The companies' commercial law that issued in 2002 requires all listed companies to prepare their financial statements according to IFRS. In Qatar, a different Surveillance Department is responsible for monitoring firms and banks' financial reporting activities. In 1999, when IAS were adopted for the first time in Qatar, the Central Bank required all banks to have at least two external auditors, from those registered with the Ministry of Commerce, to audit their financial statements and to report any non-compliance with IFRS or other regulations to the Central Bank (Al-Hussaini et al., 2008). A Banking Surveillance Department in the Qatar Central Bank is responsible for monitoring and supervising banks' compliance with IFRS, companies' law, and Central Bank's requirements relying on the external auditors reports (Al-Shammari, 2005).

In 2005, the Qatar Financial Market Authority (QFMA) was established, amended by the decree law No. (14) 2007 and the law No. (10) of 2009, as an independent supervisory and regulatory body over the financial market. In 2012, a repeal of the law of 2005 was issued to expand the authority of QFMA by giving it all the regulatory, supervisory, and control roles over the financial markets, which granted the QFMA more power to conduct its function more effectively and comprehensively through setting the financial reporting requirements (QFMA, 2017). Additionally, it has the authority to impose surveillance and enforcement activities over capital markets. However, the QSE has permitted some Islamic financial institutions to implement accounting standards issued by the Accounting and Auditing Organization for Islamic Financial Institutions (AAOIFI), along with IFRS, if the AAOIFI does not express any issues (IFRS, 2017).

The Enforcement Process in Saudi Arabia

The companies' laws that issued in 1965 obligated all companies to prepare financial statements and allowed a licensed Certified Public Accountant (CPA) auditors to audit these financial statements. In 1968, a resolution was issued by the Ministry of Commerce, which led to the establishment of a higher committee that is responsible for monitoring and supervising accounting and auditing profession in Saudi Arabia (Albader, 2015). In 1992, the Saudi Organization of Certified Public Accountants (SOCPA) was established, it operates under the authority of the Ministry of Commerce. Its main duties are to improve the knowledge and the proficiency of accounting practices in Saudi Arabia and to review and develop the implementation of accounting and auditing standards (SOCPA, 2017). Since the establishment of SOCPA, it has issued 22 accounting standards and 15 auditing and accounting profession standards where all listed firms were required to comply with these standards (SOCPA, 2017). In the case of the existence of accounting issues that are not covered by Saudi Accounting Standard (SAA), SOCAP requires companies to implement IFRS (Albader, 2015).

Moreover, in 2012, SOCPA has built a plan to ensure the efficient transition from Saudi accounting standards, which were formed influenced by GAAP, toward IFRS (Albader, 2015). In this regard, SOCAP reported that in order to overcome the difficulties related to the transition procedures and to ensure an efficient and a smooth transition to IFRS two committees were established, these are Accounting Standards Committee and Auditing Standards Committee, which are responsible for resolving the appropriate procedures through the transition toward IFRS (Albader, 2015). Additionally, SOCPA approved the IFRS convergence to force all listed companies, other than financial institutions, to adopt IFRS with some modifications, such as adding more disclosure requirements, eliminating optional treatments, and adjusting IFRS requirements that contradict with Shariah or local laws (Al-Mannai and Hindi, 2015).

The Enforcement Process in the UAE

Three regulatory bodies in the UAE govern corporate sector, accounting practices, and financial reporting, these are the Ministry of Economy, the UAE Central Bank, and the Securities Commodities Authority (SCA) (Khasharmeh and Aljifri, 2010; Boshnak, 2017). All listed companies in the

UAE have to comply with the federal regulations and rules issued by the Ministry of Economy (Aljifri and Moustafa, 2007). These rules and regulations state the requirements of registration and licensing, the responsibilities and duties of auditors, penalties and disciplinary measure, and other general rules (Boshnak, 2017). The first law issued to govern accounting practices in the UAE was in 1975 entitled 'organizing accountancy and auditing' (Otman, 2014). In 1997, the UAE Accounting and Auditing Association (UAEAAA) was established to help in developing the application of the international accounting standards in the UAE, the aim of this association is to set the laws and regulations related to the performance of listed companies (UAEAAA, 2017). The UAEAAA is the national accounting body for accountants and auditors that recommends the desired accounting standards to the legislative authorities (IFRS, 2017).

The companies' law issued in 1984 did not determine the specific accounting standards or the information that should be implemented by companies in their financial statements, but it required that companies should issue a balance sheet and an income statement (Al-Zarouni, 2009). In 1988, another resolution was released, which requires companies to issue audited financial statements and to provide them to the Ministry of Commerce. Another amendment was made in the year 2000, which requires all listed companies to issue interim financial statements in addition to the annual financial statements. Later, in 2004, all companies were required to adopt IFRS (Al-Zarouni, 2009). Additionally, in 1999, all banks and financial institutions were required to prepare financial statements under IFRS to increase the understandability and comparability of financial statements (Al-Shammari, 2005).

Corporate Governance

Huge efforts were made in GCC countries toward improving their corporate governance codes to be aligned with the rapid growth of the capital markets in these countries (Qurashi, 2017). This was supported by the initiatives taken by the international institutions in helping the MENA region in developing their own corporate governance codes. More specifically, in 2005, Hawkamah, the institute of corporate governance, was established to help the MENA region in developing and implementing integrated corporate governance frameworks in order to overcome the governance gap. The main objective of Hawkamah is to "shape corporate governance practices and framework throughout the region by promoting the core values of transparency, accountability, fairness, disclosure, and responsibility" (Shehata, 2013, pp. 42–43). Another major role of Hawkamah is engaging different governments and industries in forming various corporate governance benchmarks that may be considered motives in enhancing corporate governance practices in the region (Qurashi, 2017). Additionally, a strategic partnership was established between MENA and Organization for Economic Co-operation and

Development (OECD) countries in order to share knowledge and experience about the standards and principles of a good corporate governance, the MENA-OECD program was started in 2005 aiming to enhance the investment environment and to modernize governance structures and operations throughout the MENA region (OECD, 2017).

Corporate Governance Codes in GCC Countries

In Oman, the efforts of improving the issues regarding the lack of transparency and poor internal control started in 1998 by establishing the Omani Capital Market Authority (CMA), which commenced its work in 1999, and it reports to the Minister of Commerce. Among the GCC member states, the Omani (CMA) has developed the first corporate governance code in 2002, which was amended in 2003 (Oyelere and Al-Jifri, 2011). This code was applicable to all listed companies in Muscat Stock Exchange (MSE) and requires these companies to publish a separate section about their corporate governance practices in their annual reports (Shehata, 2013). The Omani corporate governance code includes 11 sections, such as company's philosophy, board of directors, audit committee and other committees, process of nomination of directors, remuneration matters, details of non-compliance, means of communication with shareholders and investors, market price data, specific areas of non-compliance with the provisions of corporate governance and reasons for non-compliance, and professional profile of the statuary of auditor (Shehata, 2015). The Omani CMA has revised the Omani corporate governance code and updated it in 2015, which was planned to be enforced by 2016 (Qurashi, 2017). The new code includes 14 principles that govern the practices of the listed companies in MSE, and they determined the roles and duties of the board of directors, for example; this code has determined that the board of directors is responsible for hiring the higher management positions, setting the objectives of the company, and measuring the performance of board committees.

In Saudi Arabia, until 2006, the main code that was governing companies practices is the code issued in the companies' act of 1965 (Haniffa and Hudaib, 2007). Moreover, Albassam (2014) reported that this companies' act was not governing all the related internal corporate governance mechanisms, as well, the regulations related to protecting shareholders. However, in 2003, Saudi Arabia has established the Capital Market Authority (CMA) to oversight the listed companies in Saudi Arabia stock exchange (AlNodel and Hussainey, 2010). CMA has issued the corporate governance code in 2006, and this code was amended in 2009. The code is applicable to all listed companies on a comply/explain basis and recommends all companies to disclose information about their corporate governance practices in their annual reports (Albassam, 2014). Additionally, this code covers the main principles of OECD, and all listed companies have to report their compliance to this code and to provide justifications in case of non-compliance to the CMA (Hussainey and Al-Nodel, 2008). The Saudi corporate governance code includes 19 articles divided into 5 main sections, which are the following: preliminary provisions, rights of shareholders and general assembly, disclosure and transparency, board of directors, and closing provisions, additionally, in 2012, the Saudi Arabian Monetary Agency (SAMA) has issued its corporate governance practices for banks and financial institutions that operate in Saudi Arabia (Shehata, 2013).

In the UAE, the development of corporate governance was started in 2004 when the corporate governance code drafts were released by Abu Dhabi Securities Market and amended in 2005. Additionally, the Emirates Securities and Commodities Authority (ESCA) had also drafted a corporate governance code that was released in 2007; this code was mandatory and issued on a comply/penalize basis starting from 2010, in other words, listed companies were given a transition period of three years to get adjusted in order to implement and to enforce the new regulations (Shehata, 2013). This code was established to enhance corporate governance practices by companies, it requires listed companies to disclose an integral part, signed by the chairman of the board, in their annual reports describing their compliance with corporate governance code (Hassan, 2011). This part must include information related to the board of directors' duties, composition, structure, and the selection process of directors. In addition to the information related to board committees, internal control system, shareholders rights, and rules governing the external auditor appointment and discharging (Hassan, 2011). In 2009, the most recent issue of corporate governance code was published by ESCA to replace the 2007 code (Hassan, 2009). This code includes 16 articles and these were applicable to all listed domestic non-financial companies other than those wholly owned by government; the new code includes new issues related to the board structure, directors' duties and responsibilities, chief executive officer (CEO) role, and board committees; companies must report to shareholders and to the ESCA about their corporate governance practices (Shehata, 2013). Additionally, in 2009, the Central Bank of the UAE issued the corporate governance guidelines for UAE banks. In 2011, another corporate governance code was published for small and medium enterprises that includes nine corporate governance rules (Shehata, 2015).

In Kuwait, the companies' law issued in 1960 included 12 provisions that were related to corporate governance practices, these provisions were minimal; they addressed issues regarding board elections, their term of office, and the minimum number of annual meetings (Al-Shammari and Al-Sultan, 2010). The awareness of corporate governance in Kuwait is evidenced by the efforts of the Chamber of Commerce and the Union Investment Companies to organize seminars and workshops to enhance the awareness of corporate governance and to raise the need of having a good corporate governance code (Hamdan and Al-Sartawi, 2013). The corporate governance code in Kuwait started to be drafted in 2006 and were expected to be implemented in 2007, however, in 2010, the Kuwaiti Capital Standards Rating Agency had released the corporate governance code on a comply/explain basis (Shehata, 2015). This code was applicable to all listed companies and recommends companies to disclose a separate section in their annual reports about their corporate governance practices; this code includes seven principles of corporate governance, which are as follows: rights of shareholders, ownership structure, equitable treatment of shareholders, role of stakeholders, disclosure and transparency, responsibility of the board, and management effectiveness (Shehata, 2013).

In Bahrain, in order to attract international investments, authorities became aware of the importance of accepting and implementing effective corporate governance practices. Accordingly, the Ministry of Industry and Commerce (MOIC) revised and amended the commercial companies' law in 2001 to address issues related to corporate governance, such as board of directors' election, responsibilities, composition, voting rights, and obligations (Hussain and Mallin, 2002). Additionally, in 2003, the MOIC and the Central Bank of Bahrain (CBB) have funded a project to enhance the awareness of corporate governance in the corporate sector (Qurashi, 2017). In 2006, the National Steering Committee for corporate governance was established under the guidance of the MOIC and CBB in the aim of forming a corporate governance law draft, which was expected to be implemented in 2007. However, the code was not issued until 2010 by MOIC and CBB on a comply/explain basis and was applicable to all listed companies and financial institutions (Shehata, 2013). The code recommends all companies to issue a separate section in their annual reports disclosing their corporate governance practices. This code includes nine principles and five appendices, where seven principles were related to the board of directors, one of them related to the disclosure of corporate governance practices implemented by companies, and the last one was related to the Islamic principles. The five appendices were related to independent directors, audit committee, nominating committee, remuneration committee, and corporate governance disclosure (CBB, 2017).

In Qatar, the efforts of improving corporate governance practices started by the establishment of Qatar Financial Market Authority (QFMA) in 2005, which has drafted the first corporate governance code in 2006 and was expected to be implemented in 2007. Nevertheless, the corporate governance code was released in 2009 (Qurashi, 2017). This code was applicable to all listed companies that are subject to the QFMA on a comply/explain basis. The code includes 31 articles distributed into 10 sections, which are preamble, definitions and scope, compliance with corporate governance, board of directors, internal controls, external auditor, disclosure, shareholders rights, stakeholders' rights, corporate governance report, and code of enforcement; moreover, in 2008, the Central Bank of Qatar has issued the corporate governance guidelines for banks and financial institutions that include 11 sections, these are introduction, definitions, principles of the guidelines, shareholders, board of directors, executive management, internal audit, external audit, stakeholders, transparency and disclosure, and conclusion (Shehata, 2013).

Comparison of Corporate Governance among GCC Member States

In order to provide a better presentation of corporate governance codes in GCC member states, Table 2.3 provides a comparison of the main issues related to corporate governance practices among GCC countries, which are: date of issuance of corporate governance code, the institution issued such code, the legal status of the code, board independence, role of the chairman and CEO, board size, and audit committee.

From Table 2.3, it is clear that the first corporate governance code issued was in Oman in 2002, and the most recent code was in Kuwait and Bahrain. The UAE's code is the only code that issued on the comply/penalize basis. Regarding board composition, it indicates that all the six GCC countries require at least one-third of the directors to be independent and require to separate the role of board chairman and the CEO. For board size, only Bahrain and Saudi Arabia had determined the number of board members, specifically, Bahrain's code has determined that the number of board members should not be more than 15 members, while Saudi Arabia's code requires the number of members not to be less than 3 and not more than 11. Regarding audit committee, all codes require the presence of at least three non-executive members in the committee.

Summary

This chapter has described the major aspects of the environment of GCC countries that are related to the accounting standards and to the corporate governance codes implemented in these countries. It aimed to spotlight on the legislation frameworks of financial reporting as they play an important role in shaping financial reporting outlines and establishing the procedures of monitoring and enforcing accounting standards. Moreover, it described the growth of corporate governance codes issued among GCC member states to provide a comparison of the main issues of these codes.

The chapter started with the identification of the broad economy, capital markets, and legislation of the six countries. The oil export is considered the main source of revenue for all GCC countries. Lately, all GCC countries aimed to attract foreign investments to improve their economies infrastructure and diversify their income sources. Additionally, financial reporting procedures in GCC member states are governed by the companies' laws and securities market law, and in all six countries, the market laws require the board of directors of each listed company to submit annual audited financial statements to the stock exchange authorities within a specific period of time.

Table 2.3 Comparison of corporate governance codes in GCC countries

Country	*Year of Publication*	*Issuing Entity*	*Legal Status*	*Board Independence*	*Role of Chairman and CEO*	*Board Size*	*Audit Committee*
Bahrain	2010	Ministry of Industry and Commerce and Central Bank of Bahrain	Comply/explain basis	At least three independent directors. One-third should be independent in companies with a controlling shareholders	Must be separated	Not more than 15 members	At least three members, the majority independent, and the committee chair should be independent non-executive director
Oman	2002	Capital Market Authority	Comply/explain basis	At least one-third of the board members must be independent or two whichever is greater	Must be separated	Not stipulated	At least three non-executive directors, the majority independent, and the chair of the committee should be independent non-executive
Qatar	2009	Qatar Financial Authority	Comply/explain basis	At least one-third of the board members must be independent	Must be separated	Not stipulated	At least three non-executive directors, the majority independent, and the chair of the committee should be independent non-executive director if the number of available independent members is not sufficient

Saudi Arabia	2006	Capital Market Authority	Comply/explain basis	At least one-third of the board members must be independent or two members whichever is greater	Must be separated	Not less than 3 and not more than 11	At least three non-executive directors
UAE	2009	Ministry of Economy and the Securities and Commodities Authority	Comply/penalize basis	At least one-third of the board members must be independent	Must be separated	Not stipulated	At least three non-executive directors, majority independent, and the chair of the committee should be independent non-executive director
Kuwait	2010	Capital Standards Rating Agency	Comply/explain basis	At least one-third of the board members must be independent, or two members whichever is greater, and one-third for companies with controlling shareholders	Must be separated	Not stipulated	At least three non-executive members, the majority independent, and the chair of the committee should be independent non-executive director and should not be in any other committees

Source: Adapted from Shehata (2013) and Husseinali et al. (2016).

This was followed by a presentation of the accounting standards in GCC countries; IFRS were adopted as mandatory accounting standards for all listed companies in Oman, Kuwait, and Bahrain in 1986, 1991, and 1996, respectively. While Central Banks in Saudi Arabia, Qatar, and the UAE have required banks and financial institutions to adopt IFRS in 1992, 1999, and 1999, respectively. Thereafter, the enforcement and monitoring mechanisms were also discussed; in all GCC countries the Ministry of Commerce is mainly responsible for monitoring companies' compliance with both IFRS disclosure requirements and the companies' law requirements. Finally, a discussion of the growth of corporate governance codes in these countries was presented to clarify the areas of similarities and differences among these codes. Among GCC countries, Oman has developed the first corporate governance code, while Kuwait and Bahrain have developed the most recent ones.

The next chapter highlights the main aspects of the IFRS and the main theories that expressed the factors that may affect the level of compliance with IFRS disclosure requirements. Additionally, it discusses the previous studies that examined the relationship between some firm characteristics and the level of compliance with IFRS.

References

Abu Dhabi Securities Exchange (ADX) (2017). Available: https://www.adx.ae/English/Pages/default.aspx. Accessed: [01/10/2017].

Al Mutawaa, A., & Hewaidy, A.M. (2010). Disclosure level and compliance with IFRSs: An empirical investigation of Kuwaiti companies. *The International Business & Economics Research Journal, 9*(5), 33–50.

Al-Ajmi, J. (2009). Investors' use of corporate reports in Bahrain. *Managerial Auditing Journal, 24*(3), 266–289.

Albader, M. (2015). *Transition to IFRS and its implications for accounting education in Saudi Arabia* (Doctoral dissertation, Victoria University).

Albassam, W. (2014). *Corporate governance, voluntary disclosure and financial performance: Ban empirical analysis of Saudi listed firms using a mixed-methods research design* (Doctoral dissertation, University of Glasgow).

Alfaraih, M. (2009). *Compliance with international financial reporting standards (IFRS) and the value relevance of accounting information in emerging stock markets: Evidence from Kuwait* (Doctoral dissertation, Queensland University of Technology).

Al-Hussaini, A., Al-Shammari, B., & Al-Sultan, W. (2008). Development of enforcement mechanisms following adoption of international accounting standards in the gulf co-operation council member states. *Journal of International Business Strategy, 8*(3), 50–71.

Aljifri, K. (2008). Annual report disclosure in a developing country: The case of the UAE. *Advances in Accounting, 24*(1), 93–100.

Aljifri, K., & Khasharmeh, H. (2006). An investigation into the suitability of the international accounting standards to the United Arab Emirates environment. *International Business Review, 15*(5), 505–526.

Aljifri, K., & Moustafa, M. (2007). The impact of corporate governance mechanisms on the performance of UAE firms: An empirical analysis. *Journal of Economic and Administrative Sciences, 23*(2), 71–93.

Al-Mannai, E.S., & Hindi, N.M. (2015). Adoption of IFRS by listed companies in Qatar: Challenges and solutions. *International Journal of Accounting and Finance, 5*(1), 1–26.

AlNodel, A., & Hussainey, K. (2010). Corporate governance and financing decisions by Saudi companies. *Journal of Modern Accounting and Auditing, 6*(8), 1–14.

Al-Qahtani, A.K. (2005). The development of accounting regulation in the GCC: Western hegemony or recognition of peculiarity?. *Managerial Auditing Journal, 20*(3), 217–226.

Al-Shammari, B.A. (2005). *Compliance with international accounting standards by listed companies in the Gulf Co-operation Council member states: An empirical study* (Doctoral dissertation, University of Western Australia).

Al-Shammari, B., & Al-Sultan, W. (2010). Corporate governance and voluntary disclosure in Kuwait. *International Journal of Disclosure and Governance*, 7(3), 262–280.

Al-Zarouni, A. (2009). *Corporate financial disclosure in emerging markets: The case of the UAE* (Doctoral dissertation, Griffith University).

Bahrain Bourse (2017). Available: http://www.bahrainbourse.com/who-we-are. Accessed: [14/10/2017].

Basher, S.A., & Sadorsky, P. (2006). Oil price risk and emerging stock markets. *Global Finance Journal, 17*(2), 224–251.

Boshnak, H. (2017). *Mandatory and voluntary disclosures in GCC listed firms* (Doctoral dissertation, University of the West of England).

Boursa Kuwait (2017). Available: https://www.boursakuwait.com.kw/BoursaKuwait/Page.aspx?PAGE=39. Accessed: [5/10/2017].

Central Bank of Bahrain (CBB) (2017). Available: http://cbb.complinet.com/cbb/display/display.html?rbid=3274. Accessed: [10/10/2017].

Cooke, T.E., & Wallace, R.O. (1990). Financial disclosure regulation and its environment: A review and further analysis. *Journal of Accounting and Public Policy, 9*(2), 79–110.

Doupnik, T.S., & Salter, S.B. (1995). External environment, culture, and accounting practices: A preliminary test of a general model of international accounting development. *The International Journal of Accounting, 30*, 189–207.

Dubai Financial Market (DFM) (2017). Available: http://www.dfm.ae/market-data/market-data-overview. Accessed: [11/10/2017].

Haak-Saheem, W., Festing, M., & Darwish, T.K. (2017). International human resource management in the Arab Gulf States – an institutional perspective. *The International Journal of Human Resource Management, 28*(18), 2684–2712.

Hamdan, A., & Al-Sartawi, A. (2013). Corporate governance and institutional ownership: Evidence from Kuwait's financial sector. *Jordan Journal of Business Administration, 9*(1), 191–203.

Haniffa, R., & Hudaib, M. (2007). Locating audit expectations gap within a cultural context: The case of Saudi Arabia. *Journal of International Accounting, Auditing and Taxation, 16*(2), 179–206.

Hassan, M. (2009). UAE corporations-specific characteristics and level of risk disclosure. *Managerial Auditing Journal, 24*(7), 668–687.

Hassan, M., Al Shriaan, A., & k Al-Mutairi, A. (2017). An analysis of Kuwait economy 1995-2015. *Asian Social Science, 13*(12), 24–34.

Hassan, M.K. (2011). Corporate governance practices in emerging economies: Initial findings from the UAE. *China-USA Business Review, 10*(9), 856–864.

Herath, S.K., & Alsulmi, F.H. (2017). International financial reporting standards (IFRS): The benefits, obstacles, and opportunities for implementation in Saudi Arabia. *International Journal of Social Science and Business, 2*(1), 1–18.

Hossain, M., & Hammami, H. (2009). Voluntary disclosure in the annual reports of an emerging country: The case of Qatar. *Advances in Accounting, 25*(2), 255–265.

Hussain, S.H., & Mallin, C. (2002). Corporate governance in Bahrain. *Corporate Governance: An International Review, 10*(3), 197–210.

Hussainey, K., & Al-Nodel, A. (2008). Corporate governance online reporting by Saudi listed companies. *Research in Accounting in Emerging Economies, 8*, 39–64.

Husseinali, A., Fah, C.F., Ramadili, S.M., & Chowdury, T.H.S. (2016). Corporate governance reforms and financial reporting quality at Middle East stock markets. *International Journal of Economics, Commerce and Management, 4*(1), 121–138.

IFRS (2017). IFRS application around the world. Available: http://www.ifrs.org/use-around-the-world/use-of-ifrs-standards-by-jurisdiction/united-arab-emirates/. Accessed: [2/11/2017].

Joshi, P.L., Bremser, W.G., & Al-Ajmi, J. (2008). Perceptions of accounting professionals in the adoption and implementation of a single set of global accounting standards: Evidence from Bahrain. *Advances in Accounting, 24*(1), 41–48.

Joshi, P.L., & Wakil, A. (2004). A study of the audit committees' functioning in Bahrain: Empirical findings. *Managerial Auditing Journal, 19*(7), 832–858.

Khasharmeh, H.A., & Aljifri, K. (2010). The timeliness of annual reports in Bahrain and the United Arab Emirates: An empirical comparative study. *The International Journal of Business and Finance Research, 4*(1), 51–71.

Mohamed, E.K., Oyelere, P., & Al-Busaidi, M. (2009). A survey of internet financial reporting in Oman. *International Journal of Emerging Markets, 4*(1), 56–71.

Muscat Clearing and Depositary (MCD) (2017). Available: https://www.mcd.gov.om/page.aspx?i=1. Accessed: [25/10/2017].

Muscat Securities Market (MSM) (2017). Available: https://www.msm.gov.om/. Accessed: [20/10/2017].

Naser, K., & Nuseibeh, R. (2003). Quality of financial reporting: Evidence from the listed Saudi nonfinancial companies. *The International Journal of Accounting, 38*(1), 41–69.

OECD (2017). Organization for Economic Cooperation and Development (OECD). Available: http://www.oecd.org/mena/competitiveness/. Accessed: [5/12/2017].

Otman, K.A.M. (2014). *Corporate governance and firm performance in listed companies in the United Arab Emirates* (Doctoral dissertation, Victoria University).

Oyelere, P., & Al-Jifri, K. (2011). Corporate governance regulation and the timeliness of response to new disclosure requirements. *British Accounting and Finance Annual Conference*, 12–14.

Qatar Financial Market Authority (QFMA) (2017). Available: http://www.qfma.org.qa/English/Pages/default.aspx. Accessed: [15/10/2017].

Qatar Stock Exchange (QSE) (2017). Available: https://www.qe.com.qa/. Accessed: [16/10/2017].

Qurashi, M. (2017). Comparison of corporate governance codes for GCC countries with the UN best practices. *BAM Conference, UK, September, 2017.*

Saudi Organization for Certified Public Accountants (SOCPA) (2017). Available: http://www.socpa.org.sa/Socpa/Home.aspx. Accessed: [20/11/2017].

Shehata, N. (2013). *Corporate governance disclosure in the Gulf countries* (Doctoral dissertation, Aston University).

Shehata, N.F. (2015). Development of corporate governance codes in the GCC: An overview. *Corporate Governance, 15*(3), 315–338.

Strolla & Peri (2016). World Finance Review (May 2016). Available: http://www.worldfinancereview.com/issue/Oman.pdf. Accessed: [05/01/2017].

Tadawul (2017). Available: https://www.tadawul.com.sa/wps/portal/tadawul/about. Accessed: [22/02/2018].

The World Factbook (2017). Available: https://www.cia.gov/library/publications/resources/the-world-factbook/index.html. Accessed: [25/10/2017].

UAE Accounting and Auditing Association (UAEAAA) (2017). Available: http://www.aaa4uae.com/. Accessed: [20/12/2017].

3 International Financial Reporting Standards (IFRS)

Introduction

Annual reports issued by companies are considered the most important official way that companies demonstrate their performance results to the users of financial statements and all stakeholders (Kieso et al., 2010). Whittington (1993) suggested that annual reports are the essential way to deliver quantitative and qualitative data about companies to all stakeholders, which helps them in evaluating the performance of companies' managements. Therefore, given such importance of the information included in the financial statements in forming and building the decisions of the users of these statements, the quality of this information became an important issue in accounting literature.

Moreover, the separation between management and ownership has created the need to ensure the credibility of financial reporting; hence, having one set of accounting standards is essential to ensure the transparency and quality of the financial statements issued by companies as the quality of accounting data is related to the disclosure practices implemented by these companies (Barth et al., 2008). In addition, the cross countries trading and the existence of global stock markets have led to an increase in interest in examining the level of disclosed information in the financial statements (Dahawy and Conover, 2007).

In the past, several countries used their own created set of accounting standards in guiding companies' disclosure practices, which has created barriers in efficiently forming and allocating capital. This implies that to achieve a sufficient capital allocation, investors need relevant information and faithful presentation of financial and non-financial information that enable them to compare the financial statements among their desired companies (Kieso et al., 2010). Accounting standards are considered an important perspective in developing the efficiency of capital markets (Chen et al., 2001; Lin et al., 2019). Accordingly, a single and widely accepted set of high quality accounting standards is needed to achieve a sufficient comparability and to increase the value relevance of the disclosed information. The standard setters regulatory authorities around the world

DOI: 10.4324/9781003211556-3

have recognized that in order to enhance the understandability of financial statements, a single set of high-quality standards had to be developed (Kieso et al., 2010; Chen et al., 2019).

The Concept of IFRS

International financial reporting standards (IFRS) are the international accounting rules issued by the International Accounting Standard Board (IASB), which govern companies' accounting practices around the world (Ball, 2006). IASB is a private institution based in London, the United Kingdom, which is considered the main international accounting standards setting organization in the world. Since 1970s, huge efforts have been made to form one set of high-quality, understandable, and comprehensive accounting standards to serve the public needs of all users of financial statements. In particular, in 1973, the International Accounting Standards Committee (IASC) was established by professional accounting bodies from Australia, Canada, France, Germany, Japan, Mexico, Netherlands, United Kingdom and Ireland, and United States. The IASC issued a set of accounting rules in 1975, these rules were described as the International Accounting Standards (IAS) (Ball, 2006). Later, in 2001, a restructuring occurred to IASC to become IASB. In addition, IAS were restructured to be referred to as the IFRS. The constitution of IASB supported that all the previous standards issued by the previous agreements (IAS) would continue to be applicable unless they are amended or withdrawn by the board. Therefore, in this chapter, when the term IFRS is mentioned, it refers to both the International Financial Reporting Standards and International Accounting Standards.

Organizational Structure of Setting Accounting Standards

The IASB was established by an independent institution called IFRS foundation. The IFRS foundation consists of 22 trustees who provide a supervision over IASB in relation to its structure, strategy, and fund raising resources. IASB consists of 16 members for a five years renewable term, who are selected depending on their background and technical skills, from different countries (Kieso et al., 2010; Paul and Burks, 2010). Moreover, in 1973, in line with the establishment of IASC, the Standard Interpretation Committee (SIC) was established. In 2001, this committee was replaced by the International Financial Standard Interpretation Committee (IFSIC). Later, in 2010, it was renamed to be IFRS Interpretation Committee (IFRSIC). The main roles of this committee are to interpret the application of IFRS and issue guidelines for accounting cases that are not covered by IFRS. In other words, it helps in solving accounting problems as they arise before issuing a consensus to resolve these issues. Additionally, it is responsible for the convergence toward

IFRS through coordinating with national standards setters in different countries. This committee consists of 14 voting members appointed by IFRS foundation trustees (IASplus, 2016).

Furthermore, in 2001, the Standards Advisory Council (SAC) was established. In 2010, it was renamed as the IFRS Advisory Council (IFRSAC). The main objective of such council is to advise the IASB about the priorities of the board's agenda and the major standards setting projects. This council includes 30 or more members appointed by IFRS foundation's trustees for a three years renewable term. Finally, in 2009, the monitoring board was established, which acts as the formal channel between the capital market authorities and the IFRS foundation in order to enhance the foundation's public accountability; additionally, this board is responsible for appointing and monitoring the trustees of IFRS foundation to ensure the fulfilment of their responsibilities toward the IFRS foundation's constitution (IASplus, 2016).

IASB Pronouncements

IASB issues three major types of pronouncements. The first one is the International Financial Reporting Standards (IFRS), these standards aim to cover the new accounting issues that were not covered by IAS, or to amend or replace some of the previous standards issued by IASC before the establishment of IASB in 2001. Until the time we completed data collection, IASB has issued 17 of these standards, in addition to the 41 standards issued by IASC. The second type of pronouncements issued by IASB is the Conceptual Framework of Financial Reporting. This conceptual framework aims to set guidelines for the preparation of financial statements to help in resolving accounting issues that are not addressed by the international accounting standards. More specifically, in case of the absence of a standard or an interpretation applied to a new transaction or new reporting issue, this framework helps management to use its judgment to resolve these issues. Additionally, this conceptual framework defines the objectives of financial reporting and the qualitative characteristics of the disclosed financial information (Kieso et al., 2010). The third pronouncement is the International Financial Reporting Standards Interpretations, which is issued by the IFRSIC. These interpretations are also considered authoritative and must be followed, and they cover new accounting issues not addressed by IFRS and in the absence of authoritative guidance for such issues (Kieso et al., 2010).

Furthermore, regarding the process of issuing new standards, the IASB implements an international due process, which involves the following steps; after an accounting issue that is not addressed by IFRS or the conceptual framework is raised, the IASB investigates the national accounting requirements and practices of this issue, and consults with the national standards setters to decide whether to add it to the standard-setting agenda or not. Then, the IASB consults with IFRS advisory council to form an advisory working group to advise IASB. After that, the IASB publishes a discussion document for public comments followed by an exposure draft for these comments. After considering all of the comments within the specific comment period, IASB holds a public hearing and conducts field tests for additional consultation. Finally, the IASB proceeds to the ballot stage, which requires at least ten votes of the board members to issue the new standard (ACCA, 2013).

National Accounting Standards and IFRS

In the past, several countries have developed their own national accounting standards, more specifically, a number of countries have built their own standards-setting organizations to issue the accounting standards that should be implemented by companies operating in these countries (Kieso et al., 2010). For example, Canada has the Accounting Standards Board, Japan has the Accounting Standards Board of Japan, Germany has the German Accounting Standards Committee, and the United States has the Financial Accounting Standards Board (FASB). According to the literature, the country's national accounting standards are known as the Generally Accepted Accounting Principles (GAAP); in other words, GAAP refers to the common financial accounting and reporting principles that govern the accounting practices in a given environment (ACCA, 2013). The most common type of GAAP is the US GAAP, which was not just used in the United States but also in several other countries.

Notably, the idea that each country has implemented its own accounting standards has created boundaries in comparing the financial statements among companies from different countries as the disclosure practices are different under countries' national standards (Ding et al., 2007). Moreover, the national standards setters issue standards that are oriented by different perspectives; some of them are principle based, rules based, tax based, and business based. This diversity of the bases in building these standards has led to differences in their concepts and objectives (Kieso et al., 2010). Therefore, national standards setters aim to reach to a high level of convergence of their national accounting standards toward the international accounting standards (IASB, 2008).

In this regard, the IASC did two surveys to explore the adoption of IAS around the world. The first survey was conducted in 1988 using a questionnaire executed over 70 countries asking if their companies' financial statements were prepared in accordance to IAS or not, the results of this survey revealed that the majority of countries were applying accounting standards that were consistent with most of the IAS requirements. The second survey was performed in 1996 over 67 countries, and the main results of this survey showed that 56 of the 67 countries were applying IAS as the main reference of the accounting practices or had their own developed standards based on IAS. In addition, it found that only 11 countries had their own standards, which they were developed without reference to IAS (Al-Shiab, 2003). In the year 2000, the International Organization of Securities Commissions recommended securities regulators around the world to permit the use of IAS. In 2005, almost all publicly listed companies in Europe were required to prepare their financial statements in accordance to IFRS. Moreover, FASB has made huge efforts to achieve the convergence between IFRS and US GAAP (Barth et al., 2008), in particular, FASB and IASB signed the Norwalk agreement in 2002, which aimed to unify the accounting practices under both types of standards. In 2007, the Securities Exchange Commission (SEC) ensured the conversion from GAAP to IFRS, and allowed all public US companies and foreign companies the option to use IFRS instead of US GAAP (Paul and Burks, 2010).

In sum, the need for accounting standards that govern the preparation and presentation of financial statements is crucial for each country; however, relying on the national accounting standards (GAAP) for each country limits the ability to understand and compare the financial statements of companies from different countries, since national accounting standards are built depending on the country's own perspectives. Moreover, as a result of internationalization, the existence of multinational companies, and the presence of international investors, the need for one set of accounting standards, that guide the accounting practices around the world, became essential. This was proved by the establishment of IASB in 2001 by professional accounting bodies from different countries, which aimed to issue a unified set of accounting standards to be implemented around the world and to resolve new accounting issues that may appear. Since the establishment of IASB, huge efforts were made to unify the accounting standards to help investors to diversify their investments and compare the financial statements of their desired companies.

Theories Supporting Compliance with IFRS

Different theoretical frameworks have been used in accounting literature to interpret and analyze the level of compliance with IFRS disclosure requirements. Notably, there is no single theory that explains the financial disclosure practices implemented by companies (Al-Htaybat, 2005; Omar and Simon, 2011). In broad terms, each of the following theories interprets the extent of financial disclosure based on different perspectives; however, most of them are based on the fact that the degree of IFRS compliance depends on the costs and benefits of disclosing information (Cooke, 1992; Haniffa and Cooke, 2002). This section presents the main financial reporting theories delivered by previous studies, which are institutional theory, signaling theory, and legitimacy theory.

Institutional Theory

This theory contributes to the literature in terms of explaining why companies tend to adopt similar forms and characteristics (Deegan, 2013). Institutional theory is concerned with the existed values and beliefs of social and organizational life (Scott, 2001; Irvine, 2008). DiMggio and Powell (1983) expanded the concept of isomorphism as the key aspect of institutional theory. This concept assumes that people tend to follow structures and practices that are legitimate and socially accepted by others (Rodrigues and Craig, 2007). Isomorphism is concerned with the values and beliefs of a social environment that affect how companies operate (Al-Omari, 2010). DiMggio and Powell (1983) reported that institutional pressure, where all companies must have the same characteristics, will force companies to shape their activities to be similar to other organizations in the same environment. Additionally, they suggested that isomorphism pressure occurs through three mechanisms, which are coercive, mimetic, and normative isomorphism.

Firstly, coercive isomorphism is related to the expectations that shareholders have about the company, which affect its reporting practices. In other words, companies form their institutional practices as a result of the pressure enforced by stakeholders over these companies (DiMggio and Powell, 1983). Deegan (2013) stated that according to this isomorphism, companies' actions are affected by the economic, social, environmental, and ethical needs and concerns of major stakeholders. Secondly, mimetic isomorphism, which is based on the idea that companies adopt each other's practices in order to enhance their competitive advantage and reduce their level of uncertainty (DiMggio and Powell, 1983; Rodrigues and Craig, 2007). Uncertainty was reported as an effective factor that drives companies to imitate other companies' practices (DiMggio and Powell, 1983). In other words, due to uncertainty and the lack of guidance in an environment, companies tend to imitate the actions of more successful referent companies (Qu et al., 2012). Furthermore, Deegan (2013) concluded that companies will mimic the approaches implemented by the leading companies in their sectors, and this homogeneity in organizational structure enhances stakeholders' perception about the company. Pricope (2016) concluded that the process of the adoption of IFRS is significantly affected by mimetic pressure. The third mechanism is the normative isomorphism; which supports how cognitive backgrounds of individuals affect the practices of a certain profession (Hassan, 2008). This implies that individuals with similar training and education background tend to adopt the same practices, which explains the similarities in reporting approaches (DiMggio and Powell, 1983). Qu et al. (2012) and Herath and Alsulmi (2017) stated that companies' reporting trends are defined by the culture and working practices created by managers in the workplace.

According to the existing literature, developing countries are subject to the three mechanisms of isomorphism from multinational lending agencies, capital markets, the big-four audit firms, and IASB (Irvine, 2008; Judge et al., 2010). In terms of coercive isomorphism, developing countries lie under the pressure of two primary global organizations, which are the World Bank and the International Monetary Fund (Phan, 2014). Scholars have argued that these agencies have driven developing countries to implement IFRS or to develop their own national standards in accordance with IFRS (Perera and Baydoun, 2007; Hassan, 2008; Al-Omari, 2010). For mimetic isomorphism, Al-Omari (2010) suggested that it is the result of the pressure generated by multinational companies. The existence of multinational companies has increased the acceptance of implementing IFRS in the preparation of financial statements and the need for converging toward IFRS. There is evidence that countries are more likely to adopt IFRS if they have trade partners or countries, within their geographical region, that are IFRS adopters (Irvine, 2008; Ramanna and Sletten, 2009). For normative isomorphism, in developing countries' context, it is the pressure generated from professional bodies, educational institutions, and professional training programs (Phan, 2014). In addition, it has been proved by the existing literature that big-four audit companies play a very important role in spreading IFRS globally, which creates a pressure among accounting societies toward IFRS adoption (see, for example, Street and Gray, 2002; Gillis, 2011).

Accordingly, isomorphism explains why countries tend directly to implement similar forms and structures to appear similar to other countries, which supports the idea that countries favor applying the same accounting standards (Pricope, 2016). Thus, institutional theory has been used in the accounting literature to examine the level of the implementation of IFRS (Judge et al., 2010; Lasmin, 2011). This signifies that institutional factors play an important role in the adoption of IFRS, as they will force countries and organizations to be involved in the growth-enhancing process, which means that countries adopt IFRS not just to search for competitive advantage resources and develop their economic performance, but also to become legitimate and socially accepted (Rodrigues and Craig, 2007; Pricope, 2016). More specifically, institutional theory implements the idea that companies' structures and their implemented practices are the results of aiming to gain legitimacy and social acceptance (Scott, 2001). In addition, scholars support the idea that in order for companies to earn legitimacy and social acceptance, they must adopt institutional isomorphism (Rodrigues and Craig, 2007). Failure to do this will lead the company to lose its legitimacy (DiMggio and Powell, 1983; Carruthers, 1995).

Signaling Theory

Previous studies have relied on signaling theory to explain the extent of voluntary disclosure of the company (Omar and Simon, 2011; Aburaya, 2012). Signaling theory deals with the level of information that investors have about the company, and it discusses how to reduce the level of information asymmetry between managers and investors. Specifically, signaling appears as a result of information asymmetry, where managers have more information than stakeholders (Aburaya, 2012). Information asymmetry can be reduced by disclosing more information (signals) to the stakeholders (Morris, 1987). Signaling theory assumes that managers have inside information that investors do not (Kapopoulos and Lazaretou, 2007). The existence of such differences in the level of information between company insiders (such as managers and board members) and outside users (such as investors) creates signaling costs. For example, investors usually evaluate companies according to their perception, which may be higher or lower than the real value of the firm. The latter implies that, for high quality companies, investors may evaluate those companies with lower values than real, and the opposite may happen for low quality firms where investors' perception and the level of information they have may lead to evaluate these companies higher than their real values (Alfaraih, 2009). Therefore, to avoid signaling costs and low valuation of the firm, managers tend to disclose more information (Ross, 1979; Haniffa, 1999). Disclosing more information to investors will signal the company's real value and help the company to promote its high quality performance to enhance investors' perception about the company's profitability and risk (Alfaraih, 2009; Baazaoui and Zaraï, 2019).

Moreover, companies could increase the disclosed (signaled) information to differentiate themselves from other low performance companies; this implies that companies with good performance tend to disclose more information to spread signals to the users of financial statements about their success (Abd-Elsalam, 1999; Haniffa, 1999; Alves, 2011). Companies with good news are expected to disclose more information (Ross, 1979). However, the theory has been criticized for its lack of explanations in relation to some disclosure practices by companies; for example, not disclosing all of the information does not always signify bad intention; the company may hide some valuable information in order not to expose it to competitors (Okcabol and Tinker, 1993). Another criticism of this theory is that it assumes that managers are always acting according to their own interests; it suggests that managers may disclose or hide information just to serve their own benefits (Aburaya, 2012).

Legitimacy Theory

Suchman (1995) defined legitimacy as "a generalized perception or assumption that the actions of an entity are desirable, proper, or appropriate within some socially constructed system of norms, values, beliefs, and definitions" (p. 574). Lindblom (1994) defined legitimacy as "a condition or a status which exists when an entity's value system is congruent with the value system of the larger social system of which the entity is a part. When a disparity, actual or potential, exists between the two value systems, there is a threat to the entity's legitimacy" (p. 2). These definitions provide the main aspect of legitimacy theory, which assumes that there is a social contract between the organization and its society (Kent and Stewart, 2008), and companies are recognized in their societies according to the adequacy of their social activities (Nasi et al., 1997). This stands on the idea that the society has its own rules and regulations, and each company will ensure that its operations are aligned with the norms and the values of the society, and companies will avoid violating the contract in order to avert losing its legitimacy (Branco and Rodrigues, 2006; Alves, 2011).

The main idea of legitimacy theory is that in order for companies to survive they have to operate within the framework of the norms and values of the society that they exist in (Aburaya, 2012). In other words, this theory relies on two main factors, the first one states that companies always tend to perform in accordance with the values and norms of their society. Companies, as a member in the society, are expected not to violate the regulations issued by these societies (Wilmshurst and Frost, 2000). It suggests that companies will always aim to avoid legitimacy costs, which refer to the penalties enforced by the community (Brown and Deegan, 1998). Moreover, legitimacy costs appear if there is a gap between the company's performance and the expectations of the society. Therefore, in order for a company to maintain its legitimacy, it should match its activities with the expectations and the perception of the society (Alves, 2011).

The second factor is that, in order to ensure a company's commitment, a disclosure of the activities implemented by the company to meet its social responsibility should be conducted (Dowling and Pfeffer, 1975). According to Ashforth and Gibbs (1990), disclosing information to the relevant stakeholders is a way for companies to legitimate their activities and their existence. Furthermore, since this theory is concerned with how the company reacts in relation to the expectations of the external environment (Guthrie and Parker, 1989), it looks to financial disclosure as a way to establish a company's legitimacy, and it proposes a relationship between corporate disclosure practices and the community's expectations (Deegan, 2013). Additionally, ensuring that the company is committed to the norms and expectations of the society is another motivation to disclose more information (Deegan and Blomquist, 2006). In other words, this theory supports the idea that the disclosure practices implemented by the company are motivated by gaining social acceptance and meeting the needs of the external users (Hassaan, 2012). Scott (2001) stressed that countries adopt IFRS not just to gain economic benefits but also to earn legitimacy and acceptance in the global markets.

In conclusion, all the previous theories support the idea that disclosing information will help companies to gain major benefits from their relationship with their communities. These theories deal with the image about the company that stakeholders have in their minds. Institutional theory and legitimacy theory are concerned mainly with how the norms, traditions, and values of the society form the disclosure practices implemented by companies, and how usually companies assure that they are not violating these rules and regulations. Meanwhile, signaling theory focuses on disclosing information as a method to differentiate companies with high-quality performance from other companies, and to improve the investors' perception about the company to avoid misevaluation.

Motivations Toward the Adoption of IFRS

As discussed earlier, the convergence toward IFRS has become a crucial issue for accounting standards setters around the world; lately, approximately 130 countries have adopted or committed to adopt IFRS (Pricope, 2016). Hence, several researchers have attempted to examine the benefits of implementing a single set of international accounting standards and reported that applying unified accounting standards is beneficial in serving the public interests of users of financial statements; for instance, they supported that the adoption of one set of accounting standards decreases the variations in national practices that resulted from the diversification of institutional and cultural dimensions (see, for example, Armstrong et al., 2010). Moreover, the IFRS convergence improves market performance, and that's why it is expected that all companies will adopt IFRS in preparing and presenting their financial statements (Edogbanya and Kamardin, 2014). Thus, this section highlights the main aspects of the motivations that justify the need for adopting IFRS.

Accounting Harmonization

According to literature, the main benefit of having one set of international accounting standards is to enhance accounting harmonization among countries, which makes the comparison between companies from different countries easier for the users of financial statements. Accounting harmonization could be defined as the practice of improving the comparability of accounting procedures through minimizing the variations in these procedures (Nobes and Parker, 2008). This implies that the adoption of IFRS enhances the understandability and comparability of financial statements among companies in the same country and among companies from different countries. In this vein, Larson (1993) stated that having one set of accounting practices helps the potential investors in comparing the financial statements issued by their desired companies. Street et al. (1999) and Brown (2006) supported that the adoption of IFRS eliminates the confusion resulted from using different accounting practices and measurements by companies, which provides a comprehensive understanding of evaluating their performance. Isabel and Mariela (2009) and Pichler et al. (2018) asserted that internationalization and globalization are the most important motives for the harmonization of financial statements preparation and presentation. According to Leuz (2003) and Barth (2008), it is easier and less costly for the users of financial statements to understand financial information prepared under one set of international standards in comparison with cost of understanding statements prepared under different domestic standards.

Additionally, accounting harmonization is essential for both local and international users of financial statements who seek for useful financial data about their targeted companies. This stands on the idea that financial information is not limited only for domestic users, but it could also be used by foreign ones. In this respect, Tyrrall et al. (2007) concluded that the existence of one set of accounting standards helps in attracting investors across borders. Moreover, Pricope (2016) asserted that as a result of globalization, the expansion of trade, and the openness to foreign capital markets, investment decisions became not limited only to local users; but also international users may need to access the financial information, which confirms the need to have one set of international accounting standards. Cai and Wong (2010) and Herath and Alsulmi (2017) reported that the adoption of IFRS helps the global financial markets to function more effectively, and they revealed a higher integration among these markets after the adoption of IFRS in comparison with the period before the adoption. Brown (2006) expressed that such adoption reduces the cost of processing the information included in the financial statements and increases the efficiency of capital markets. Street et al. (1999) supported the idea that the adoption of IFRS reduces the boundaries to international investments.

Financial Reporting Quality

Another aspect of the motivations for the adoption of IFRS is the improvements of the quality of financial information, this stands on the fact that the adoption of high-quality standards leads to a higher quality financial reporting, which signifies that financial reports prepared under IFRS are more informative and have higher quality (Barth et al., 2008; Hlel and Nafti, 2019; Mbir et al., 2020). Barth et al. (2008) assessed the effect of the adoption of IAS on the quality of financial reporting, they examined this relation over 21 countries and found that companies which applied IAS evidenced less earnings management and more value relevant information in comparison with non-adopters. In addition, they pointed out that companies implementing IAS showed a comparatively higher level of improvements in the quality of their financial information in the period after the adoption of IFRS than before. Moreover, Wirtanen (2009) reported that there were positive effects of the adoption of IFRS in Finnish companies, and IFRS are considered a comprehensive information package that makes accessing information by management easier for decision-making processes. Additionally, the author suggested that the mandatory adoption of IFRS enhanced accounting information quality. Verriest et al. (2013) supported the idea that the adoption of IFRS gives companies the opportunity to offer a more transparent information to investors.

On the other hand, Jeanjean and Stolowy (2008) conducted research to test the effect of the adoption of IFRS on the quality of financial information in France, the United Kingdom, and Australia. They reported contradictory results; they stressed that after the adoption of IFRS, the level of earnings management in France increased and remained the same in the United Kingdom and Australia, which signifies that there were no real benefits of adopting IFRS on the quality of accounting data in the United Kimgdom and Australia. Barth (2008) suggested that there is no compelling enhancement in the quality of financial reporting system for companies that adopted IFRS in the United States. Paananen and Lin (2009) tested the effect of IFRS on the quality of accounting information in Germany, and they reported that the quality of accounting data decreased after the mandatory adoption of IFRS in Germany. Wang and Campbell (2012) revealed that IFRS implementation did not deter earnings management in Chinese companies.

The justification of the absence of the improvements in the quality of financial information depends on different perspectives, the first one stands on the idea that IAS may be lower quality than domestic standards (Barth et al., 2008). Secondly, the benefits of IFRS adoption are associated with the full compliance with IFRS, not partial compliance (Queku, 2016). Thirdly, having different alternatives of the accounting procedures enables managers to choose among these alternatives, which gives them the opportunity to manipulate accounting numbers. In this vein, Ashbaugh and Pincus (2001) suggested that limiting such alternatives increases the quality of financial reporting through decreasing managers' opportunities to manipulate earnings. Devalle et al. (2016) concluded that the low level of disclosure may be related to the debate that there are too many mandatory disclosure requirements included in IFRS, which gives companies the chance to decide which disclosure requirements are relevant and which are not, subjectively. To resolve this issue, IASC and IASB have issued a set of principle-based standards that aim to remove the allowable alternatives to assure accounting treatments that reflect firms' performance accurately (Barth et al., 2008).

Value Relevance of Accounting Information

The adoption of IFRS has been proved to have an effect in improving the value relevance of information which affects the analysts' forecasting accuracy (Alfaraih, 2009). Christensen et al. (2009) argued that the restatement from the UK GAAP to IFRS provided more relevant information to investors. As well, Wang and Welker (2011) revealed that in both Europe and Australia the restatement from GAAP to IFRS helped companies to provide more relevant information to the users of financial statements. Accounting standards are considered an important feature in developing the efficiency of capital markets (Chen et al., 2001). McKinsey and Company (2002) reported that investors are willing to invest more in companies with sufficient accounting disclosure. The IASB, when setting the accounting standards, ensured that disclosure requirements would make financial reporting more beneficial for investors (Susan, 2011). According to Brown (2006), the adoption of IFRS is useful for small investors when trading with professional investors, this implies that improving the quality of financial information helps those investors in getting the same level of information in comparison to professional ones. Moreover, Hope (2003) argued that the adoption of IFRS enforces companies to apply the rules and regulations of these standards, which helps to detect the level of uncertainty of financial analysts' expectations. In particular, the study found a significant negative relationship between the level of disclosure and the dispersion of forecast errors, additionally, it reported that the high level of disclosure decreases the level of uncertainty of forecasted earnings. The same results were revealed by Myring and Shortridge (2010); who stressed that the adoption of IFRS increases the accuracy of analysts' forecasts. Hodgdon et al. (2008) showed a negative relation between the level of disclosure and analysts' forecasting errors.

In conclusion, having one set of accounting standards has major benefits for all related parties of companies. The internationalization and the increase in number of cross-listed companies in different capital markets require the unification of accounting practices to ease the comparison among companies from different countries. Accounting harmonization helps in reducing the cost of understanding and processing the disclosed information by the users of financial statements, and this enhances the possibility of improving the efficiency of capital markets through attracting foreign investors across borders and reducing the boundaries of international investments. Several scholars have assured that improving the disclosure practices by companies plays a significant role in improving the quality of financial information and decreasing the level of earnings management practices. Meanwhile, some researchers agreed that in order to experience the positive effects of adopting IFRS, a full compliance with all of the disclosure requirements of these standards is a must. Moreover, improving the quality for financial information and improving the level of disclosed information help financial analysts in building their expectations about companies' earnings more precisely.

IFRS Compliance

The disclosure practices implemented by companies are governed by the accounting standards that the company uses as guidelines in preparing its financial statements. Accordingly, a variety of studies have attempted to evaluate the level of the adoption of IFRS in developed and developing countries through examining the extent of disclosure practices applied by companies. According to the literature, there are two types of disclosure: the first one is mandatory disclosure, which could be defined as the obligatory disclosure required by laws and regulations. The existence of such regulations, which force companies to provide information to the users of financial statements, reduces the opportunities for companies to hide information that may be useful to those users (Darrough, 1993). Furthermore, according to Healy and Palepu (2001), mandatory disclosure helps to reduce the information asymmetry between management and the users of accounting data. The second type of disclosure is voluntary disclosure, which is defined as the additional or the optional disclosure motivated by management, which may be advantageous and relevant for decision makers (Graham et al., 2005). Additionally, Depoers (2000) defined voluntary disclosure as the right of shareholders that more information should be disclosed.

Given the importance and the benefits of compliance with IFRS disclosure requirements, this section aims to explore the efforts made by previous researchers to interpret the compliance with IFRS through evaluating the extent of both types of disclosure, mandatory and voluntary. Researchers reported that there are variations in the level of compliance with IFRS; thus, a discussion of the factors that influence the level of compliance with international accounting standards will be highlighted in both developed and developing countries.

IFRS Compliance in Developed Countries

The interest in measuring the level of disclosure adopted by companies started in 1960s; Cerf (1961) could be considered as the pioneering study that attempted to examine this issue. He developed an index of how to measure the extent of a company's disclosure. Later, studies became concerned with developing a theoretical framework that provides a basis of how to explain the disclosure practices of financial information implemented by companies (see, for example, McNally et al., 1982; Cooke, 1989a). The third perspective of the literature was focused on testing the level of compliance with one set of accounting rules (IFRS), and the applicability of these rules to different cultures and environments.

The spread of the international accounting standards among countries and the increase in the number of companies that implemented these standards motivated researchers to examine the level of compliance with IAS/IFRS, especially for companies that claimed to use these standards in preparing their financial statements. More specifically, scholars were interested in testing whether companies that claimed to be IFRS adopters were really complying with all of the disclosure requirements of these standards or not (Glaum and Street, 2003). In this regard, Cairns (1999) investigated the adoption of IAS and revealed nine categories in accordance to the level of compliance of the sampled companies, ranging from full compliance to unqualified description of differences. Examples of these categories are as follows: full IAS compliance, full IAS compliance with exceptions specified in accounting policies, and full IAS compliance with exceptions in the notes of financial statements. Moreover, Street et al. (1999) pointed out that even if the company's accounting footnotes or the auditor's opinion show that the company complied with most or all of the IAS, there were remarkable examples of non-compliance with some measurements and disclosure requirements of individual IAS. In another work, Street and Bryant (2000) examined the level of compliance with IAS of the US companies that claimed to use IAS. Their results showed a compelling level of compliance for companies that disclose in the footnote that they are IAS followers, especially if there was an audit opinion supporting that the financial statements were prepared under IAS. In addition, they suggested that a company should not refer to the usage of IAS unless it applied every single disclosure requirement in the IAS.

Empirically, different studies have tested the level of compliance with the international accounting standards in developed countries; most of these studies showed a low level of compliance with IFRS. For instance, McNally et al. (1982) revealed a low level of voluntary disclosure in New Zealand. Street et al. (1999) examined the level of compliance with IAS in 12 different countries for the year of 1996 using a sample of 49 companies; they found a significant low level of compliance with IAS, and they reported that only 41% of the sampled companies complied with all IAS. Later, Street and Gray (2002) used a larger sample of 279 firms in 32 different countries for the year of 1998 to measure the level of compliance and non-compliance with disclosure and footnotes of IAS; their results showed a non-compliance level with IAS disclosure requirements; the average of compliance was 74%. Tsalavoutas (2011) investigated the level of compliance with IFRS in Greece at the first year of the transition from GAAP into IFRS, and showed that the level of compliance was relatively low. Furthermore, Devalle et al. (2016) conducted a study to test financial statements prepared under IFRS for 189 Italian companies for the year 2010 in order to examine the level of adopting the mandatory disclosure requirements of intangible assets. Their results revealed that there was a low level of compliance with these disclosure requirements.

Moreover, before the mandatory adoption of IFRS in Europe in 2005, some companies voluntarily adopted IFRS while some others were using their countries' own built standards. Thus, some scholars aimed to compare between the level of compliance with IFRS and the level of compliance with GAAP. For example, Glaum and Street (2003) conducted a comparison between the level of compliance with IAS and the level of compliance with German GAAP for a sample of 200 companies in Germany for the year 2000; the sample included 100 companies applying IAS and another 100 companies applying GAAP. The results showed that the level of compliance lay between 41.6% and 100%, with an average of 83.7% for both types of standards. In addition, their results stated that the level of compliance with IAS was lower than the level of compliance with GAAP, in particular, they found that the level of compliance for the companies that use GAAP was 86.6%, and 80.9% for the companies that implemented IAS. Moreover, using a sample of all listed manufacturing and construction companies on the Athens stock exchange in 2004, Apostolou and Nanopoulos (2009) assessed the level of compliance with IAS and the level of compliance with Greek disclosure requirements using two disclosure indices; the first index includes mandatory items according to Greek domestic standards, and the second index includes some items of the international accounting standards requirements. They revealed a significant level of non-compliance with both IAS and domestic standards.

In conclusion, despite the benefits of the adoption of IFRS discussed earlier, there is no evidence for the full compliance with all of the disclosure requirements of IFRS, even for companies that claim to be IFRS adopters. Therefore, scholars have become interested in examining the reasons behind the non-compliance with IFRS. The following section presents a discussion of the main factors reported by previous studies to have an effect on the extent of disclosure implemented by companies in developed countries.

Determinants of IFRS Compliance

Beside the literature that attempted to examine the level of compliance with IFRS, several studies aimed to explore the factors that control the level of compliance with these standards. In broad terms, previous researchers have shown that the variations in the level of compliance are linked to some factors, such as cultural related factors, education, internationality, and the level of proficiency of the accounting profession (see, for example, Zeghal and Mhedhbi, 2006; Daske et al., 2008). In addition, some concluded that the characteristics of companies, such as firm size, firm age, listing status, liquidity, profitability, and industry type also play an important role in determining the level of the adoption of IFRS (Hassaan, 2012). Moreover, Haniffa and Cooke (2002) examined the factors that may affect the level of compliance with IAS, they categorized these factors into five groups: economy, capital markets, accounting and regulatory framework, enforcement mechanisms, and culture. Morris and Gray (2007) conducted a study to examine the level of compliance with IFRS of 519 firms in 12 different countries in 2002; they found that country level variables and firm level variables affected the level of the adoption of IFRS. Additionally, they reported that country level variables, such as the rules and regulations of the accounting practices and the enforcement level over these regulations had a higher effect than the firm level variables. Consequently, this section highlights the main determinants of the level of compliance with IFRS discussed by the previous studies, these include listing status, firm size, industry type, culture and environment, cost-benefit analysis, and cost of capital.

Listing Status

One of the factors that discussed by authors to have an effect on companies' disclosure practices is the listing status (Firth, 1979). In this regard, Cerf (1961) designed a study to examine the determinants of the extent of the company's disclosure using a sample of listed and non-listed US companies; it reported that listed companies have a higher level of disclosure than non-listed companies. The same results were expressed by Singhvi and Desai (1971); they conducted a study of 100 listed companies in the United States, and found that the company's level of disclosure is related to its listing status.

Furthermore, Cooke (1989b) revealed that there is a significant relationship between the listing status of the company and the level of voluntary disclosure. Specifically, he examined the effect of three different types of listing status on disclosure; he divided the sampled companies into three categories according to their listing status, these are listed companies in Stockholm only, non-listed companies, and multiple listed companies. He concluded that non-listed companies practice lower level of disclosure than companies listed in Stockholm only, and the level of disclosure of the companies listed only in Stockholm market is lower than the multiple listed companies, as the latter follow both domestic and foreign regulations. In another work, Cooke (1991) conducted a study using a sample of 48 listed and non-listed Japanese companies for the year 1988, it was asserted that listing status is positively associated with the level of voluntary disclosure. The same results were reported by (Cooke, 1993) in a study performed in Japan for the year 1993.

Additionally, Cooke (1992) reported that publically and cross listed companies lie under the eyes of investors, agents, and other users of accounting information, which enforces these companies to disclose more information, while the pressure over domestic and non-listed companies is relatively lower and that's why they disclose less. Later, Street and Bryant (2000) examined the level of compliance with IAS for companies that claimed to use IAS for a sample of US listed companies and US non-listed companies, their results showed a higher level of disclosure for US listed companies in comparison with the level of disclosure for non-listed companies. On the other hand, Buzby (1975) asserted that there is no association between listing status and the level of financial disclosure in a study conducted using 44 listed and non-listed companies in the United States for the period of 1970–1972.

Firm Size

Another factor that influences the level of disclosure is firm size (Cooke, 1991). In this vein, Cerf (1961) reveled that firm size is the main factor that affects the level of disclosure of the US companies. Likewise, Singhvi and Desai (1971), Buzby (1975), and Arcay and Vazquez (2005) reported that firm size plays an important role in determining the level of disclosure. In the United Kingdom, Firth (1979) conducted a study for the year 1976 in order to investigate the effect of the size of the firm on the level of disclosure; he asserted that there is a positive relationship between firm size and the level of voluntary disclosure. As well, Cooke (1992) pointed out that the bigger the size of the firm the more the disclosed information. In another work, Depoers (2000) conducted a study to review the level of voluntary disclosure of French companies for the year 1992, using a sample of 102 industrial and commercial companies; it was reported that managers tend to disclose more information when the size of the company is bigger and if the company has foreign activities. Alves et al. (2012) have built a disclosure index to examine the determinants of the disclosure practices of Portuguese and Spanish firms, they reported that firm size is one of the main determinants of the level of disclosure. In contrast, McNally et al. (1982) performed a study in New Zealand using a sample of 103 companies for the period of 1974–1979 to examine the level of voluntary disclosure and the effect of some firm characteristics on companies' disclosure practices; they concluded that there is no relation between voluntary disclosure and firm size.

Industry Type

The type of the industry that the company belongs to was one the factors that asserted by scholars to have an effect on the level of compliance with IFRS (Cooke, 1991). Cooke (1992) found that manufacturing companies significantly disclose more information than other types of companies. Industry type affects the level of disclosure from different perspectives. The first one, in the case of high competitive sectors, companies may avoid disclosing information in order not to be exposed to competitors (Omar and Simon, 2011). Moreover, Depoers (2000) reported that companies tend to hide information if it will affect their competitive advantages. The second perspective, in some cases there could be dominant companies in the industry that may lead the disclosure practices of other companies (Omar and Simon, 2011). In addition, Abd-Elsalam (1999) expressed that companies in the same industry tend to adopt the same disclosure policies. On the other hand, McNally et al. (1982), Cooke (1989b) and Anderson and Daoud (2005) reported that there is no association between industry type and the level of disclosure.

Culture and Environment

Environmental and institutional factors of each country were proved by the existing literature to have an effect on the level of compliance with IFRS (see, for example, Zeghal and Mhedhbi, 2006). Some researchers suggested that culture affects the level of compliance with IFRS from two perspectives. Firstly, the differences in cultural backgrounds of the financial statements preparers and users have created different levels of awareness about the importance of financial disclosure (Saudagaran and Meek, 1997). According to Gray (1988), one of the cultural values, depending on Hofstede's (1980) cultural dimensions model, that affects the level of compliance with IFRS is the secrecy versus transparency; the latter implies that companies in general tend to keep confidential information restricted only for the users who are closely involved in managing and financing the company. Moreover, Perera (1989) suggested that the tendency of secrecy affects the extent of disclosure in the accounting reports. Secondly, culture affects the formulation and the enforcement of the laws and regulations settled by authorities at the country level, this signifies that even if the accounting standards are the same, the level of enforcement and the monitoring procedures over the compliance with these standards vary according to countries' cultural backgrounds (Nobes, 2006). Tsalavoutas (2011) pointed out that the high level of non-compliance exposes the need of improving the enforcement mechanisms over the adoption of IFRS. Rahman (1999) reported that as a result of the absence of appropriate enforcement mechanisms in the country, companies may ignore international standards and adopt the accounting practices that suit their own purposes.

Furthermore, Ball et al. (2003) and Daske et al. (2008) argued that for the adoption of IFRS to be effective in enhancing the quality of financial reporting, institutional environment should provide incentives, at the country level, for IFRS adopters. Qu et al. (2012) investigated the level of corporate voluntary disclosure for 297 Chinese companies for the period of 1995–2006; they expressed that companies reacted positively to the enforcements made by market regulatory authorities. In particular, they reported that the level of disclosure increased through the period of the study, as well as, the level of transparency of financial statements. Also, they found that companies tend to adopt high level of disclosure to achieve institutional legitimacy in the economy that they are operating in. Recently, Pricope (2016) stressed that countries adopt IFRS as a result of pressure spread over by economic, social, and political factors. Moreover, she reported that institutional factors play an important role in the adoption of IFRS, relying on the fact that institutions will force countries and organizations to be involved in the growth-enhancing process, which implies that countries adopt IFRS not just to improve their competitive advantage resources or to develop their economics performance, but also to become legitimate and socially accepted.

Cost-Benefit Analysis

Cost and benefit analysis of disclosure practices affects the extent of disclosure in the financial statements (Levinsohn, 2001). In this regard, Depoers (2000) defined this analysis as the trade-off between the incentives to withhold and the incentives to disclose information.

Tsalavoutas (2011) reported a low level of compliance with IFRS in Greece at the first year of the transition from GAAP into IFRS; he suggested that this low level of compliance refers to the high cost of implementing the new standards in comparison with cost of implementing GAAP, and that the new standards require measurements that are different form GAAP's requirements, thus, implementing these requirements increases the cost of disclosing information.

Moreover, some researchers have justified the low level of compliance with the international accounting standards by the existence of some problematic standards. In this respect, Street et al. (1999) reported that the low level of the adoption of IAS could be justified by the existence of some problematic standards to comply with, such as IAS 2 (Inventory in Relation to LCM), IAS 8 (Requirements of Disclosing Profit and Loss for Extraordinary Items), IAS 16 (Disclosure Requirements for Revaluation of Property Plant and Equipment), and IAS 22 (Business Combination). In the same vein, Cairns (2001) reported some problematic standards, such as IAS 12 (Income Tax), IAS 14 (Segment Reporting). As well, Street and Gray (2002) reported some problematic standards, such as IAS 12, IAS 14, IAS 16, IAS 32, and IAS 33. Glaum and Street (2003) have also expressed some problematic standards to apply, such as standards related for pension, leasing, financial instruments, provisions, and contingencies.

Cost of Capital

Cost of capital refers to the ability of the company to acquire capital in case of issuing new shares, Brown and Martinsson (2014) stressed that there is a positive relationship between the level of transparency and the ability of acquiring capital; the more transparent the financial statements the higher the availability of external capital and the lower the cost of capital. Applying full disclosure helps the company to reduce the information asymmetry between managers and investors, which reduces the cost of capital (Diamond and Verrecchia, 1991; Abad et al., 2018). In other words, to decrease the cost of capital the company should provide more information to enhance its market value; users of accounting data need information to evaluate the performance of the firm, specially investors, they need to evaluate their investments in order to decide if the amount they will pay for acquiring the shares worth or not. This may result them to pay lower amount than the real value of the shares, which affects the market value of the firm. Investors are eager to pay higher amount for the shares of companies that disclose more information (Mckinsey and Company, 2002). Thus, companies are motivated to disclose more information to avoid the undervaluation of their shares (Alfaraih, 2009). In addition, not providing full disclosure of information creates information asymmetry and makes the company's shares unattractive to investors, which affects the liquidity of the company in case of issuing new shares (Petersen and Plenborg, 2006).

In conclusion, the level of compliance with IFRS is determined by two types of factors, some of them are internal factors such as firm size, the level of accounting proficiency of financial statements preparers, and the cost of implementing the new standards. External factors, such as culture, industry type, enforcement mechanisms, and users' perception about the company. Culture and rules and regulations were proved to have a significant influence in determining the commitment of companies to prepare their financial statements in accordance to the requirements of IFRS. Moreover, culture and enforcement level justify the variations in the level of IFRS adoption among countries, where cultural backgrounds of financial statements issuers and the users affect the quality of the disclosed information. Firm size and listing status also have major effects on the extent of disclosed information. According to prior studies, big companies tend to provide higher level of disclosure. In addition, listed companies disclose more information as they are under the eyes of the users of financial statements, and multi listed companies have a higher level of disclosure due to the fact that they are committed to follow the rules and regulations of their domestic countries and foreign ones. Furthermore, the image of the company that investors have determine its trend of disclosure practices, this implies that companies disclose more information to avoid the misevaluation of their shares. Finally, cost-benefit analysis derives how the company reacts to the implementation of the new standards.

IFRS Compliance in Developing Countries

As discussed previously, the adoption of IFRS has major benefits for all users of financial statements in developed countries; however, some researchers suggested that it is not necessary that users of financial statements in developing countries will gain the same rewards from applying one set of accounting standards. For example, Irvine and Lucas (2006) argued that IFRS were designed for high-income countries, therefore, they may not be beneficial for local users of financial statements in developing countries. Likewise, Kapaya (2000) reported that these international accounting standards could not be considered an effective tool of enhancing the quality of accounting practices in developing countries.

Furthermore, Al-Shiab (2003) expressed that IFRS is hard to be implemented in developing countries because they are settled upon the experience of developed countries. Pricope (2016) suggested that IFRS were created by high-income countries and common law legal systems, which makes the implementation of IFRS in countries with different cultures and different regulations debatable. Moreover, the shortened capabilities of applying IFRS in these countries may lead to the possibility of not experiencing the desired economic benefits and outcomes of implementing these standards (Dahawy and Conover, 2007). According to Irvine and Lucas (2006), this lack of relevance, for some economic situations in developing countries, is related to the high cost of the adoption of IFRS. Chamisa (2000) supported that the limited applicability of IFRS in developing countries is the result of the differences in their cultural backgrounds, their geographical locations, and their development stages.

On the other hand, Peasnell (1993) argued that since developing countries do not have a strong accounting structure, it would be very beneficial for these countries to apply IAS. Chamisa (2000) stated that the adoption of IAS in developing countries is not to reach for accounting harmonization, but it is mainly to improve the accounting practices in these countries. Moreover, Alsaqqa and Sawan (2013) examined the effect of moving from the adoption of GAAP to IFRS in the UAE. They tested the advantages and challenges of adopting these standards in Abu Dhabi and Dubai stock markets; they reported that such adoption enhances the relevancy, reliability, comparability, and understandability of accounting reports, which improves investors' confidence in companies' managements. In addition, they expressed that IFRS provide more disclosure details than GAAP, which improves the decision-making process.

Empirically, the results of the previous studies that examined the level of compliance with IFRS in developing countries revealed general results. For example, Fekete et al. (2008) used a sample of Hungarian companies and reported that the level of compliance for these companies is on average 62%. Abdullah et al. (2012) examined the level of compliance with IFRS in Malaysian companies through testing the annual reports of public listed companies and meeting with accounting practitioners; their results showed that none of the sampled companies comply fully with IFRS requirements, and the most problematic standards are the following: IAS 36 (Impairment of Assets), IAS 17 (Leases), and IAS 19 (Employees Benefits). In another study that was applied in the Nigerian context, Edogbanya and Kamardin (2014) found a high level of compliance with IFRS in Nigerian financial institutions. Hasan et al. (2013) also showed that the level of disclosure has been improved in Bangladeshi listed firms, but it is still below the expectations and there is still a need to improve the level of reliability and transparency of the financial reporting of these companies.

Consequently, researchers attempted to examine the factors that affect the level of disclosure in developing countries. Cooke and Wallace (1990) pointed out that accounting practices and disclosure insights in developing countries are more influenced by external factors. Culture was one of the major factors that researchers linked to the variations in the level of compliance between developed and developing countries. These variations are the results of the differences in their national cultural and the desired outcomes for these countries (Alsaqqa and Sawan, 2013). Moreover, Pricope (2016) investigated the effect of institutional factors on the level of compliance with IFRS using a sample of 97 developing countries for the year 2013; it was reported that the adoption of IFRS is driven by the institutional isomorphism not by the economic benefits.

Moreover, the effectiveness of the regulatory bodies plays a significant influence in guiding the disclosure practices in developing countries. According to Abd-Elsalam and Weetman (2003), there is a high possibility of non-compliance with disclosure requirements of IFRS in developing countries due to the inadequate regulatory framework, weak enforcement mechanisms, and the existence of inefficient markets in these countries; thus, enhancing the role of these regulatory bodies is essential. Al-Shiab (2003) asserted that the low enforcement levels and the low level of accounting knowledge of accounting users make these standards hard to be implemented in developing countries. Furthermore, firm size has a significant influence on governing the disclosure practices of companies; Fekete et al. (2008) concluded that big companies experience the benefits of IFRS adoption more than small companies, hence, they tend to disclose more information. Industry type also was evidenced to hinder the extent of disclosure in the financial statements, Fekete et al. (2008) reported that high tech companies showed better compliance than other types of companies in Hungary.

IFRS Compliance in the Middle East

The studies that examined the level of compliance with IFRS in the Middle East revealed an acceptable level of adopting the mandatory disclosure requirements and a significant non-compliance level with the voluntary disclosure requirements, and most of them have demonstrated that the level of compliance has been improved during the recent years (Al-Akra et al., 2010). For example, Abdelrahim et al. (1997) conducted a study on 22 Kuwaiti listed companies to examine the extent of IAS adoption by these companies in 1995; they tested the level of compliance with the disclosure requirements of three standards, which are IAS 16 (accounting for property, plant, and equipment), IAS 20 (accounting for government grants and disclosure of government assistance), and IAS 23 (borrowing costs); they found that companies fully comply with the mandatory requirements of these standards but not with the voluntary ones. In the same context, Alfaraih (2009) performed a study in Kuwait to test the level of compliance with IFRS for all listed companies in the country for the year 2006; it was found that the average level of compliance of Kuwaiti companies lay between 49% and 92% with an average of 72.6%. Additionally, the study revealed that most of Kuwaiti companies comply with mandatory requirements of IFRS and there is no firm fully complied with all of IFRS requirements. Furthermore, Al Mutawaa and Hewaidy (2010) used 48 listed companies in Kuwait to examine the level of disclosure in the financial statements for the year 2006; they found that the overall compliance level for these companies was 69% of the disclosure requirements that they examined.

Furthermore, using a sample of 168 listed companies in Turkey for the year 2011, Demir and Bahadir (2014) revealed that the level compliance with IFRS requirements for these companies lay between 64% and 94% with an average of 79%. In Jordan, Omar and Simon (2011) reported that the level of compliance was 69%, and it has been increased in comparison with the results of the previous studies. In another work, Al-Akra et al. (2010) examined the level of compliance with the mandatory disclosure requirements of companies listed in Amman Stock Exchange for the years 1996 and 2004; they found that the level of compliance with the mandatory disclosure requirements significantly increased through the period of study.

Dahawy and Conover (2007) conducted a study to examine the level of the adoption of the mandatory market requirements of the Capital Market Authority (CMA) in Egypt; they stated that the level of disclosure averaged 61% of these requirements. In another work, Samaha et al. (2012) reviewed the level of disclosure for listed companies in Egypt and found a high level of compliance with the mandatory disclosure requirements and low level with voluntary disclosure requirements. Joshi and Al-Mudhahki (2013) used a sample of 37 listed companies in Bahrain and reported a fair level of adoption of the disclosure requirements of IAS 1 (presentation of financial statements). Shankaraiah and Rao (2002) examined the practices of accounting standards in Oman; they pointed out that accounting disclosure policies are implemented by almost all of the sampled companies. In the same context, Al-Jabri and Hussain (2012) stated that Omani listed companies do not fully comply with the requirements of IFRS, and the average of the level of compliance, among the sampled companies, was 79% and the lowest level of compliance was 41%. Apart from the studies that examined the level of compliance with IFRS in one country, Al-Shammari (2005) performed a cross countries study, he attempted to test the level of compliance with IFRS in GCC member states for the period of 1996–2002, using a sample of 137 companies. He concluded that the average level of compliance among all of the sampled firms was 75%. Additionally, he found that the level of compliance increased during the period of the study from 68% in 1996 to 82% in 2002. In another work, Boshnak (2017) reported that the level of compliance with IFRS in GCC countries increased between the years 2010 and 2013 from 72% to 74%.

In conclusion, the studies that examined the level of compliance with IFRS in the Middle East showed a compelling level, and they reported that the level of adoption of IFRS has been increased during the years. However, none of them revealed that companies fully complied with all of the disclosure requirements of IFRS. Following is a discussion of the factors that affect the level of adopting IFRS disclosure requirements in the Middle East.

Determinants of IFRS Compliance in the Middle East

A number of studies were conducted to examine the factors that affect the level of adopting the disclosure requirements of IFRS in the Middle East. Firm size, cultural dimensions, industry type, and cost of implementing these standards were proved to have major roles in governing the extent of disclosure practices. Hence, following is a discussion of the empirical results of the previous studies that examined the effect of these factors on the level of compliance with IFRS mandatory disclosure requirements in the Middle East.

FIRM SIZE

Firm size is considered the main feature among other firm characteristics that affect the level of disclosure (Hassan, 2009; Al Mutawaa and Hewaidy, 2010; Demir and Bahadir, 2014). Al-Shammari (2005) and Alfaraih (2009) found that there is a significant relationship between company's size and the level of compliance with IFRS. Alsaqqa and Sawan (2013) reported that small-sized companies tend not to comply with IFRS due to the difficulty and high cost of implementing these standards in comparison with big-sized companies. Al-Shiab (2003), Omar and Simon (2011), and Alhazaimeh et al. (2014) examined the effect of some firm characteristics on the extent of disclosure in Jordan; they reported that firm size has a significant positive impact on the level of disclosure. In addition, they pointed out that firm size is the main factor that explains the variations in disclosure practices of Jordanian companies, relying on the idea that investment decisions motivate large companies to disclose more information than smaller firms as the former need to attract more capital. Similarly, Al-Jabri and Hussain (2012) concluded that large companies in Oman tend to show more compliance with IFRS to increase their marketability and to enhance their abilities in obtaining capital. Joshi and Al-Mudhahki (2013) divided their sampled companies according to their size, and found that larger companies have a higher level of compliance and tend to disclose more information. However, Al-Moataz and Hussainey (2012) did not detect a significant association between firm size and disclosure practices.

CULTURE AND ENVIRONMENT

According to the existing literature, cultural perspectives and the level of enforcement in the Middle Eastern countries have a significant influence on the level of the adoption of IFRS. In this regard, Dahawy and Conover (2007) asserted that culture makes companies selective in choosing the standards to comply with, and the low level of compliance with IFRS disclosure requirements of the listed companies in Egypt can be justified based on the idea that international accounting standards, to some limit, are inconsistent with the Egyptian culture and with the needs of Egyptian investors. Shankaraiah and Rao (2002) reported that the adoption of IAS in Oman without looking into their relevance in the context of Oman creates domestic problems and indigenousness; they suggested that for IAS to be effective when implemented, a study of the relevance of the context where they will be applied is important. Moreover, they pointed out that there are some disclosure requirements depend on personal judgments of the financial statements prepares, for example, some standards require to disclose all material amounts, and what is material and immaterial is a matter of relativity, which differs according to the personal judgment. Thus, the existence of the variations in personal judgments, which depends on the values, experience, and accounting proficiency level of financial statements prepares, create a doubt in the quality of financial reporting and affect the comparability among companies. In the same vein, Alsaqqa and Sawan (2013) revealed that the adoption of IFRS is influenced by the level of users' education and their level of knowledge about the international accounting standards. Meanwhile, they reported that the lack of knowledge about accounting profession generates difficulties in implementing IFRS in relation to increasing the costs needed by companies to train their accounting staff to be familiar with the requirements of these standards and to keep them updated with new amendments of these standards.

Moreover, culture influences the formulation and the enforcement of laws and regulations in the country (Al-Omari, 2010). Therefore, the extent of enforcement strategies was tested by scholars to examine its effect on the adoption of IFRS. For example, Alsaqqa and Sawan (2013) reported that compliance with IFRS is determined by the competence level of enforcement bodies. Moreover, Demir and Bahadir (2014) reported that the average of compliance of Turkish companies is lower than the average compliance of other Middle Eastern countries, and they pointed out that this is due to the low level of enforcement mechanisms in Turkey. Samaha et al. (2012) concluded that the low level of voluntary disclosure requirements in Egypt is due to the inadequate framework. In Jordan, Omar and Simon (2011) revealed that the level of compliance in Jordanian companies increased as a result of the changes in the Jordanian economy, represented by the establishment of new regulatory agencies aiming to enhance the ability of achieving investment goals and to establish a well-planned investment environment. In Oman, Al-Jabri and Hussain (2012) reported that non-compliance is the result of the inadequate enforcement mechanisms. Al-Shammari (2005) asserted that the variations in the level of compliance in GCC countries refer to the differences in their institutional frameworks and regulations.

INDUSTRY TYPE

Industry type also was one of the factors that reported by prior studies to have an effect on companies' disclosure practices (Al-Shammari, 2005). Al-Shiab (2003) reported that, in Jordan, companies operating in mining industry and building equipment industry disclose more information than other industries, and he explained this fact relying on the idea that companies in these industries are involved heavily in foreign investments and they lie under the pressure of foreign investors; therefore, they tend to disclose information more than other types of companies. Using a sample of 145 listed companies in Amman Stock Exchange for the year 2003, Omar and Simon (2011) also reported that industrial companies disclose more information than services companies and this is attributed to the idea that their nature and activities complexity are different from services companies, and there are some standards that are applicable only for manufacturing companies. In Kuwait context, Alfaraih (2009) reported that there are significant differences in the level of compliance with IFRS among the five industry categories, which implies that the type of the industry where the company operates affects its level of compliance with the disclosure requirements of IFRS. In the same context, Al Mutawaa and Hewaidy (2010) sated that there is a significant positive association between the level of compliance with IFRS and the type of industry. Haddad et al. (2015) pointed out that companies operating in certain types of industries disclose more information in their annual reports than others, which implies that industry type is significantly associated with the level of disclosure.

COST-BENEFIT ANALYSIS

The cost of adopting some standards was also another factor that has been examined by scholars. Shankaraiah and Rao (2002) suggested that it is better to make some accounting standards easier to implement in order to achieve the desired benefits of adopting these standards. Alfaraih (2009) found that the level of compliance varies among the measured accounting standards, and this could refer to the cost and difficulty of implementing some standards. Omar and Simon (2011) reported that companies disclose more information if the benefits of presenting information exceed the cost of hiding it.

Moreover, Al-Jabri and Hussain (2012) addressed that the lack of compliance with IFRS is the result of the difficulties in understanding some standards' requirements or it is due to the lack of resources needed to keep financial statements preparers updated with the changes in these standards. Furthermore, they concluded that non-compliance also might be justified by the cost-benefit analysis of implementing and non-implementing these standards; in other words, if the cost of compliance is higher than the cost of non-compliance, in terms of penalties, companies will choose not to implement these standards. Al-Shammari (2005) expressed a deviation in the level of compliance among standards, the highest level of compliance (the average is higher than 80%) was for IAS 1, IAS 16, IAS 18, IAS 23, IAS 24, IAS 27, and IAS 30, while the lowest level of compliance (the average is lower than 50%) was for IAS 14, and IAS 37, and he referred the high level of compliance with some standards to the fact that they are less difficult to implement and require lower cost.

In conclusion, the variations in the cultural values are considered the main reason behind the differences in the extent of disclosure practices between companies and among countries. The existence of personal judgments in some standards has created difficulties in comparing between companies as they vary according to the cultural values and the level of accounting knowledge of both users and preparers of financial statements. In addition, firm size also has a significant influence in determining the level of implementing the disclosure requirements; it was proved that big companies tend to disclose more information than small ones. Furthermore, the high cost of implementing some disclosure requirements and the existence of some problematic standards have led to limit the adoption of IFRS in the Middle East. Additionally, it was evidenced that companies' disclosure practices differ according to the type of industry that they are operating in.

Table 3.1 summarizes the previous studies that have examined financial disclosure and IFRS compliance, including the author(s) and the year of each study, the country where the research was conducted, the sample size, the variables tested, and the main findings of each study.

Summary

This chapter has provided an extensive overview of the existing literature that attempted to examine the level of compliance with IFRS. It aimed to highlight the main aspects of the disclosure practices among companies in order to provide the needed framework to form our propositions, and help in interpreting the results regarding the level of compliance with IFRS.

The chapter started with providing an overview of the concept of IFRS and the organizational structure of the agencies who are responsible for issuing these standards. This was followed by a differentiation between the countries' national accounting standards (which are called GAAP) and IFRS, and the benefits of convergence from GAAP toward IFRS.

Thereafter, this chapter delivered an overview of the previous studies that examined the level of compliance with IFRS in both developed and developing countries and the major factors that affect such a compliance. The previous literature of IFRS compliance revealed variations in the level of compliance with IFRS among countries and asserted that the level of disclosure has to be improved. Moreover, they revealed that there is a low level of the full compliance with all of the disclosure requirements of IFRS.

In both developed and developing countries, previous studies have showed that the level of compliance varies among companies because of two types of factors; internal factors, such as firm size, the level of accounting proficiency of financial statements preparers, and the cost of implementing these standards. The other type is external factors, such as listing status, industry type, and culture. Cultural structure was proved to have the main impact on the variations in the level of compliance among countries as the level of compliance with IFRS is significantly related to the national culture and country's regulations that form the enforcement mechanisms of the disclosure requirements of IFRS.

Table 3.1 A chronological summary of empirical studies relates to financial disclosure and IFRS compliance

Author(s) Year	*Country*	*Sample*	*Independent Variables (measures)*	*Findings*
McNally et al. (1982)	New Zealand	103	Firm size Industry type Growth Audit type Rate of return	The level of disclosure is very low. Firm size has a significant influence on the level of compliance with mandatory disclosure requirements. The other independent variables have insignificant influence.
Cooke (1989a)	Sweden	93	Listing status Firm size Industry type	Listing status and firm size have a significant influence on the extent of disclosure. 60% of the disclosure is explained by the independent variables.
Cooke (1989b)	Sweden	90	Firm size Industry type Listing status	Only listing status and firm size have significant effect.
Cooke (1991)	Japan	48	Firm size Listing status Industry type	All the independent variables have a positive influence on the level of voluntary disclosure.
Cooke (1992)	Japan	35	Firm size Listing status Industry type	Large companies, multi listed companies and manufacturing companies disclose more information.
Cooke (1993)	Japan	48	Listing status	Multiple listed companies disclose more information.
Abd-Elsalam (1999)	Egypt	72	Firm size Listing status Audit firm size	Firm size, listing status, audit firm size are positively related to the level of mandatory disclosure.
Street et al. (1999)	12 countries	49		The degree of compliance by companies that claim to adopt IFRS is very mixed. Important areas of noncompliance with the measurement and disclosure of IAS.

				National standard setters and regulator need to work more closely to eliminate the significant differences between national accounting guidelines.
Chamisa (2000)	Zimbabwe	NA		The benefits of the adoption of IFRS in developing countries depend on the needs and ends expected from such adoption and the specific national environment where they will be applied. IFRS are more irrelevant for countries where the public sector is the dominant while it is more relevant for countries where the private sector dominates and there capital markets exists.
Street and Bryant (2000)	United States	82		The level of disclosure is high for US listed companies. The existence of audit opinion or the existence of footnote that express that the company is using IFRS in preparing it financial statements are highly associated with high level of adoption of IFRS.
Street and Gray (2002)	United States	279	Auditor size Listing status	There is a significant effect of the listing status on the level of disclosure. Companies audited by big audit firms disclose more information.
Ball et al. (2003)	Hong Kong, Malaysia, Singapore, and Thailand	2726		To avoid the idea that the adoption of IAS does not guarantee high-quality financial information, IAS adopters should drastically alter their enforcement mechanisms, political, legal, and economic institutions affecting reporting incentives.
Glaum and Street (2003)	Germany	200	Audit firm size Listing status Firm size	There is a low level of compliance for companies that apply IAS in comparison with companies that apply US GAAP. Audit firm size, listing status have a positive effect on the level of compliance

(Continued)

Table 3.1 (Continued)

Author(s) Year	*Country*	*Sample*	*Independent Variables (measures)*	*Findings*
				Firm size doesn't have a significant influence on the disclosure practices.
Zeghal and Mhedhbi (2006)	NA	64 developed countries	Economic growth Education level The degree of external economic openness Cultural membership in a group of countries The existence of capital markets	Education level, the existence of capital markets, and cultural membership have a significant positive effect on the adoption of IFRS. While for no significant effect of economic growth, and external economic openness on the adoption of IFRS.
Dahawy and Conover (2007)	Egypt	15	NA	Low level of compliance with IAS. The extent of disclosure range from 52% to 76% with an average of 62%.
Daske et al. (2008)	26 countries	656 country-month observations		Mandatory adopters of IFRS face a significant increase in their market liquidity and Tobin's q after IFRS became mandatory and a decrease in there cost of capital.
Fekete et al. (2008)	Hungary	18	Corporate size Industry type	Both independent variables are significantly associated with the extent of compliance with IFRS disclosure requirements. Big high tech companies comply best with IFRS.
Alfaraih (2009)	Kuwait	163	Leverage Profitability Firm size	The average compliance with IFRS mandatory disclosure requirements is 72.6% for the year 2006. Leverage, profitability, and firm size are positively related to the level of compliance with IFRS disclosure requirements.

Al Mutawaa and Hewaidy (2010)	Kuwait	48	Company size Profitability Leverage Liquidity Type of industry Type of auditor Company age	The average level of compliance is 69% of the disclosure requirements of the 12 standards tested by the researchers. Firm size and industry type are significantly positively related with IAS disclosure requirements. Other independent variables are statistically insignificant.
Armstrong et al. (2010)	European Countries	3265		The adoption of IFRS in European countries increased the quality of information and decreased the information asymmetry.
Omar and Simon (2011)	Jordan	145	Firm size Leverage Profitability Number of shareholders Listing status Industry type	All the independent variables have a significant effect on the aggregate level of disclosure.
Tsalavoutas (2011)	Greece	153	Auditor firm size	The average level of compliance with IFRS mandatory disclosure requirements is approximately 80%. Audit firm size and big audit are positively related to the level of compliance with IFRS.
Abdullah et al. (2012)	Malaysia	225		The overall level of compliance in Malaysian companies is 88% using dichotomous method and 84% using partial compliance method. None of the Malaysian companies comply fully with IFRS. There are some problematic standards and they found that this low level of compliance resulted from the high cost of implementing such standards, some financial statements preparer ignore some disclosure requirements, norms in business practices.

(*Continued*)

Table 3.1 (Continued)

Author(s) Year	*Country*	*Sample*	*Independent Variables (measures)*	*Findings*
				Despite the noncompliance of IFRS Malaysian companies still receive clean audit reports which indicates the low level of enforcement mechanisms. The adoption of IFRS does not necessary leads to increase the quality of financial reporting because of the different incentives in the adoption of IFRS.
Al-Jabri and Hussain (2012)	Oman	94		Omani companies don't fully comply with IAS requirements because of the lack of the proper enforcement level. The average level of compliance is 79%. The lack of compliance is also the result of low non-compliance costs and of the difficulties to interpret some accounting standards. Although they found differences in the level of compliance among individual companies because of (1) small companies don't have the required resources to implement accounting standards and (2) large companies tend to show more compliance with IAS to increase it marketability in capital markets in order to enhance their abilities to obtain capital.
Alves et al. (2012)	Spain and Portugal	140	Firm size Growth opportunities Organizational performance The presence of large shareholders Board compensation	All the independent variables affect the level of voluntary disclosure

Qu et al. (2012)	China	297	Listing status	Listed firms disclose more information. Companies adopt disclosure requirements to earn institutional legitimacy.
Alsaqqa and Sawan (2013)	UAE	245 Questionnaire was distributed to 20 banking sector 131 listed firms 45 external auditor 49 financial analysts		The benefits of adopting IFRS exceeds their cost and difficulties. The adoption of IFRS has improved the quality of financial information which helped in attracting more investors to UAE.
Joshi and Al-Mudhahki (2013)	Bahrain	37	Firm size	There is a high level of compliance with the disclosure requirement of IAS 1 in respect of components of financial statements, comparability, compliance, and stock information. Lager companies tend to disclose more information.
Devalle et al. (2016)	Italy	189		Low compliance with the intangible assets mandatory disclosure requirements. May be there are too many disclosure requirements in the current versions of IFRS which gives companies too much subjectivity to decide which items are relevant and which are not.

(*Continued*)

Table 3.1 (Continued)

Author(s) Year	*Country*	*Sample*	*Independent Variables (measures)*	*Findings*
Pricope (2016)	97 developing countries	NA	Institutional pressures	The process of IFRS compliance in developing countries is influenced by mimetic pressures. While coercive and normative pressures are not significant determinants of IFRS adoption.
Mbir et al. (2020)	Ghana	23	Firm size Leverage	The sampled companies did not attain the desired level of financial reporting quality after the adoption of IFRS. The lack of proper enforcement over the implementation of IFRS will limit the compliance with IFRS and improving the quality of financial reporting. Leverage and firm size have a negative relationship between firm size and financial reporting quality.

Source: Developed by the authors.

The next chapter highlights the main aspects of the corporate governance and the main corporate governance codes that companies have to implement in both developed and developing countries.

References

Abad, D., Cutillas-Gomariz, M.F., Sánchez-Ballesta, J.P., & Yagüe, J. (2018). Does IFRS mandatory adoption affect information asymmetry in the stock market? *Australian Accounting Review, 28*(1), 61–78.

Abdelrahim, A.M., Hewaidy, A.M., & Mostafa, G.N. (1997). The relevance of international accounting standards to the evaluation of fixed assets in Kuwait corporations. *Arab Journal of Administrative Sciences, 5*(1), 53–96.

Abd-Elsalam, O.H. (1999). *The introduction and application of international accounting standards to accounting disclosure regulations of a capital market in a developing country: The case of Egypt* (Doctoral dissertation, Heriot-Watt University).

Abd-Elsalam, O.H., & Weetman, P. (2003). Introducing International Accounting Standards to an emerging capital market: Relative familiarity and language effect in Egypt. *Journal of International Accounting, Auditing and Taxation, 12*(1), 63–84.

Abdullah, M., Sulaiman, N.A., Ismail, K., & Sapiei, N.S. (2012). Compliance with International Financial Reporting Standards (IFRSs) in a developing country: Evidence from Malaysia. *Journal of Accounting Perspectives, 5*(1), 23–34.

Aburaya, R. (2012). *The relationship between corporate governance and environmental disclosure: UK evidence* (Doctoral dissertation, Durham University).

ACCA (2013). Diploma in International Financial Reporting. *Becker Professional Education.*

Al Mutawaa, A., & Hewaidy, A.M. (2010). Disclosure level and compliance with IFRSs: An empirical investigation of Kuwaiti companies. *The International Business & Economics Research Journal, 9*(5), 33–50.

Al-Akra, M., Eddie, I.A., & Ali, M.J. (2010). The association between privatisation and voluntary disclosure: Evidence from Jordan. *Accounting and Business Research, 40*(1), 55–74.

Alfaraih, M. (2009). *Compliance with international financial reporting standards (IFRS) and the value relevance of accounting information in emerging stock markets: Evidence from Kuwait* (Doctoral dissertation, Queensland University of Technology).

Alhazaimeh, A., Palaniappan, R., & Almsafir, M. (2014). The impact of corporate governance and ownership structure on voluntary disclosure in annual reports among listed Jordanian companies. *Procedia-Social and Behavioral Sciences, 129*, 341–348.

Al-Htaybat, K. (2005). *Financial disclosure practices: Theoretical foundation, and an empirical investigation on Jordanian printed and internet formats* (Doctoral dissertation, University of Southampton).

Al-Jabri, H., & Hussain, M.M. (2012). Compliance with international accounting standards requirements among Omani listed companies. *Journal of Administrative and Economics Science, 5*(2), 75–105.

Al-Moataz, E., & Hussainey, K. (2012). Determinants of corporate governance disclosure in Saudi companies. *Journal of Economics and Management, 5*(1), 52–84.

Al-Omari, A.M. (2010). The institutional framework of financial reporting in Jordan. *European Journal of Economics, Finance and Administrative Sciences, 22*(1), 32–50.

Alsaqqa, I., & Sawan, N. (2013). The advantages and the challenges of adopting IFRS into UAE stock market. *International Journal of Business and Management, 8*(19), 1–23.

Al-Shammari, B.A. (2005). *Compliance with international accounting standards by listed companies in the Gulf Co-operation Council member states: An empirical study.* (Doctoral dissertation, University of Western Australia).

Al-Shiab, M. (2003). *Financial consequences of IAS adoption: The case of Jordan* (Doctoral dissertation, Newcastle University).

Alves, H.R.A.M., Rodrigues, A.M., & Canadas, N. (2012). Factors influencing the different categories of voluntary disclosure in annual reports: An analysis for Iberian Peninsula listed companies. *Tékhne, 10*(1), 15–26.

Alves, H.S.A. (2011). *Corporate governance determinants of voluntary disclosure and its effects on information asymmetry: An analysis for Iberian Peninsula listed companies* (Doctoral dissertation, Universidade de Coimbra, Portugal).

Anderson, M., & Daoud, M. (2005). *Corporate governances disclosure by Swedish listed corporations* (Master thesis, Jonkoping International Business School, Jonkoping University, Sweden).

Apostolou, A.K., & Nanopoulos, K.A. (2009). Voluntary accounting disclosure and corporate governance: Evidence from Greek listed firms. *International Journal of Accounting and Finance, 1*(4), 395–414.

Arcay, M.R.B., & Vazquez, M.F.M. (2005). Corporate characteristics, governance rules and the extent of voluntary disclosure in Spain. *Advances in Accounting, 21*, 299–331.

Armstrong, C.S., Barth, M.E., Jagolinzer, A.D., & Riedl, E.J. (2010). Market reaction to the adoption of IFRS in Europe. *The Accounting Review, 85*(1), 31–61.

Ashbaugh, H., & Pincus, M. (2001). Domestic accounting standards, international accounting standards, and the predictability of earnings. *Journal of Accounting Research, 39*(3), 417–434.

Ashforth, B.E., & Gibbs, B.W. (1990). The double-edge of organizational legitimation. *Organization Science, 1*(2), 177–194.

Baazaoui, H., & Zaraï, M.A. (2019). The effect of firm characteristics on the disclosure of IAS/IFRS information: The cases of Tunisia, France and Canada. *International Business and Accounting Research Journal, 3*(2), 124–153.

Ball, R. (2006). International Financial Reporting Standards (IFRS): Pros and cons for investors. *Accounting and Business Research, 36*(supl. 1), 5–27.

Ball, R., Robin, A., & Wu, J.S. (2003). Incentives versus standards: Properties of accounting income in four East Asian countries. *Journal of Accounting and Economics, 36*(1), 235–270.

Barth, M.E. (2008). Global financial reporting: Implications for US academics. *The Accounting Review, 83*(5), 1159–1179.

Barth, M.E., Landsman, W.R., & Lang, M.H. (2008). International accounting standards and accounting quality. *Journal of Accounting Research, 46*(3), 467–498.

Boshnak, H. (2017). *Mandatory and voluntary disclosures in GCC listed firms* (Doctoral dissertation, University of the West of England).

Branco, M., & Rodrigues, L. (2006). Communication of corporate social responsibility by Portuguese banks: A legitimacy theory perspective. *Corporate Communications: An International Journal, 11*(3), 232–248.

Brown, A.M. (2006). The financial milieu of the IASB and AASB. *Australian Accounting Review, 16*(38), 85–95.

Brown, J.R., & Martinsson, G. (2014). *Financial Disclosure, Corporate Transparency, and Innovation.* Working paper, Iowa State University, January 14.

Brown, N., & Deegan, C. (1998). The public disclosure of environmental performance information—a dual test of media agenda setting theory and legitimacy theory. *Accounting and Business Research, 29*(1), 21–41.

Buzby, S.L. (1975). Company size, listed versus unlisted stocks, and the extent of financial disclosure. *Journal of Accounting Research, 13*(1), 16–37.

Cai, F., & Wong, H. (2010). The effect of IFRS adoption on global market integration. *International Business & Economics Research Journal (IBER), 9*(10), 25–34.

Cairns, D. (1999). Degrees of compliance. *Accountancy: International Edition, 124*(1273), 114–118.

Cairns, D. (2001). *International accounting standards survey 2000: An assessment of the use of IAS in the financial statements of listed companies.* David Cairns International Financial Reporting: Henley on Thames.

Carruthers, B.G. (1995). Accounting, ambiguity, and the new institutionalism. *Accounting, Organizations and Society, 20*(4), 313–328.

Cerf, A.R. (1961). *Corporate reporting and investment decisions.* Public Accounting Research Program, Institute of Business and Economic Research, University of California.

Chamisa, E.E. (2000). The relevance and observance of the IASC standards in developing countries and the particular case of Zimbabwe. *The International Journal of Accounting, 35*(2), 267–286.

Chen, C., Lee, E., Lobo, G.J., & Zhu, J. (2019). Who benefits from IFRS convergence in China? *Journal of Accounting, Auditing & Finance, 34*(1), 99–124.

Chen, C.J., Chen, S., & Su, X. (2001). Is accounting information value-relevant in the emerging Chinese stock market? *Journal of International Accounting, Auditing and Taxation, 10*(1), 1–22.

Christensen, H.B., Lee, E., & Walker, M. (2009). Do IFRS reconciliations convey information? The effect of debt contracting. *Journal of Accounting Research, 47*(5), 1167–1199.

Cooke, T.E. (1989a). Disclosure in the corporate annual reports of Swedish companies. *Accounting and Business Research, 19*(74), 113–124.

Cooke, T.E. (1989b). Voluntary corporate disclosure by Swedish companies. *Journal of International Financial Management & Accounting, 1*(2), 171–195.

Cooke, T.E. (1991). An assessment of voluntary disclosure in the annual reports of Japanese corporations. *The International Journal of Accounting, 26*(3), 174–189.

Cooke, T.E. (1992). The impact of size, stock market listing and industry type on disclosure in the annual reports of Japanese listed corporations. *Accounting and Business Research, 22*(87), 229–237.

Cooke, T.E. (1993). Disclosure in Japanese corporate annual reports. *Journal of Business Finance & Accounting, 20*(4), 521–535.

Cooke, T.E., & Wallace, R.O. (1990). Financial disclosure regulation and its environment: A review and further analysis. *Journal of Accounting and Public Policy, 9*(2), 79–110.

Dahawy, K., & Conover, T. (2007). Accounting disclosure in companies listed on the Egyptian stock exchange. *Middle Eastern Finance and Economics, 1*(1), 5–20.

Darrough, M.N. (1993). Disclosure policy and competition: Cournot vs. Bertrand. *Accounting Review, 68*(3), 534–561.

Daske, H., Hail, L., Leuz, C., & Verdi, R. (2008). Mandatory IFRS reporting around the world: Early evidence on the economic consequences. *Journal of Accounting Research, 46*(5), 1085–1142.

Deegan, C. (2013). *Financial accounting theory*. McGraw-Hill Education Australia.

Deegan, C., & Blomquist, C. (2006). Stakeholder influence on corporate reporting: An exploration of the interaction between WWF-Australia and the Australian minerals industry. *Accounting, Organizations and Society, 31*(4-5), 343–372.

Demir, V., & Bahadir, O. (2014). An investigation of compliance with International Financial Reporting Standards by listed companies in Turkey. *Accounting and Management Information Systems, 13*(1), 4–34.

Depoers, F. (2000). A cost benefit study of voluntary disclosure: Some empirical evidence from French listed companies. *European Accounting Review, 9*(2), 245–263.

Devalle, A., Rizzato, F., & Busso, D. (2016). Disclosure indexes and compliance with mandatory disclosure—the case of intangible assets in the Italian market. *Advances in Accounting, 35*, 8–25.

Diamond, D.W., & Verrecchia, R.E. (1991). Disclosure, liquidity, and the cost of capital. *The Journal of Finance, 46*(4), 1325–1359.

DiMggio, P., & Powell, W. (1983). The iron cage revisited: Institutional isomorphism and collective rationality in organizational fields. *American Sociological Review, 48*(2), 147–160.

Ding, Y., Hope, O.K., Jeanjean, T., & Stolowy, H. (2007). Differences between domestic accounting standards and IAS: Measurement, determinants and implications. *Journal of Accounting and Public Policy, 26*(1), 1–38.

Dowling, J., & Pfeffer, J. (1975). Organizational legitimacy: Social values and organizational behavior. *Pacific Sociological Review, 18*(1), 122–136.

Edogbanya, A., & Kamardin, H. (2014). Adoption of international financial reporting standards in nigeria: Concepts and issues. *Journal of Advanced Management Science, 2*(1), 72–75.

Fekete, S., Matis, D., & Lukac, J. (2008). Factors influencing the extent of corporate compliance with IFRS: The case of Hungarian listed companies. *Annales Universitatis Apulensis Series Oeconomica, 1*(10), 1–12.

Firth, M. (1979). The impact of size, stock market listing, and auditors on voluntary disclosure in corporate annual reports. *Accounting and Business Research, 9*(36), 273–280.

Gillis, P.L. (2011). *The Big Four in China: Hegemony and counter – hegemony in the development of the accounting profession in China* (Doctoral dissertation, Macquarie University Sydney, Australia).

Glaum, M., & Street, D.L. (2003). Compliance with the disclosure requirements of Germany's new market: IAS versus US GAAP. *Journal of International Financial Management & Accounting, 14*(1), 64–100.

Graham, J.R., Harvey, C.R., & Rajgopal, S. (2005). The economic implications of corporate financial reporting. *Journal of Accounting and Economics, 40*(1), 3–73.

Gray, S.J. (1988). Towards a theory of cultural influence on the development of accounting systems internationally. *Abacus, 24*(1), 1–15.

Guthrie, J., & Parker, L.D. (1989). Corporate social reporting: A rebuttal of legitimacy theory. *Accounting and Business Research, 19*(76), 343–352.

Haddad, A.E., AlShattarat, W.K., AbuGhazaleh, N.M., & Nobanee, H. (2015). The impact of ownership structure and family board domination on voluntary disclosure for Jordanian listed companies. *Eurasian Business Review, 5*(2), 203–234.

Haniffa, R.M. (1999). *Culture, corporate governance and disclosure in Malaysian corporations* (Doctoral dissertation, University of Exeter).

Haniffa, R.M., & Cooke, T.E. (2002). Culture, corporate governance and disclosure in Malaysian corporations. *Abacus, 38*(3), 317–349.

Hasan, M.S., Hossain, S.Z., & Swieringa, R.J. (2013). Corporate governance and financial disclosures: Bangladesh perspective. *Research Journal of Finance and Accounting, 4*(1), 109–119.

Hassaan, M. (2012). *Corporate governance and compliance with International Financial Reporting Standards (IFRSs): Evidence from two MENA stock exchanges* (Doctoral dissertation, Aston University).

Hassan, M. (2008). The development of accounting regulations in Egypt: Legitimating the International Accounting Standards. *Managerial Auditing Journal, 23*(5), 467–484.

Hassan, M. (2009). UAE corporations-specific characteristics and level of risk disclosure. *Managerial Auditing Journal, 24*(7), 668–687.

Healy, P.M., & Palepu, K.G. (2001). Information asymmetry, corporate disclosure, and the capital markets: A review of the empirical disclosure literature. *Journal of Accounting and Economics, 31*(1), 405–440.

Herath, S.K., & Alsulmi, F.H. (2017). International financial reporting standards (IFRS): The benefits, obstacles, and opportunities for implementation in Saudi Arabia. *International Journal of Social Science and Business, 2*(1), 1–18.

Hlel, K., & Nafti, I.K. (2019). Board characteristics, IFRS adoption and voluntary disclosure: Evidence from management forecasts accuracy in France. *International Journal of Management and Enterprise Development, 18*(1/2), 41–62.

Hodgdon, C., Tondkar, R.H., Harless, D.W., & Adhikari, A. (2008). Compliance with IFRS disclosure requirements and individualanalysts' forecast errors. *Journal of International Accounting, 17*(1), 1–13.

Hofstede, G. (1980). *Culture's consequences: International differences in work-related values.* Newbury Park, CA: Sage.

Hope, O.K. (2003). Accounting policy disclosures and analysts' forecasts. *Contemporary Accounting Research, 20*(2), 295–321.

IASplus (2016). IFRS Interpretations Committee. Available: https://www.iasplus.com/en-gb. Accessed: [2/10/2016].

International Accounting Standards Board (IASB) (2008). *International accounting standards and SIC interpretations.* London: IASC.

Irvine, H. (2008). The global institutionalization of financial reporting: The case of the United Arab Emirates. *Accounting Forum, 32*(2), 125–142.

Irvine, H.J., & Lucas, N. (2006). *The rationale and impact of the adoption of International Financial Reporting Standards: The case of the United Arab Emirates* (University of Wollonglon Australia).

Isabel, S., & Mariela, I. (2009). Implementation of IFRS for non-financial companies and its impact on financial stability and monitoring at the Central Bank of Chile. *Central Bank of Chile, SDFP*, 1–26.

Jeanjean, T., & Stolowy, H. (2008). Do accounting standards matter? An exploratory analysis of earnings management before and after IFRS adoption. *Journal of Accounting and Public Policy, 27*(6), 480–494.

Joshi, P.L., & Al-Mudhahki, J. (2013). Empirical study of compliance with international accounting standards (IAS-1) by stock exchange listed companies in Bahrain. *Journal of Financial Management & Analysis, 26*(2), 43–54.

Judge, W., Li, S., & Pinsker, R. (2010). National adoption of international accounting standards: An institutional perspective. *Corporate Governance: An International Review, 18*(3), 161–174.

Kapaya, G. (2000).'International Accounting Standards and Accounting in Developing/Emerging Nations-How About Fresh Start?'. *Discussion Paper Series: Accounting and Finance*. No. 9. September. Middlesex University Business School.

Kapopoulos, P., & Lazaretou, S. (2007). Corporate ownership structure and firm performance: Evidence from Greek firms. *Corporate Governance: An International Review, 15*(2), 144–158.

Kent, P., & Stewart, J. (2008). Corporate governance and disclosures on the transition to international financial reporting standards. *Accounting & Finance, 48*(4), 649–671.

Kieso, D.E., Weygandt, J.J., & Warfield, T.D. (2010). *Intermediate accounting: IFRS edition* (Vol. 2). John Wiley & Sons.

Larson, R.K. (1993). International accounting standards and economic growth: An empirical investigation of their relationship in Africa. *Research in Third World Accounting, 2*(24), 165–179.

Lasmin, D. (2011). An institutional perspective on international financial reporting standards adoption in developing countries. *Academy of Accounting and Financial Studies Journal, 15*(2), 61–71.

Leuz, C. (2003). IAS versus US GAAP: Information asymmetry–based evidence from Germany's new market. *Journal of Accounting Research, 41*(3), 445–472.

Levinsohn, A. (2001). FASB weighs the value of voluntary disclosure. *Strategic Finance, 82*(9), 73–74.

Lin, S., Riccardi, W.N., Wang, C., Hopkins, P.E., & Kabureck, G. (2019). Relative effects of IFRS adoption and IFRS convergence on financial statement comparability. *Contemporary Accounting Research, 36*(2), 588–628.

Lindblom, C.K. (1994). The implications of organizational legitimacy for corporate social performance and disclosure. In *Critical Perspectives on Accounting Conference, New York* (Vol. 120).

Mbir, D.E.G., Agyemang, O.S., Tackie, G., Abeka, M.J., & Ntim, C.G. (2020). IFRS compliance, corporate governance and financial reporting quality of GSE-listed non-financial firms. *Cogent Business & Management,* 7(1), 1–18.

McKinsey & Company, J. (2002). *Global investor opinion survey: Key findings*. London: McKinsey & Company.

McNally, G.M., Eng, L.H., & Hasseldine, C.R. (1982). Corporate financial reporting in New Zealand: An analysis of user preferences, corporate characteristics and disclosure practices for discretionary information. *Accounting and Business Research, 13*(49), 11–20.

Morris, R.D. (1987). Signalling, agency theory and accounting policy choice. *Accounting and Business Research, 18*(69), 47–56.

Morris, R.D., & Gray, S.J. (2007). Corporate transparency differences in the Asian region: The feasibility of global standardization in practice. In *AFAANZ Conference, Gold Coast, July*.

Myring, M., & Shortridge, R.T. (2010). Corporate governance and the quality of financial disclosures. *The International Business & Economics Research Journal, 9*(6), 103.

Nasi, J., Nasi, S., Phillips, N., & Zyglidopoulos, S. (1997). The evolution of corporate social responsiveness: An exploratory study of Finnish and Canadian forestry companies. *Business & Society, 36*(3), 296–321.

Nobes, C. (2006). The survival of international differences under IFRS: Towards a research agenda. *Accounting and Business Research, 36*(3), 233–245.

Nobes, C., & Parker, R.H. (2008). *Comparative international accounting*. Pearson Education.

Okcabol, F., & Tinker, T. (1993). Dismantling financial disclosure regulations: Testing the Stigler-Benston hypothesis. *Accounting, Auditing & Accountability Journal, 6*(1), 10–38.

Omar, B., & Simon, J. (2011). Corporate aggregate disclosure practices in Jordan. *Advances in Accounting, 27*(1), 166–186.

Paananen, M., & Lin, H. (2009). The development of accounting quality of IAS and IFRS over time: The case of Germany. *Journal of International Accounting Research, 8*(1), 31–55.

Paul, A., & Burks, E. (2010). Preparing for international financial reporting standards. *Journal of Finance and Accountancy, 4*, 1–8.

Peasnell, K.V. (1993). Accounting in developing countries: The search for appropriate technologies. *Research in Third World Accounting, 2*, 1–16.

Perera, H., & Baydoun, N. (2007). Convergence with international financial reporting standards: The case of Indonesia. *Advances in International Accounting, 20*, 201–224.

Perera, M.H.B. (1989). Towards a framework to analyze the impact of culture on accounting. *The International Journal of Accounting, 24*(1), 42–56.

Petersen, C., & Plenborg, T. (2006). Voluntary disclosure and information asymmetry in Denmark. *Journal of International Accounting, Auditing and Taxation, 15*(2), 127–149.

Phan, D. (2014). What factors are perceived to influence consideration of IFRS adoption by Vietnamese policymakers? *Journal of Contemporary Issues in Business and Government, 20*(1), 27–40.

Pichler, S., Cordazzo, M., & Rossi, P. (2018). An analysis of the firms-specific determinants influencing the voluntary IFRS adoption: Evidence from Italian private firms. *International Journal of Accounting, Auditing and Performance Evaluation, 14*(1), 85–104.

Pricope, C.F. (2016). The role of institutional pressures in developing countries. Implications for IFRS. *Theoretical and Applied Economics, 22*(2), 27–40.

Qu, W., Cooper, B.J., Wise, V., & Leung, P. (2012). Voluntary disclosure in a changing regulatory environment – evidence from Chinese stock market. *International Journal of Economics and Finance, 4*(4), 30.

Queku, I., (2016) Review of compliance measure in empirical accounting literature: Perspective of international financial reporting standards. *Research Journal of Finance and Accounting*, 7(14), 59–66.

Rahman, M.Z. (1999). *The role of accounting disclosure in the East Asian financial crisis: Lessons learned?* Geneva: United Nations Conference on Trade and Development.

Ramanna, K., & Sletten, E. (2009). Why do countries adopt international financial reporting standards? *Harvard Business School Accounting & Management Unit Working Paper*, (09-102).

Rodrigues, L.L., & Craig, R. (2007). Assessing international accounting harmonization using Hegelian dialectic, isomorphism and Foucault. *Critical Perspectives on Accounting, 18*(6), 739–757.

Ross, S. (1979). Disclosure regulation in the financial markets: Implications of modern finance theory and signaling theory in Edwars F., 1979. *Issues in Financial Regulation.* New York: Mc Graw Hill, 177–202.

Samaha, K., Dahawy, K., Hussainey, K., & Stapleton, P. (2012). The extent of corporate governance disclosure and its determinants in a developing market: The case of Egypt. *Advances in Accounting, 28*(1), 168–178.

Saudagaran, S.M., & Meek, G.K. (1997). A review of research on the relationship between international capital markets and financial reporting by multinational firms. *Journal of Accounting Literature, 16*, 127–159.

Scott, W.R. (2001). *Institutions and organizations* (2nd ed.). Thousand Oaks, CA: SAGE Publications.

Shankaraiah, K., & Rao, D.N. (2002). Corporate governance and accounting standards in Oman: An empirical study on practices. Available at SSRN 480522.

Singhvi, S.S., & Desai, H.B. (1971). An empirical analysis of the quality of corporate financial disclosure. *The Accounting Review, 46*(1), 129–138.

Street, D.L., & Bryant, S.M. (2000). Disclosure level and compliance with IASs: A comparison of companies with and without US listings and filings. *The International Journal of Accounting, 35*(3), 305–329.

Street, D.L., & Gray, S.J. (2002). Factors influencing the extent of corporate compliance with International Accounting Standards: Summary of a research monograph. *Journal of International Accounting, Auditing and Taxation, 11*(1), 51–76.

Street, D.L., Gray, S.J., & Bryant, S.M. (1999). Acceptance and observance of international accounting standards: An empirical study of companies claiming to comply with IASs. *The International Journal of Accounting, 34*(1), 11–48.

Suchman, M.C. (1995). Managing legitimacy: Strategic and institutional approaches. *Academy of Management Review, 20*(3), 571–610.

Susan, M. (2011). *Research in Social Problems and Public Policy*. Emerald Group Publishing Limited.

Tsalavoutas, I. (2011). Transition to IFRS and compliance with mandatory disclosure requirements: What is the signal?. *Advances in Accounting, 27*(2), 390–405.

Tyrrall, D., Woodward, D., & Rakhimbekova, A. (2007). The relevance of International Financial Reporting Standards to a developing country: Evidence from Kazakhstan. *The International Journal of Accounting, 42*(1), 82–110.

Verriest, A., Gaeremynck, A., & Thornton, D.B. (2013). The impact of corporate governance on IFRS adoption choices. *European Accounting Review, 22*(1), 39–77.

Wang, S., & Welker, M. (2011). Timing equity issuance in response to information asymmetry arising from IFRS adoption in Australia and Europe. *Journal of Accounting Research, 49*(1), 257–307.

Wang, Y., & Campbell, M. (2012). Corporate governance, earnings management, and IFRS: Empirical evidence from Chinese domestically listed companies. *Advances in Accounting, 28*(1), 189–192.

Whittington, G. (1993). Corporate governance and the regulation of financial reporting. *Accounting and Business Research, 23*(supl. 1), 311–319.

Wilmshurst, T.D., & Frost, G.R. (2000). Corporate environmental reporting: A test of legitimacy theory. *Accounting, Auditing & Accountability Journal, 13*(1), 10–26.

Wirtanen, J. (2009). *The influence of IFRS implementation on business management in Finnish born globals* (M.S. thesis, Helsinki school of Economics).

Zeghal, D., & Mhedhbi, K. (2006). An analysis of the factors affecting the adoption of international accounting standards by developing countries. *The International Journal of Accounting, 41*(4), 373–386.

4 Corporate Governance

Introduction

The separation between ownership and management has created the agency problem; eliminating such a problem and protecting shareholders' interests can be done through enhancing companies' corporate governance practices, which will eliminate the conflict of interests between management and shareholders (Fama and Jensen, 1983; Karamanou and Vafeas, 2005). Having a good corporate governance ensures that companies are responsibly managing their affairs (Aly et al., 2022) and serves the benefits of all of the stakeholders from different perspectives. First, it protects the owners' rights by detecting managers' opportunities to manipulate the resources of the company and by increasing shareholders' trust in managers. Second, a good corporate governance enhances the confidence of investors in companies' managers, which provides the company with the needed capital to achieve the desired economic development through attracting more investors (Jensen and Meckling, 1976; Haniffa, 1999).

The Concept of Corporate Governance

Corporate governance is defined as the process of setting the strategies for achieving the company's objectives in the long run, planning how to achieve these objectives, and ensuring that these plans are followed (Tricker, 1984). In addition, Tricker concluded that corporate governance includes monitoring and supervising management's performance and disclosure, and that corporate governance represents the accountability toward parties who made legitimate claims to the company. Furthermore, corporate governance involves 'a set of relationships between a company's management, its board, its shareholders, and other stakeholders. Corporate governance also provides the structure through which the objectives of the company are set, and the means of attaining those objectives and monitoring performance are determined' (OECD, 2015: p. 9). In the same vein, corporate governance is defined as a 'set of principles that concerning governing companies and how these principles are disclosed or communicated externally' (Parum, 2005: p. 702).

DOI: 10.4324/9781003211556-4

According to OECD (2015), there are two sets of factors that affect management activities and corporate performance. First, internal corporate factors, which are related to the effectiveness of the interaction among management, board of directors, shareholders, and other stakeholders. Such factors include board of director characteristics, such as board size, board composition, chief executive officer (CEO) duality, ownership structure, and audit committee. Second, external corporate governance factors that play a significant role in supporting and encouraging good corporate governance. These factors include laws, regulations, and external auditor quality.

Corporate Governance Principles

The Organization for Economic Co-operation and Development (OECD) has made remarkable efforts in reviewing and improving the effectiveness of corporate governance; these efforts started in the mid of 1999s through setting the principles of corporate governance to enhance the legal and institutional framework. These principles were related to the identification of corporate governance practices that should be implemented in both public and private companies in order to improve the efficiency of capital markets and the stability of the entire economy (Tariff, 2006; Shanikat and Abbadi, 2011). In 2004, the OECD has revised these principles and issued another version in order to help countries in developing their legal, institutional, and regulatory frameworks (Otman, 2014). Later, the current revision of these principles was released in 2015.

The existence of such principles is advantageous from different aspects; first, these principles help in protecting the rights of shareholders and limiting the expropriation of the company's resources by management. Second, the implementation of these principles assists companies in improving their reputations and competitive advantages. Third, a good corporate governance eases the company's accessibility to the needed resources (Hassaan, 2012). These principles were designed to be adaptable to different cultural and institutional aspects, and they provide the needed guidelines for countries to help them in implementing these principles (Jesover and Kirkpatrick, 2005). Therefore, all corporate governance practices followed by companies are based on the following six corporate governance principles demonstrated by OECD; these principles assist companies to gain credibility in confirming the application of the internationally accepted principles (Hassaan, 2012). These principles could be summarized as follows:

Ensuring the Basis for Effective Corporate Governance

'The corporate governance framework should promote transparent and fair markets, and the efficient allocation of resources. It should be consistent with the rule of law and support effective supervision and enforcement' (OECD, 2015: p. 13). This principle emphasizes importance of corporate governance in ensuring the transparency of financial reporting and reaching the best allocation of the company's assets through presenting the best distribution of responsibilities among authorities. In addition, this principle focuses on the importance of having a suitable legal and regulatory environment and the usefulness of the presence of an institutional framework to guarantee the effectiveness of corporate governance. Moreover, it suggests that the effectiveness of implementing corporate governance principles depends mainly on the country's corporate governance framework; in other words, rules and the regulatory frameworks affect the validity of applying these principles. More specifically, companies' law, securities regulations, accounting and auditing standards, insolvency law, contract law, labor law, and tax law are very important factors in determining the degree of usefulness of such principles. Furthermore, in order to improve the enforcement policies and procedures over exercising corporate governance practices in the country, the responsibilities of the regulatory authorities should be clearly identified and designed to serve the public interests (OECD, 2015).

The Rights of Shareholders and Key Ownership Functions

> The corporate governance framework should protect and facilitate the exercise of shareholders' rights and ensure the equitable treatment of all shareholders, including minority and foreign shareholders. All shareholders should have the opportunity to obtain effective redress for violation of their rights. (OECD, 2015: p. 19)

This principle is related to the basic rights of shareholders to have secure methods of ownership registration and transfer. It asserts on the right of shareholders in exercising their ownership benefits, such as participating in decision-making process during shareholders meetings, voting and electing board members, obtaining relevant and material information about the company on a timely and regular basis, and sharing the profit of the corporation. Additionally, this principle is concerned with the idea that in order to achieve the needed improvements and suitable functioning of capital markets, investors' rights should be protected against the misuse or expropriation of the company's resources by board members and controlling shareholders. It is the responsibility of the regulatory authorities and policy makers to protect the rights of minority shareholders against violation (OECD, 2015).

Institutional Investors, Stock Markets, and Other Intermediaries

'The corporate governance framework should provide sound incentives throughout the investment chain and provide for stock markets to function in a way that contributes to good corporate governance' (OECD, 2015: p. 31). This principle focuses on the involvement of shareholders and investors in corporate governance of the firm, it suggests that the investment chain is very long and includes a lot of intermediaries that stand between the company and stakeholders. Thus, this principle encourages companies to implement strategies and activities that enhance the involvement of shareholders, particularly institutional investors, in corporate governance. Since the number of institutional investors increased, the company has to disclose the codes related to how institutional shareholders can use their rights, such as voting rights at shareholders meetings and the ability to have a direct contact with the company's management. Moreover, this principle spots light on the importance of the institutional investors in determining the effectiveness and credibility of the company's corporate governance practices in regard of the degree of incentives they have to exercise their ownership rights, their ability to inform the use of their ownership rights, and how they will effectively exercise their ownership functions. In other words, this principle encourages institutional investors to disclose their plans in respect to corporate governance and how they intend to exercise their ownership rights (OECD, 2015).

The Role of Stakeholders in Corporate Governance

'The corporate governance framework should recognize the rights of stakeholders established by law or through mutual agreements and encourage active co-operation between corporations and stakeholders in creating wealth, jobs, and the sustainability of financially sound enterprises' (OECD, 2015: p. 37). This principle is concerned with the idea that the rights of stakeholders settled by laws and regulations should be respected. It recommends that corporate governance framework should identify the rights of stakeholders, recognize their contributions in achieving the strategic objectives of the company, and transparently show their rights to obtain effective redress in case of the violation of their rights. Furthermore, this principle is related to the relationship between the company and its stakeholders; it focuses on the rights of stakeholders to access the needed information in a regular and timely basis when they participate in corporate governance process. Additionally, it focuses on the rights of employees to be a part in corporate governance practices implemented by companies, such as the right of having employee representation in the board and the existence of work councils to consider their points of views in specific company's decisions. Finally, this principle ensures that an effective and efficient insolvency framework and compelling enforcements of creditors' rights should be included in the corporate governance practices of the company (OECD, 2015).

Disclosure and Transparency

'The corporate governance framework should ensure that timely and accurate disclosure is made on all material matters regarding the corporation, including the financial situation, performance, ownership, and governance of the company' (OECD, 2015: p. 41). This principle is considered the core principle of this book; as it deals with the information that should be disclosed by companies. This principle suggests that information should be prepared and disclosed in accordance with high-quality standards of financial and non-financial reporting. In addition, it suggests that an annual auditing should be conducted by an independent, competent, and qualified auditor in order to provide an external and objective assurance to the board and shareholders that financial statements are fairly representing the company's financial position and performance in all material aspects. It deals mainly with the disclosure of both financial and non-financial information through summarizing the type of information that should exist in the company's annual reports. Moreover, this principle focuses on the right of shareholders to be provided with all of the required material information on a timely basis. More specifically, this principle deals with the channels of disseminating information to the users of financial statements in order to ensure providing them with equal, timely, and cost-efficient access to the disclosed information (OECD, 2015).

The Responsibilities of the Board

'The corporate governance framework should ensure the strategic guidance of the company, the effective monitoring of management by the board, and the board's accountability to the company and the shareholders' (OECD, 2015: p. 51). This principle is related to the structure of the board of directors and its main functions, which include reviewing corporate strategy, selecting and compensating management, and ensuring the integrity of the company's accounting and financial reporting systems. The board should apply high ethical standards and should take into consideration the interests of all the stakeholders. According to this principle, board of directors is responsible for avoiding the conflict of interests and fairly dealing with all stakeholders' interests through making objective and independent decisions. This also includes the necessity of an equal and fair treatment of the rights of all shareholders. Furthermore, this principle discusses the role of the board of directors in risk management and internal audit strategies, and it deals with the improvements and trainings backgrounds of board members to establish specialized board committees in different areas, such as remuneration committee, audit committee, and risk management committee. For large companies, it is better to have a special committee that deals with remuneration policy and the contracts of the board members (OECD, 2015).

In conclusion, the review of the OECD corporate governance principles reveals that these principles describe the essential framework of forming good corporate governance practices. Additionally, these principles demonstrated the basis of the board of directors' responsibilities in achieving the best interests of the company and serving the benefits of all stakeholders.

As well, they provided a scheme of how to protect the rights of stakeholders. It is notable that these principles focus on the importance of disclosure and transparency, and on the role of the board of directors in overseeing and monitoring companies' disclosure practices (Al-Akra et al., 2010; Samaha and Dahawy, 2010).

The Implementation of Corporate Governance Codes

As presented earlier, the OECD has issued a set of corporate governance codes that companies should implement in order to ensure the effectiveness of their corporate governance practices. The corporate governance codes have been introduced for developed countries and they are recently presented in developing countries. Therefore, a number of studies have attempted to examine the level of compliance with these codes, the effect of implementing these codes on improving companies' performance, and the factors that affect the level of compliance with these codes. According to Albassam (2014), corporate governance codes are essential to improve the company's transparency and accountability, which enhances the confidence of financial statements users in companies' managers. Given the importance of adopting the corporate governance codes in improving corporate governance practices, following is a presentation of the studies that endeavored to examine the compliance with corporate governance codes and the factors that affect the compliance with such codes in both developed and developing countries.

Corporate Governance in Developed Countries

Previous researchers who examined the level of the implementation of corporate governance codes revealed a high level of compliance in developed countries, and they reported an apparent increase in the level of compliance with these codes. For example, Conyon (1994) concluded that there was a noticeable enhancement in the level of compliance with corporate governance codes in UK companies in a survey performed from the year 1988 to 1993. He reported that 77% of companies separated the CEO role in the year 1993 in comparison with 57% in 1988. Furthermore, he reported that 94% of the sampled companies activated remuneration committees in 1993 in comparison of 54% in 1988.

As well, Conyon and Mallin (1997) conducted a study to examine the degree of the implementation of the recommendations of Cadbury Committee report by UK listed firms, they reported a high level of commitment with these recommendations and an increase in the number of firms operated both audit and remuneration committees. Additionally, they found an increase in the number of non-executive members in the board, which could be considered an evidence of the improvement in the level of compliance with corporate governance principles. Using a sample of 408 listed companies in Germany, Werder et al. (2005) structured a study to examine the level of the acceptance of corporate governance codes that issued in 2002 in Germany; they reported a high level of compliance with these codes in the year 2003 and suggested that this level will increase in the future. The same results were reported by Cromme (2005) that 75% of companies in Germany have applied the corporate governance codes in the year 2003. Chalevas (2011) concluded that the level of compliance with corporate governance codes improved in Greek companies during the period of 2000–2003. In Italy, Allegrini and Greco (2013) conducted a study to investigate the extent of applying corporate governance codes issued in 2007 and found a high level of compliance with these codes. Similarly, Salterio et al. (2013) investigated the level of the adoption of 16 corporate governance recommendations issued by the Canadian Securities Administrators of 472 Canadian firms; they revealed that on average 82% of the sampled companies adopted some of these 16 recommendations, while only 39% of these companies fully complied with all of the 16 recommendations.

Furthermore, scholars have attempted to test the factors that may affect the extent of compliance with corporate governance principles. Ownership structure and listing status were proved to affect the effectiveness of corporate governance practices. In this regard, Arcay and Vazquez (2005) conducted a study in Spain to review the effect of some firm characteristics on the goodness of corporate governance practices in Spanish companies; they reported that ownership structure has a significant influence in determining the extent of the company's governance practices. More specifically, their findings showed that ownership concentration has a negative relationship with the adoption of good corporate governance practices; the latter implies that companies with concentrated ownership do not reach the same level of compliance in comparison to wide spread ownership companies. Additionally, they expressed that there is a significant positive relationship between listing status and the quality of corporate governance; their results showed that cross-listed Spanish firms tend to apply a corporate governance system that matches both the local rules and regulations of governance practices and those in the foreign markets in where they are listed. In relation to the impact of firm size on the adoption of corporate governance codes, scholars revealed mixed results; for instance, Werder et al. (2005) proved that firm size plays an important role in determining the level of compliance with corporate governance codes. While Arcay and Vazquez (2005) did not detect any relationship between firm size and the compliance with corporate governance rules.

Culture and regulatory framework are also evidenced to have an effect on both the forming of corporate governance models and the implementation of corporate governance principles. Scholars have presented two models for corporate governance. The first one is the one-tier board model, which suggests that governance is limited only to owners, and the role of the board of directors is just to monitor the performance of the company and regularly report to those owners. The second model is the two-tier board model, which suggests that there are two boards, the first one is to supervise and the second one is to manage the companies' day-to-day activities. Under this model the supervisory board is not involved in managing the company (Haniffa, 1999; Mavrommati, 2008). Haniffa (1999) suggested that the model of corporate governance relies on the country's culture and its corporate environment. The existence of these models is the result of the variety of the roles of the board of directors in the company, the leadership structure, and the organizations' structure (Maassen, 2002). Furthermore, the effectiveness of corporate governance is a matter of the conditions that exist in countries, such as cultural values, past experience, and the needs of all users of financial statements (Hassaan, 2012). According to Verriest et al. (2013), the effectiveness of corporate governance is a function of three complementary factors, which are the enforcement toward the transparency among capital markets, investors' protection, which affects the independence of board members, and some firm specific factors, such as the existing complementarities over corporate governance practices.

Corporate Governance in Developing Countries

Lately, corporate governance in developing countries has attracted the attention of scholars due to the weakness of corporate governance in these countries, which had led to economic crises that affected these countries (Oman et al., 2004). It is held that corporate governance is very important in establishing a suitable investment environment in emerging markets (Hassaan, 2012). In comparison with the level of compliance with corporate governance codes in developed countries, the extent of corporate governance results varies in developing countries. In other words, the results of the previous studies that examined the level of compliance with corporate governance codes in emerging markets revealed disparity in such compliance among these countries. For example, Krambia-Kapardis and Psaros (2006) investigated the compliance with corporate governance codes by companies listed in Cyprus stock exchange; they reported that only a small number of companies comply with significant aspects of corporate governance codes and a large number of companies did not implement any, which implies that the reforms to improve corporate governance practices were not successful. Tsamenyi et al. (2007) used a sample of 22 listed firms in Ghana to test the level of compliance with corporate governance codes from 2001 to 2002; they built a corporate governance index and found that the average compliance with these codes is 52%. In another work, Campbell et al. (2009) examined the level of compliance with Polish codes of Corporate Governance Best Practices for the year 2005; they reported that despite the high level of overall compliance with these codes, there are some codes faced with high level of non-compliance, such as the codes that are related to board independence, board size, the composition of board committees, and the appointment of the auditor. Moreover, using a sample of 100 listed Chinese companies for the period from 2004 to 2006, Cheung et al. (2010) revealed that corporate governance practices implemented by Chinese companies have been improved. Black et al. (2010) examined the corporate governance practices in Brazilian context and found that the main weakness in the level of compliance among the sampled companies was related to the independence of the board; companies do not have independent directors at all or they had a small number of independent directors. Ntim et al. (2012) constructed a corporate governance index that includes 50 provisions in order to test the level of compliance with corporate governance codes in South Africa for the period between 2002 and 2006, they reported that the level of compliance increased through the period of the study; more specifically, the level of compliance has improved form 47% in 2002 to 69% in 2006. In addition, some studies examined the effectiveness of corporate governance across countries; for instance, Patel et al. (2002) investigated the level of the adoption of corporate governance codes in 19 developing counties using a sample of 354 firms for the period between 1998 and 2000; they found a high level of transparency and disclosure of corporate governance practices in these firms, particularly in Asian emerging markets and South Africa.

Corporate Governance in the Middle East

A number of studies have examined the degree of compliance with corporate governance codes in the Middle Eastern context; most of the results of these studies revealed that the level of compliance with these codes should be improved. For instance, Hussain and Mallin (2002) studied the effectiveness of corporate governance practices in Bahrain and reported that despite the fact that most of the sampled companies have structural features of corporate governance, there is still a need for further improvements. Similarly, Aljifri and Moustafa (2007) revealed that corporate governance codes in the UAE should be improved to be matched with the UAE business environment and they recommended the implementation of OECD principles.

Shanikat and Abbadi (2011) examined the implementation of OECD principles in the rules and regulation in the Jordanian context and claimed mixed results. They found that some areas of these principles were fully served, while there are some aspects still need to be improved. Specifically, they reported that the basic decision-making rights of shareholders are protected except for large decisions, such as assets sales, and they recommended that the equitable treatment of shareholders needs to be improved because sometimes controllers may use information to serve their own benefits. Additionally, they expressed that Jordanian companies' law has protected the rules and rights of stakeholders in corporate governance codes, and also noticed that boards of directors were effective in performing their responsibilities as defined in the companies' law. Using a constructed corporate governance index that includes nine corporate governance provisions, Al-Moataz and Hussainey (2012) examined the level of compliance with corporate governance codes using a sample of 52 Saudi listed firms and reported that the level of compliance with these codes is on average of 53% for the years 2006 and 2007.

In relation to the factors that affect the degree of the implementation of corporate governance in the Middle Eastern context, industry type was found to have an effect on the degree of compliance with corporate governance codes. For instance, Hussainey and Al-Nodel (2008) tested the level of the disclosure about corporate governance practices in the company's website for a sample of listed companies in Saudi Arabia. They revealed that the level of disclosure of these practices varied among industry sectors; in particular, they reported that banks have the highest level of disclosure. Meanwhile, Hassan (2011) attempted to explore corporate governance practices in the UAE; the study cross-checked the differences in these practices between financial and non-financial sectors. It was reported that there is a gap between the companies' corporate governance practices and the UAE required corporate governance codes. Additionally, the author expressed that in terms of ownership structure and audit practices, there is no significant differences among both types of companies, while board and management structure practices were significantly different among the two sectors.

Furthermore, to enhance the implementation of good corporate governance practices, authors suggested that the enforcement over the implementation of corporate governance codes should be enhanced. In this respect, Ararat and Ugur (2003) investigated the convergence of corporate governance codes in Turkish companies and revealed that failure of supervision and weak enforcement mechanisms have led to the low level of compliance with these codes. As well, Hussainey and Aljifri (2012) asserted that in order to improve the efficiency and effectiveness of the UAE capital markets, an effective enforcement over the implementations of corporate governance codes should exist. They assured that corporate governance mechanisms are very essential in shaping the company's financial policies, and that managers have to improve their awareness about the benefits of implementing effective internal and external corporate governance mechanisms.

Moreover, Mubarak (2012) conducted a study to examine the differences in the degree of compliance with corporate governance codes in Egypt and the UAE for the year 2010; the results showed that UAE listed companies experienced more compliance with these codes than Egyptian companies; additionally, UAE companies have a higher level of disclosure of their corporate governance practices. The author justified these findings standing on the fact that the level of compliance in Egypt is associated with the diversity in the industry and the lower degree of foreign operations, whereas UAE companies have a higher level of foreign operations; the highest level of compliance was recorded for banks and financial companies since they are regulated by the central bank.

In conclusion, despite of the existence of corporate governance codes issued by OECD to be implemented by countries around the world, there are variations in the level of the adoption of these codes due to the regional, cultural, and organizational differences among countries. In developed countries, the review of the previous studies has showed a satisfactory level of commitment with corporate governance practices by companies and they showed an improvement in this commitment over the years. This can be attributed to the strong legal, cultural, and economical systems applied in these countries (Salterio et al., 2013). However, Bozec et al. (2010) reported that there is a weak legal system in developing countries; therefore, the level of the adoption of corporate governance codes in these countries is lower than developed countries. Thus, developing countries tend to implement good corporate governance practices in order to earn legitimate position, attract investors, and decrease the cost of capital. In respect to the factors that affect the implementation of corporate governance codes, ownership structure, industry type, and listing status were proved to have an effect on the level of the adoption of corporate governance codes. Additionally, culture and corporate environment play important roles in determining the extent of corporate governance practices. Last, contradictory results were revealed regarding the impact of firm size on the corporate governance practices.

Summary

This chapter has provided an extensive overview of different perspectives related to corporate governance. The chapter started with the identification of corporate governance concept, this has been followed by a discussion of the main principles issued by OECD and the implementation of these principles in both developed and developing countries, revealing that developed countries comply with corporate governance principles better than developing countries due to the variations in the effectiveness of the cultural, legal, and economical systems among these countries. Notably, a further improvement of the enforcement mechanisms in developing countries is needed.

The next chapter demonstrates the main theories that discussed the relationship between corporate governance and financial disclosure. In addition, it reviews the prior studies that examined the relationship between corporate governance and financial disclosure.

References

Al-Akra, M., Eddie, I.A., & Ali, M.J. (2010). The influence of the introduction of accounting disclosure regulation on mandatory disclosure compliance: Evidence from Jordan. *The British Accounting Review*, *42*(3), 170–186.

Albassam, W. (2014). *Corporate governance, voluntary disclosure and financial performance: Ban empirical analysis of Saudi listed firms using a mixed-methods research design* (Doctoral dissertation, University of Glasgow).

Aljifri, K., & Moustafa, M. (2007). The impact of corporate governance mechanisms on the performance of UAE firms: An empirical analysis. *Journal of Economic and Administrative Sciences, 23*(2), 71–93.

Allegrini, M., & Greco, G. (2013). Corporate boards, audit committees and voluntary disclosure: Evidence from Italian listed companies. *Journal of Management & Governance, 17*(1), 187–216.

Al-Moataz, E., & Hussainey, K. (2012). Determinants of corporate governance disclosure in Saudi companies. *Journal of Economics and Management, 5*(1), 52–84.

Aly, D., Abdelqader, M., Darwish, T.K., & Scott, K. (2022). The impact of healthcare board characteristics on NHS trust performance. *Public Money & Management*, 1–8. https://doi.org/10.1080/09540962.2021.2022272

Ararat, M., & Ugur, M. (2003). Corporate governance in Turkey: An overview and some policy recommendations. *Corporate Governance: The international Journal of Business in Society, 3*(1), 58–75.

Arcay, M.R.B., & Vazquez, M.F.M. (2005). Corporate characteristics, governance rules and the extent of voluntary disclosure in Spain. *Advances in Accounting, 21*, 299–331.

Black, B.S., De Carvalho, A.G., & Gorga, E. (2010). Corporate governance in Brazil. *Emerging Markets Review, 11*(1), 21–38.

Bozec, R., Dia, M., & Bozec, Y. (2010). Governance–performance relationship: A re-examination using technical efficiency measures. *British Journal of Management, 21*(3), 684–700.

Campbell, K., Jerzemowska, M., & Najman, K. (2009). Corporate governance challenges in Poland: Evidence from "comply or explain" disclosures. *Corporate Governance: The International Journal of Business in Society, 9*(5), 623–634.

Chalevas, C.G. (2011). The effect of the mandatory adoption of corporate governance mechanisms on executive compensation. *The International Journal of Accounting, 46*(2), 138–174.

Cheung, Y.L., Jiang, P., Limpaphayom, P., & Lu, T. (2010). Corporate governance in China: A step forward. *European Financial Management, 16*(1), 94–123.

Conyon, M., & Mallin, C. (1997). A review of compliance with Cadbury. *Journal of General Management, 22*, 24–37.

Conyon, M.J. (1994). Corporate governance changes in UK companies between 1988 and 1993. *Corporate Governance: An International Review, 2*(2), 87–100.

Cromme, G. (2005). Corporate governance in Germany and the German corporate governance code. *Corporate Governance: An International Review, 13*(3), 362–367.

Fama, E.F., & Jensen, M.C. (1983). Separation of ownership and control. *The Journal of Law & Economics, 26*(2), 301–325.

Haniffa, R.M. (1999). *Culture, corporate governance and disclosure in Malaysian corporations* (Doctoral dissertation, University of Exeter).

Hassaan, M. (2012). *Corporate governance and compliance with International Financial Reporting Standards (IFRSs): Evidence from two MENA stock exchanges* (Doctoral dissertation, Aston University).

Hassan, M.K. (2011). Corporate governance practices in emerging economies: Initial findings from the UAE. *China-USA Business Review, 10*(9), 856–864.

Hussain, S.H., & Mallin, C. (2002). Corporate governance in Bahrain. *Corporate Governance: An International Review*, *10*(3), 197–210.

Hussainey, K., & Aljifri, K. (2012). Corporate governance mechanisms and capital structure in UAE. *Journal of Applied Accounting Research*, *13*(2), 145–160.

Hussainey, K., & Al-Nodel, A. (2008). Corporate governance online reporting by Saudi listed companies. *Research in Accounting in Emerging Economies*, *8*, 39–64.

Jensen, M.C., & Meckling, W.H. (1976). Theory of the firm: Managerial behavior, agency costs and ownership structure. *Journal of Financial Economics*, *3*(4), 305–360.

Jesover, F., & Kirkpatrick, G. (2005). The revised OECD principles of corporate governance and their relevance to non-OECD countries. *Corporate Governance: An International Review*, *13*(2), 127–136.

Karamanou, I., & Vafeas, N. (2005). The association between corporate boards, audit committees, and management earnings forecasts: An empirical analysis. *Journal of Accounting Research*, *43*(3), 453–486.

Krambia-Kapardis, M., & Psaros, J. (2006). The implementation of corporate governance principles in an emerging economy: A critique of the situation in Cyprus. *Corporate Governance: An International Review*, *14*(2), 126–139.

Maassen, G. (2002). *An international comparison of corporate governance models – a study on the formal independence and convergence of one-tier and two-tier corporate boards of directors in the United States of America, the United Kingdom and the Netherlands* (3rd ed.). (PhD Series in General Management. Rotterdam School of Management. Netherlands).

Mavrommati, K. (2008). *A contribution to the study of corporate governance in the context of the Greek legal order* (Doctoral dissertation, University of Warwick).

Mubarak, A. (2012). Compliance to corporate governance code by listed companies in Egypt and the UAE. *International Journal of Innovation, Management and Technology*, *3*(5), 619–624.

Ntim, C.G., Opong, K.K., Danbolt, J., & Thomas, D.A. (2012). Voluntary corporate governance disclosures by post-apartheid South African corporations. *Journal of Applied Accounting Research*, *13*(2), 122–144.

OECD (2015). Organization for Economic Cooperation and Development (OECD). Available: http://www.oecd.org/mena/competitiveness/. Accessed: [5/12/2017].

Oman, C., Fries, S., & Buiter, W. (2004). *Corporate governance in developing, transition and emerging-market economies*. OECD Publishing.

Otman, K.A.M. (2014). *Corporate governance and firm performance in listed companies in the United Arab Emirates* (Doctoral dissertation, Victoria University).

Parum, E. (2005). Does disclosure on corporate governance lead to openness and transparency in how companies are managed? *Corporate Governance: An International Review*, *13*(5), 702–709.

Patel, S.A., Balic, A., & Bwakira, L. (2002). Measuring transparency and disclosure at firm-level in emerging markets. *Emerging Markets Review*, *3*(4), 325–337.

Salterio, S.E., Conrod, J.E., & Schmidt, R.N. (2013). Canadian evidence of adherence to "comply or explain" corporate governance codes: An international comparison. *Accounting Perspectives*, *12*(1), 23–51.

Samaha, K., & Dahawy, K. (2010). An empirical analysis of corporate governance structures and voluntary corporate disclosure in volatile capital markets: The Egyptian experience. *International Journal of Accounting, Auditing and Performance Evaluation*, 7(1-2), 61–93.

Shanikat, M., & Abbadi, S.S. (2011). Assessment of corporate governance in Jordan: An empirical study. *Australasian Accounting Business & Finance Journal, 5*(3), 93.

Tariff, J. (2006). Corporate governance in the Middle East and North Africa (MENA) region. *Arab Bank Review, 8*(1), 31–36.

Tricker, R.I. (1984). *Corporate governance: Practices, procedures, and powers in British companies and their boards of directors*. Gower Pub Co.

Tsamenyi, M., Enninful-Adu, E., & Onumah, J. (2007). Disclosure and corporate governance in developing countries: Evidence from Ghana. *Managerial Auditing Journal, 22*(3), 319–334.

Verriest, A., Gaeremynck, A., & Thornton, D.B. (2013). The impact of corporate governance on IFRS adoption choices. *European Accounting Review, 22*(1), 39–77.

Werder, A., Talaulicar, T., & Kolat, G.L. (2005). Compliance with the German corporate governance code: An empirical analysis of the compliance statements by German listed companies. *Corporate Governance: An International Review, 13*(2), 178–187.

5 Corporate Governance and IFRS Compliance

Introduction

After the numerous financial and economic crises and the failure of financial reporting in serving the needs of financial statements users, scholars became interested in expressing the importance of corporate governance in improving the company's performance (Haniffa, 1999; Sellami and Fendri, 2017). They reported that these collapses have stressed the significance of improving corporate governance around the world, as well, promoting the financial reporting quality (Pergola, 2005). In broad terms, the idea of testing the effect of corporate governance on financial disclosure is based on the agency problem. Shareholders cannot take the full control over their companies, therefore, they have to delegate this responsibility to managers, but they still need to monitor those managers' activities. As a consequent result, scholars suggested that enhancing corporate governance may be considered one of the tools that limits managers' opportunities in manipulating companies' earnings (Jensen and Meckling, 1976). This conflict of interests is obvious because managers will always have the incentives to take actions that serve their own benefits, which may reduce the credibility of financial reporting (Bouchareb et al., 2014).

Theoretical Perspectives of Corporate Governance and Financial Disclosure

There is no one single theory that can explain the relationship between corporate governance and financial disclosure; thus, several researchers have relied on more than one theory (see for example, Fiedler and Deegan, 2002; Al-Htaybat, 2005; Brennan, 2007; Shehata, 2013). In other words, the relationship between financial disclosure and corporate governance has been studied and explained based on different theoretical strands. Therefore, this section presents the most common theories that are related to the association between corporate governance and both financial reporting quality and the level of compliance with IFRS. These theories are agency theory, stakeholder theory, stewardship theory, and resource dependency theory.

DOI: 10.4324/9781003211556-5

Agency Theory

Most of the previous studies that discussed the relationship between corporate governance and the extent of disclosure were mainly developed based on the agency theory. Agency theory explains the relationship between principals (owners) and agents (managers) in the business (Al-Shammari and Al-Sultan, 2010). The main idea of this theory is related to the separation between ownership and management, where shareholders (principals) of the company will delegate the control of the day-to-day activities to managers (agents), and this separation has led to raise the possibility of increasing the conflict of interests between them (Jensen and Meckling, 1976; Al-Janadi et al., 2013).

The main assumption of the agency theory is that the interests of principals and the interests of agents are not the same; the conflict of interests occurs as both parties, shareholders and managers, will attempt to maximize their own benefits at the same time, and managers are presumed not to always act in the best of the shareholders' interests (Al-Shammari and Al-Sultan, 2010). Muth and Donaldson (1998) stated that the separation between ownership and control has enhanced the power of managers, and as a consequent result, managers are always have the motivation to make decisions and manage the company's earnings in order to serve their own benefits despite of the benefits of shareholders. Alanezi and Albuloushi (2011) suggested that agency theory adopts the idea that humans' behaviors are based on self-serving actions, and company's executives may sacrifice the benefits of shareholders to maximize their own economic benefits. Prior work has introduced how managers could use the company's resources to serve their own benefits, for example, managers could utilize insider information for their own investment decisions (Jensen and Meckling, 1976; Chalevas, 2011). Secondly, managers could pay themselves excessively in terms of salaries and bonuses (Ntim et al., 2012). Thirdly, managers could use companies' resources to serve their luxury appearance in the company, such as having big offices (Jensen and Meckling, 1976).

Agency theory suggests that the conflict of interests between managers and shareholders that resulted from the separation between ownership and management arises the agency cost (Jensen and Meckling, 1976; Kelton and Yang, 2008). More specifically, agency cost includes three types of costs, which are monitoring costs, bonding costs, and residual losses (Jensen and Meckling, 1976). Monitoring costs are the costs needed to monitor the performance of managers and limit their abnormal activities (Jensen and Meckling, 1976; Shehata, 2013). Bonding costs include financial and non-financial costs incurred to ensure that managers are acting in the best interests of all stakeholders in order to avoid the conflict of interests (Jensen and Meckling, 1976; Arnold and De Lange, 2004; Shehata, 2013). Residual losses refer to the cost-benefit analysis of monitoring and bonding costs incurred, residual loss occurs if the cost of monitoring managers' performance exceeds the benefits acquired form such actions; in other words, residual loss appears in case of failure of the monitoring and bonding costs or in case of the lack of assurance that managers are acting in the best interest of owners (Fama and Jensen, 1983, Omar, 2007).

Agency theory aims to reduce the conflict of interests between managers and shareholders, and it also aims to reduce the expropriation of shareholders' wealth (Albassam, 2014). Consequently, several scholars attempted to introduce how to decrease the agency cost; some of them suggested that corporate governance could be an effective mechanism in aligning the benefits of managers with the benefits of shareholders. For example, Fama and Jensen (1983) and Ho and Wong (2001) suggested that in order to minimize agency cost, the power of managers should be monitored and controlled, which may be achieved by having good corporate governance practices. The role of corporate governance is to save the interests of shareholders by monitoring the performance of managers, which mitigates the agency cost (McKnight and Weir, 2009).

Another aspect of decreasing the agency cost is reducing the level of information asymmetry between managers and shareholders. Information asymmetry occurs because principals and agents can access different levels of information (Omar, 2007; Mallin and Ow-Yong, 2009). Morris (1987) and Chau and Gray (2002) argued that in order for managers to reduce the agency cost and the conflict of interests, they can disclose more information. This signifies that disclosing more information helps to ensure that managers are not utilizing the company's resources into their own benefits (Haniffa, 1999). Moreover, some studies reported that voluntary disclosure could help to mitigate the agency cost; the latter means that if the company disclosed more information, this will decrease the level of asymmetry of information between financial statements' users and managers, which also helps in decreasing the monitoring costs (Barako et al., 2006; Baazaoui and Zaraï, 2019).

Stakeholder Theory

Stakeholders could be defined as the wide range of individuals and institutions who may affect or be affected by companies' operations (Freeman, 2010). Gray et al. (1996) defined stakeholders as "any human agency that can be influenced by, or can itself influence, the activities of the organization in question" (p. 33). This theory implicates the recognition and identification of the relationship between the company's activities and its stakeholders (Ansoff, 1965). It stands on the fact that the reputation of the company depends on its relationship with stakeholders and on its social responsibility, the latter implies that stakeholder theory is concerned with all the parties related to the organizations' performance rather than just focusing on shareholders (Haniffa, 1999). This is justified based on the idea that since stakeholders are involved in the company, they deserve a return for their involvement (Crowther and Jatana, 2007). Additionally, having the stakeholders' support and meeting their expectations are very essential for the continued existence of the firm (Cotter and Najah, 2011).

Stakeholder theory assumes that the main objective of the company is not just to serve the financial benefits of shareholders, but also to serve the benefits of its related broader community (Kiel and Nicholson, 2003; Chen and Roberts, 2010). This signifies that the company is responsible for serving the interests of all stakeholders, including shareholders (Clarke, 1998). Stakeholder theory further suggests that the needs of shareholders cannot be satisfied unless the needs of stakeholders were met (Foster and Jonker, 2005; Jamali, 2008).

However, this theory has been criticized from three perspectives: firstly, it is hard for the company to align the interests of all stakeholders at the same time, and stakeholder theory does not provide guidelines in regard of how to balance the interests of shareholders and other parties (Hassaan, 2012). This is because that the interests of stakeholders are not the same, for example, shareholders expect rewarding dividends, while creditors expect the company to have a strong financial position (Albassam, 2014). Secondly, Sternberg (1997) concluded that applying stakeholder theory is not well-matched with the idea of having a good corporate governance, since there is no clear measurable objectives of managers' actions, which makes it hard to evaluate their performance (Haniffa, 1999; Mallin and Ow-Yong, 2009). Thirdly, this theory mainly focuses on the social responsibility of the firm more than its main objective, which is to maximize the wealth of its owners, and this puts the benefits of the stakeholders in competition with the benefits of the managers (Sternberg, 1997). Meeting the benefits of a wider stakeholders group resulted that the focus on shareholders' benefits to become less evident (Mallin and Ow-Yong, 2009). Additionally, the assumptions of this theory contradict with the agent principal relationship, which suggests that the company is accountable only for its shareholders (Sternberg, 1997).

The normative aspect of this theory is that all stakeholders have specific minimum rights that should not be violated and should be satisfied despite the power of the stakeholders involved (Aburaya, 2012). Deegan (2013) reported that in order to confirm that all stakeholders' rights were met, a sufficient information about the company's activities should be provided to them. Aburaya (2012) suggested that the company can manage its relationship with the stakeholders by providing them more information and enhancing its social and environmental disclosure, which helps in getting their support and approval.

Stewardship Theory

Stewardship theory also discusses the relationship between shareholders and managers; nevertheless, it looks at managers as stewards, not agents, and suggests that organizations need a structure that enhances and facilitates management performance rather than monitor and control it; it looks to the board of directors as a tool to assist management rather than a monitoring tool (Albrecht et al., 2004). Stewardship theory is the contrast of the agency theory since it assumes that principals' benefits are aligned with the agents' benefits, and there is no conflict of interests between owners and managers (Donaldson, 1990; Davis et al., 1997). In other words, this theory assumes that there is no agency conflict based on the mutual benefits of principals and agents (Davis et al., 1997; Nicholson and Kiel, 2007).

Moreover, it suggests that managers are not motivated by personal interests but they are motivated by shareholders' objectives, and it assumes that managers always aim to utilize the resources of the firm to improve its value (Davis et al., 1997). Stewardship theory suggests that managers are not only driven by external factors such as benefits and compensations, but there are other internal factors can motivate them to utilize the company's resources in achieving the organizational goals, such as their reputation and career path (Donaldson and Davis, 1991), as failing to employ these resources in serving the benefits of shareholders affects their reputation and career prospects (Conyon and He, 2011). Thus, this theory supports the idea that managers are trustworthy and there is no need to monitor them (Davis et al., 1997; Letza et al., 2004), and it assumes that since managers' interests are aligned with shareholders' interests, the former will choose to voluntarily disclose more information (Boshnak, 2017).

Resource Dependency Theory

Resource dependency theory is concerned with the ability of the firm to access external resources, such as expertise and capital (Marashdeh, 2014). This theory considers the board of directors an important channel to tie the company with the outside resources, and it recognizes the board of directors not just as a monitoring tool but also as a provider of the needed resources (Nicholson and Kiel, 2007; Chen, 2011). It looks at the board of directors not as a monitoring tool but as an essential link between the company and the external environment (Haniffa and Cooke, 2002). Moreover, the theory suggests that the board of directors is an effective mechanism in serving the benefits of all the stakeholders to enhance the company's competitive advantages (Nicholson and Kiel, 2007; Chen and Roberts, 2010).

Additionally, this theory states that the structure of the board of directors affects the company's access to the financial and non-financial resources needed to improve the company's performance (Pfeffer, 1973). More specifically, proponents of this theory prefer the existence of a high number of outside directors, since they have a wider experience and more external knowledge that they can share with other board members (Haniffa and Cooke 2002; Haniffa and Hudaib, 2006). Pearce and Zahra (1992) revealed that the diversification of board members helps the company to maximize the usage of the benefits from the exchange of the company's resources with the external environment resources. In addition, their existence improves the interacting with other company's strategic environment (Haniffa and Cooke, 2002; Chen and Roberts, 2010). Therefore, non-executive directors improve the company's access to the external resources, which assists the company to have cheaper resources (Nicholson and Kiel, 2007). It suggests that the selection of board members should be according to their ability to ease the company's access to the needed resources (Marashdeh, 2014).

In conclusion, the main theoretical aspects of the relationship between corporate governance and the level of compliance with the mandatory disclosure requirements and the quality of financial reporting were discussed. The existing literature indicates that there is no single theory that can explain such a relation. In other words, it has been suggested that each of the previous theories has limited ability to provide a sufficient explanation of the role of corporate governance mechanisms in interpreting the variations in the levels of disclosure between countries (Nicholson and Kiel, 2007; Ntim and Soobaroyen, 2013). Each of these theories has been faced with critics, therefore, implying them together helps in providing the needed explanation of the relationship between corporate governance practices and the extent of disclosure practices.

Corporate Governance and IFRS Compliance

The loose of financial reporting credibility, the spread of earnings management, and the geographical dispersion of shareholders have enhanced the need of an effective control mechanism to monitor the company's performance (Macdonald and Beattie, 1993). Corporate governance concerns with directing and controlling companies, which is the main responsibility of the board of directors, consequently, week corporate governance may lead to the misconduct of management practices that may continue without detection (Ararat and Ugur, 2003). Bouchareb et al. (2014) reported that the failure of financial reporting is the result of weak internal control over opportunistic managers. Moreover, examining the importance of the quality of financial information disclosed by companies stands on the idea that poor quality of financial statements will mislead the users of financial statements, thus, several researchers have tested the reasons behind the failure of financial disclosure and agreed that in order to mitigate this failure a good corporate governance should be settled to improve the control over managers' actions (Petra, 2007; Firth et al., 2007). Therefore, the effectiveness of corporate governance in directing the disclosure practices have attracted the attention of several researchers.

The review of the previous studies will include the findings of the research that tested the effect of corporate governance on the compliance with IFRS. However, due to the lack of the number of studies that examined the effect of corporate governance on the level of compliance with

IFRS, a discussion of the previous results that linked corporate governance with the financial reporting quality will also be presented standing on the fact that governing financial reporting practices aims mainly to detect management's actions against shareholders' interests (Watts and Zimmerman, 1983). Kothari (2000) suggested that the quality of financial reporting is a reflection of the quality of the accounting standards, and the enforcement mechanisms over these standards. Moreover, IFRS implementation implies that companies have to commit with the disclosure requirements of these standards and IFRS compliance literature could be considered as a part of the financial disclosure research (Fekete et al., 2008). Consequently, a discussion of the literature that examined the effect of corporate governance on the extent of disclosure practices will also be conducted.

Accordingly, this section highlights the results of the prior studies that examined the relationship between corporate governance and the compliance with IFRS, financial reporting quality, and the level of disclosure in developed countries. Additionally, a discussion of such relations will be presented for each of the corporate governance mechanisms. Finally, a review of the previous studies that tested the relationship between corporate governance and financial reporting practices in developing countries will also be implemented focusing on the Middle Eastern context.

Corporate Governance and Financial Reporting in Developed Countries

A number of studies have examined the effect of corporate governance on the quality of financial reporting and the level of disclosure implemented by companies standing on the fact that the quality of information disclosed to shareholders is the main aspect of corporate governance (Mallin, 2002). For example, Hermanson (2003) supported the idea that good corporate governance helps in reducing the problems of financial reporting and bad accounting outcomes. Likewise, Hasan et al. (2013) revealed that good corporate governance improves financial disclosure, which enhances the confidence of shareholders in managers' performance. Arcay and Vazquez (2005) argued that the adoption of good corporate governance practices has a significant effect on the level of voluntary disclosure. Verriest et al. (2013) supported that the stronger the corporate governance the more transparent the IFRS restatements, which implies a high level of disclosure.

Furthermore, the idea of having one set of accounting standards aimed mainly to improve the disclosure practices of companies, as mentioned previously, the adoption of IFRS improved the quality of financial reporting and the level of disclosure. Accordingly, several studies attempted to examine the effect of the adoption of IFRS on the effectiveness of corporate governance in guiding the disclosure practices of companies. In this regard, Cormier (2014) reviewed the effect of the adoption of IFRS on the role of corporate governance in improving the quality of data offered by companies; positive effect of both corporate governance and IFRS implementation in reducing the information asymmetry between managers and investors was reported. Furthermore, it was found that the convergence from Canadian GAAP to IFRS enhanced the value relevance of earnings in companies with strong corporate governance. Bouchareb et al. (2014) examined the effect of corporate governance on the quality of financial reporting after the adoption of IFRS in the year 2005 in France; they found that adopting IFRS and having good corporate governance practices decreased the level of earnings management in comparison with the period before the implementation of IFRS. Additionally, Marra and Mazzola (2014) revealed that the effectiveness of corporate governance in decreasing earnings management is higher around the period of transition toward IFRS in Italian companies, but the effectiveness of corporate governance decreased as drifting away from the year 2005.

In the following subsections, a discussion of the relationships between internal and external corporate governance factors and the company's financial disclosure practices will be presented. These factors are board independence, board size, CEO duality, ownership structure, audit committee, and external auditor. The discussion of each of these factors starts with briefly referring to the relevant theoretical literature about each one of them in order to show the definition of each of these factors. Then, the applicable international empirical results relating to each factor will be discussed.

Board Independence

The importance of board independence in corporate governance effectiveness has been assured by OECD which recommended the existence of independent members in the board (OECD, 2015). Generally speaking, there are two main structures of the board of directors, the first one, is the board that is structured only from executive directors. The second one is the board that includes both executive and non-executive directors. Executive directors are the directors who work in the company and monitor its day-to-day activities, while non-executive directors are the board members from outside the company who do not work in the company, but they attend the meetings of the board. Accordingly, board independence could be defined as the percentage of outside directors to the total number of directors (Shamser and Annuar, 1993; Laing and Weir, 1999).

Having both types of directors, executives and non-executives, generates two major benefits for the company. First, from an agency theory point of view, the presence of outside directors minimizes the agency cost as outside directors are needed to enhance monitoring and controlling executive directors (Jensen and Meckling, 1976). Moreover, independent non-executive directors are seen useful because they can monitor and control the actions of the opportunistic executive directors, which helps in resolving the conflicts between managers and shareholders (Fama, 1980; Fama and Jensen, 1983). Beasley (1996) resulted that the greater proportion of outside directors significantly reduces the probability of financial statements fraud. Similarly, Klein (2002) and Bouchareb et al. (2014) concluded that the independence of the board of directors reduces the chances of earnings management. The existence of outside directors improves the independence of the board, and the greater the number of independent directors the more efficient performance (Beekes et al., 2004; Dharmadasa, et al., 2014). Moreover, Wang and Campbell (2012) reported that for state ownership companies, non-executive board members do not have an effect in decreasing the level of earnings management, while in companies with insignificant state ownership, independent board members have a significant influence in decreasing the level of earnings management. Having such results, they concluded that in case of non-state ownership it is very important for companies to increase the number of independent members, and having at least one-third of the total number of members from outside directors is effective in deterring earnings management for private companies. Second, from a resource dependency theory perspective, the presence of non-executive directors provides firms with connections to the external environment due to their knowledge and experience (Haniffa and Cooke, 2002). Non-executive directors may be considered experts who link the company with the external environment since they may work in different industries and they have different experiences that they can share with executive directors (Fama and Jensen, 1983).

Furthermore, independent board members play an important role in determining the strength of the corporate governance in the company. In this regard, Barako et al. (2006) reported that independent directors enhance the performance of board committees through supporting these committees by their knowledge and experience. However, Patton and Baker (1987) suggested that the presence of non-executive directors reduces the effectiveness of the board's controlling function over the firm, because of their lack of knowledge about the day-to-day activities in comparison with the level of knowledge that executive directors have. Likewise, Muth and Donaldson (1998) supported that executive directors have a higher level of knowledge and more access to the company's operations than outside directors.

The idea of examining the effect of board independence on the level of disclosure practices implemented by companies relies on the facts that the board of directors is responsible for the extent of the company's disclosure practices and that the structure of the board plays an important role in determining these practices (Gibbins et al., 1990). The existence of independent members forces the company to meet the disclosure requirements of accounting standards, which limits the chances of withholding information from outside users (Haniffa and Cooke, 2002). An independent board monitors the flow of information to the stakeholders (Biondi et al., 2009). Similarly, independent board members enhance corporate governance practices through improving the quality of the disclosed information and ensuring that stakeholders are getting the information they need (Beekes et al., 2004). Arcay and Vazquez (2005) conducted a study in Spain using a sample of 91 firms to examine the effect of corporate governance mechanisms on the extent of disclosed information; they reported that having independent directors in the board strengthens the monitoring function of the board over the firm, and this makes the company more responsive to stakeholders' demands of information, which aligns both managers' interests and shareholders' interests through reducing the reluctance of disclosing more information.

Empirical studies indicated mixed results in regard of the relationship between board independence and the level of disclosure. Vafeas (2005), Firth et al. (2007), Dimitropoulos and Asteriou (2010), and Verriest et al. (2013) confirmed that information quality is positively related to the percentage of outside directors in the board. In addition, Donnelly and Mulcahy (2008) and Chau and Gray (2010) revealed a positive relationship between the existence of non-executive directors and the level of voluntary disclosure. Kelton and Yang (2008) examined the relationship between corporate governance and the transparency of information disclosed through the Internet financial reporting; they found that the higher the number of independent members in the board, the more the tendency for companies to implement Internet financial reporting. Bouchareb et al. (2014) reported that board independence has a significant impact on reducing the level of earnings management and improving the quality of financial statements. Using a sample of 63 Canadian listed companies, Mnif and Znazen (2020) reported that board independence positively affects the level of compliance with IFRS. In contrast to the previous results, some studies found a negative relationship between board independence and the level of disclosure. For instance, Eng and Mak (2003) concluded that the increase in the number of outside directors reduces corporate disclosure in a study conducted in Singapore. Likewise, Huafang and Jianguo (2007) claimed that the low level of voluntary disclosure is associated with the increase in the number of independent members in the board. Additionally, some studies suggested that the independence of directors is not enough to control the quality of financial statements, and earnings informativeness is not related to the percentage of outside directors serving in the board (see, for example, Ahmed et al., 2006). Finally, some researchers did not find an influence of board independence on the level of disclosure. For example, Ibadin et al. (2012) and Hasan et al. (2013) asserted that board independence is not meaningfully associated with financial disclosure. Using a sample of 450 listed firms for the period of 2006–2007, Matolcsy et al. (2012) examined the effect of board independence on the level of financial disclosure and found that there is no relationship between board independence and the level of mandatory disclosure. Allegrini and Greco (2013) reported that there is no relationship between the existence of independent board members and corporate governance practices in a study conducted on Italian firms.

Board Size

Board size is an important feature of board structure, and it must meet the needs and objectives of the company (Noor and Fadzil, 2013). Researchers who examined the role of board size in determining the effectiveness of the board of directors revealed two different perspectives. Proponents of small board size suggested that smaller sized boards are more effective in their monitoring function and they imply a high degree of coordination and communication among board members and between the board and managers (Lipton and Lorsch, 1992; Jensen, 1993). Kao and Chen (2004) have also claimed that bigger sized boards reduce their functionality because of the inefficient communications between board members. Furthermore, Arcay and Vazquez (2005) argued that limiting the number of board members is an indication of a good corporate governance. In contrast, opponents of small board size supported that larger boards are more effective for companies; for example, Tricker (1984), Klein (2002), and Haniffa and Cooke (2002) suggested that having more members in the board brings more experience and knowledge for companies, which enhances its monitoring and controlling functions. Large firms tend to have a large board of directors in order to improve their desired functions (Coles et al., 2008).

Findings of the previous studies about the relationship between board size and the quality of disclosure are mixed. Ahmed et al. (2006) examined the relation between board size and financial reporting quality and reported a negative relationship between the board of directors' size and the quality of financial reporting. Beasley (1996) confirmed that as the number of board members decreases, the possibility of financial statement fraud decreases. In addition, Bradbury et al. (2006) found that large board size reduces the information content of earnings. On the other hand, Kent and Stewart (2008) investigated the relationship between corporate governance and mandatory disclosure requirements in Australia and found a positive relationship between board size and the disclosure quality. Using a sample of 177 Italian companies for the year 2007, Allegrini and Greco (2013) reported that board size has a positive relationship with corporate voluntary disclosure. Gao and Kling (2012) concluded that board size positively affects the level of mandatory disclosure. Finally, some scholars did not notice an influence of board size on the level of disclosure. In this respect, Arcay and Vazquez (2005) reported that board size is not associated with the provision of voluntary disclosure. Hasan et al. (2013) similarly pointed out that board size does not have a significant relationship with financial disclosure. Bouchareb et al. (2014) also reported that board size does not have an effect on the level of fraud practices in companies.

Chief Executive Officer Duality

Chief executive officer (CEO) duality means that the CEO of the company acts as the chairman of the board of directors, and good corporate governance requires the separation between CEO and board chairman positions (OECD, 2015). The CEO is responsible for managing the operations of the entire company, making major decisions to maximize the value of the firm, and she/he is supposed to report to the board of directors. Therefore, acting as the CEO and the chairman of the board of directors at the same time leads to a conflict of interests and reduces the efficiency of the board of directors as an internal control tool (Coombes and Wong, 2004). For example, the board of directors has to make decisions regarding the benefits and compensations of managers, and holding both positions by the same person mitigates the objectivity in evaluating decisions related to her/his own benefits and compensations. Also, the board of directors evaluate the performance of managers; again, she/he has to evaluate themselves which cannot be objectively done (Jensen, 1993; Petra, 2007). In addition, agency theory supports splitting the roles of CEO and chairman of the board to avoid the concentration of authority in the hands of one person (Hashim and Devis, 2009). Hence, the separation between CEO and the chair of board of directors is needed to avoid the conflict of interests and improve the independence of the board of directors (Jensen, 1993). Moreover, Dahya and Travlos (2000) revealed that having a chairman from outside the company links it with the external environment and brings to it external percepts, which help in achieving its goals and objectives. While from stewardship theory point of view, some researchers supported the idea that combining both positions enhances the decision-making process relying on the idea that having the same person acting as the CEO and the chairman of the board improves the concentration over achieving the objectives of the company (Eisenhardt, 1989).

In regards of the effect of CEO duality on the quality of financial disclosure, authors suggested that the segregation between these two positions enhances the controlling and monitoring functions of the board and limits the chances of reserving information, which lead to improve the quality of financial reporting (Forker, 1992; Jensen, 1993). Dechow et al. (1996) reported that CEO duality increases the possibility of violating accounting principles. In the same context, Beekes et al. (2004) and Firth et al. (2007) found that accounting information is more relevant for companies that separate between the CEO and the chairman of board of directors. Huafang and Jianguo (2007) analyzed the effect of CEO duality on the level of voluntary disclosure and stressed that CEO duality is associated with low level of voluntary disclosure. Chau and Gray (2010) revealed a positive relationship between having an independent chairman and the level of voluntary disclosure. Furthermore. Allegrini and Greco (2013) and Marra and Mazzola (2014) found a negative impact of CEO duality on voluntary disclosure. Conversely, Arcay and Vazquez (2005) suggested that CEO duality is not associated with the provision of voluntary disclosure. As well, Ahmed et al. (2006) and Petra (2007) did not find a significant relationship between CEO duality and financial reporting quality. In Canada, Mnif and Znazen (2020) reported that CEO duality is not significantly related to IFRS compliance.

Ownership Structure

Ownership structure is formed by the number of shares owned by one individual investor whether if it is a person or an institution (Denis and McConnell, 2003). As the existing literature alerts us, there are two main types of ownership structure: concentrated ownership and dispersed ownership. Concentrated ownership exists when a specific group holds most of the shares of the company, which signifies that they will have the highest level of influence over the company's decisions among other shareholders. While dispersed ownership exists when the ownership of the company's shares is spread over a large number of shareholders, and for this type of ownership structure, management and ownership will be separated (Haniffa, 1999).

Usually, a high level of ownership concentration improves the monitoring power of shareholders over managerial decisions, because shareholders with large ownership percentages have higher incentives to track the company's performance and its strategic decisions in comparison with shareholders who have low ownership percentages. Board of directors and managers will take into their consideration the desires and interests of large shareholders. Additionally, in companies with dispersed ownership, the probability that managers could utilize firm's resources into their own benefits is greater than companies with concentrated ownership (Maher and Andersson, 2000; Lee and Yeh, 2004). In this respect, Arcay and Vazquez (2005) reported that ownership structure may affect the level of disclosure indirectly. Specifically, they suggested that ownership concentration affects the adoption of good corporate governance practices, which influences the extent of the firm's disclosure practices.

Empirical findings of the prior studies about the relationship between these two types of ownership structure and the level of disclosure revealed mixed results. Beekes et al. (2004) pointed out a negative relationship between earnings management and ownership concentration. Similarly, Bouchareb et al. (2014) concluded that the concentration of ownership reduces the level of earnings management in the period of IFRS adoption. In contrast, having a large proportion of public ownership enforces the company to disclose more information (Hasan et al., 2013); the more detailed information to be provided for the users the higher the level of disclosure implemented (Apostolou and Nanopoulos, 2009). As well, Hossain et al. (1994) reported a positive relationship between disclosure and the structure of ownership as they found that widely held companies have a higher level of disclosure than closely held companies. They justified this result relying on the idea that the separation between ownership and control, in widely held companies, ensures the need to disclose more information in order to decrease the information asymmetry between managers and investors. Chau and Gray (2002) suggested that the level of financial reporting quality is positively related to the dispersion of ownership and they found a negative relationship between controlled firms and financial reporting quality. In the same vien, Fan and Wong (2002) and Donnelly and Lynch (2002) revealed that financial statements for firms with high level of ownership concentration have lost credibility to their users. Laidroo (2009) examined the relationship between ownership structure and public announcements disclosure and found a negative relationship between ownership concentration and the level of disclosure. Finally, some researchers reported that ownership structure has no effect on the level of disclosure (see, for instance, Depoers, 2000; Uyar, 2011). Anderson and Daoud (2005) also stated that there is no relationship between ownership concentration and the level of disclosure.

Besides the concentrated ownership and dispersed ownership, there are other types of ownership structure that have been tested by previous researchers, these include managerial ownership, institutional ownership, and family ownership. In relation to managerial ownership, Li and Qi (2008) used the data of 100 listed companies in Shanghai Shenzhen stock exchange and found that the higher the managerial ownership, the higher the level of voluntary disclosure. Conversely, Huafang and Jianguo (2007) reported that managerial ownership is not related to the level of voluntary disclosure. Regarding family-owned companies, Chau and Gray (2010) conducted a study to examine the effect of family ownership on the extent of voluntary disclosure and found that the level of disclosure is lower for the companies with high level of family shareholders. They pointed out that the existence of an independent chairman can detect the effect of family ownership on the level of disclosure. The same results were reported by Li and Qi (2008) that family owners usually prefer to implement lower level of voluntary disclosure. Lastly, institutional ownership has been evidenced to have an effect of the level of disclosure implemented by companies. In this regard, Laidroo (2009) examined the relationship between ownership structure and public announcements disclosure and found a positive relation between the level of disclosure and institutional ownership. Likewise, Barako et al. (2006) expressed that the existence of institutional owners significantly affects the effectiveness of monitoring companies' level of disclosure. Gao and Kling (2012) also asserted that the level of institutional ownership positively affects the level of mandatory disclosure. However, Huafang and Jianguo (2007) reported that state ownership is not related to the level of voluntary disclosure.

Audit Committee

To improve the effectiveness of the board of directors' role in monitoring managerial performance in the company, the board of directors is usually divided into smaller committees, and one of the most important committees is the audit committee, which helps the company to achieve its strategic goals (Fama and Jensen, 1983). Audit committee plays an important role in advising and assisting the board of directors on main accounting issues, such as the preparation of financial statements and ensuring that they are issued in compliance with accounting rules and regulations (Brennan, 2007). Another major role of the audit committee is to provide a formal communication channel between board members, internal control system, and the external auditor (Bradbury et al., 2006).

The review of the empirical studies revealed that there is a significant influence of the effectiveness of the audit committee on the level of disclosure implemented by companies. Arcay and Vazquez (2005) reported that having a good performance of the audit committee enhances monitoring firm's management and this prevents the company from hiding information that may serve the benefits of the stakeholders. Kelton and Yang (2008) examined the relationship between corporate governance and the transparency of information through the internet financial reporting; they found that the higher the number of audit committee members the more tendency for companies to implement a high level of Internet financial reporting. Moreover, Allegrini and Greco (2013) expressed a positive relationship between audit committee and the level of voluntary disclosure. Verriest et al. (2013) asserted that the more the effective audit committee the higher the quality of financial information and the low level of earnings management. Meanwhile, some researchers suggested that the adoption of IFRS improved the effectiveness of the audit committee. In this regard, Bouchareb et al. (2014) found that the existence of the audit committee reduced the level of earnings management significantly in the period of the adoption of IFRS. Likewise, Marra and Mazzola (2014) found that the higher level of the audit committee effectiveness was around the year of transition toward IFRS but after that it decreased. However, Mnif and Znazen (2020) stated that audit committee size and its meeting frequency do not have a significant impact on the level of compliance with IFRS in Canada.

External Auditor

As discussed earlier, agency cost occurs when there is a conflict between managers' interests and shareholders' interests; however, the existence of the external auditor plays an important role in eliminating this cost through reducing such a conflict (see Hossain et al., 1994; Anderson and Daoud, 2005; Barako et al., 2006). More specifically, having an independent external auditor helps to eliminate the opportunities for managers to manipulate earnings (Chung et al., 2003). In addition, the role of the external auditor is very essential in monitoring managers' actions to guarantee the integrity of financial reporting (Hasan et al., 2013). In this regard, Brennan (2007) reported that beside the needs to monitor and control managers' performance, shareholders still need another type of expert assurance about the quality of financial reporting and this is the role of the external auditor. The latter implies that the opinion expressed by the auditor about the level of reliability of the disclosed information enhances the level of assurance for shareholders about managers' performance.

Empirically, scholars expressed that the opinion of the external auditor has been evidenced to have an effect on the extent of the disclosed information in financial statements due to her/his ability to detect material errors in the financial statements (DeAngelo, 1981; Gao and Kling, 2012). Additionally, a positive relationship between the quality of the external auditor and the level of financial disclosure is documented. In this vein, Singhvi and Desai (1971) conducted a study on 100 listed companies in the United States and reported a positive relationship between the quality of external audit and the extent of disclosure. Likewise, Chung et al. (2003) and Riccardi (2019) concluded that the quality of financial reporting is positively related to the quality of external auditor. Bouchareb et al. (2014) found that the quality of external auditor in the period of the adoption of IFRS helps to improve the quality of financial statements.

The quality of the external auditor has been expressed by prior studies from two different perspectives. In relation to the first perspective, some studies linked the quality of the external audit with the size of the audit firm. In this regard, Ahmed and Nicholls (1994) reported that there is a positive relation between the size of the audit firms and the level of disclosure of their clients, depending on the idea that large audit firms tend to be associated with clients who provide better disclosure practices. Similarly, Malone et al. (1993) pointed out that due to the low market share of small audit firms they may be affected by their clients' needs, which may lead to lower level of disclosure for the clients of these firms. In addition, the findings of Kent and Stewart (2008) showed that there is a positive relationship between the size of the external auditor and the level of mandatory disclosure in Australian companies. The second aspect to measure the quality of external auditor refers to whether the auditing firm is recognized as one of the big-four auditing companies in the world or not (Brown et al., 2010). Becker et al. (1998) suggested that accounting information is more reliable for big-four audit firms' clients in comparison to other audit firms. Moreover, Tsalavoutas (2011) reported that having a big-four audit firm increases the level of compliance with IFRS. In contrast, some studies did not detect any relationship between auditor quality and the level of financial disclosure. For instance, Firth (1979) found that the type of the auditor is not significantly related to the level of voluntary disclosure in a study conducted in UK listed firms for the year 1976. Depoers (2000) reported that audit firm's size does not affect the extent of voluntary disclosure. Furthermore, Anderson and Daoud (2005) and Barako et al. (2006) revealed that there is no relation between external auditor size and the level of disclosure.

In conclusion, good governance ensures that companies are performing better and having better relationships with all stakeholders. Notably, companies generally have a little incentive to voluntarily disclose information, and applying good corporate governance practices ensures that companies will serve the benefits of all stakeholders, which enhances the extent of disclosure for these companies. The previous section has provided an extensive overview of the studies that examined the effect of some internal and external corporate governance mechanisms, such as board independence, board size, CEO duality, ownership structure, audit committee, and external auditor on the degree of disclosure in the financial statements. The revision of the previous studies regarding the effect of corporate governance mechanisms on the degree compliance with disclosure requirements of the international accounting standards revealed mixed results, for all of these mechanisms, scholars' findings varied among these three conclusions, which are positive relationship, negative relationship, and non-significant relationship.

Corporate Governance and Financial Reporting in Developing Countries

The improvement of corporate governance is essential in developing countries to ensure the success of companies' performance and create a suitable investment environment (Hassaan, 2012). Accordingly, scholars aimed to examine the effect of the improvements of corporate governance on the extent of disclosure in these countries. In this respect, Sanan and Yadav (2011) conducted a study to test the effect of corporate governance principles on the level of disclosure in Indian companies using standard and poor transparency survey; they found that even with the notable corporate governance improvements, there is a moderate level of disclosure in these companies, and they suggested that the enforcement level over corporate governance codes' implementation should be enhanced to increase the level of financial reporting quality. Conversely, using a sample of 20 listed companies in Ghana, Aboagye-Otchere et al. (2012) examined the effect of corporate governance on the level of disclosure for the period of 2003–2007; they reported that the level of mandatory disclosure has been improved through the years, and that the existence of accounting experts in the audit committee improves the disclosure practices. Consequently, this section presents a preview of the studies that aimed to examine the effect of corporate governance mechanisms on the level of the implementation of accounting standards' disclosure requirements in developing countries, followed by a section that discusses such effect in the Middle East.

One of the main corporate governance mechanisms that has been examined by scholars is board composition. In this vein, Chakroun and Matoussi (2012) investigated the effect of some internal and external mechanisms of corporate governance on the level of voluntary disclosure in Tunisian firms for the period between 2003 and 2008; they stated that the composition of the board of directors has an influence on the level of voluntary disclosure. Luthan and Satria (2016) conducted a study to test the effect of good corporate governance mechanisms on earnings management of 65 sampled companies in Indonesia; they found that board independence and audit committee have negative impact on earnings management before and after the period of convergence to IFRS. However, Akhtaruddin and Haron (2010) used a sample of 124 of public listed companies in Malaysia to examine the effect of some corporate governance mechanisms on the level of disclosure; they reported that there is a weak relationship between the percentage of non-executive directors in the audit committee and the level of voluntary disclosure.

Ownership structure is another mechanism implemented by scholars to test its effect on the level of disclosure. Hossain et al. (1994), Huafang and Jianguo (2007), and Chakroun and Matoussi (2012) reported a positive relationship between ownership structure and the level of financial disclosure. Using a sample of 22 listed companies in Ghana stock exchange, Tsamenyi et al. (2007) found that ownership structure and dispersion of shareholding have a significant effect on company's disclosure. Barako (2007) examined the factors that may affect the level of voluntary disclosure in the annual reports of Kenyan listed companies between the years 1992 and 2001; it was found that voluntary disclosure is influenced by ownership structure and corporate governance attributes. In the same vein, Luthan and Satria (2016) tested the relationship between ownership structure and earnings management before and after the mandatory adoption period of IFRS in Indonesia and they reported a negative relationship before the mandatory adoption and a non-significant relation after the adoption. Furthermore, Rouf and Harun (2011) tested the effect of ownership structure on the level of voluntary disclosure using a sample of 94 Bangladeshi companies in 2007; they reported that the level of disclosure is negatively related to the percentage of management ownership and positively related to institutional ownership structure. Finally, for the effect of the external auditor on the extent of disclosure in developing countries, Hasan et al. (2013) revealed that external auditor has a significant influence on the level of disclosure for a sample of 20 Bangladeshi listed firms. As well, Luthan and Satria (2016) found that the quality of external auditor has a negative relationship with earnings management before and after the convergence to IFRS.

Corporate Governance and Financial Reporting in the Middle East

The Asian financial crisis in 1997/1998 has exposed the substantial need of increasing the number of firms that practice good corporate governance among countries to rebuild investors' confidence in financial reporting (Alzoubi, 2012). The previous studies that examined the effect of corporate governance on the disclosure practices in the Middle East yielded general results. For example, Al-Janadi et al. (2013) used a sample of 87 listed companies in Saudi Arabia for the years 2006 and 2007; it was found that both external and internal corporate governance mechanisms play an efficient role in providing a high-quality level of voluntary disclosure. Aksu and Espahbodi (2016) concluded that the level of transparency and the level of disclosure are high in Turkey. Additionally, they compared the level of transparency and disclosure between the voluntary adopters of IFRS in 2003 and 2004, and the mandated adopters in 2005; they revealed that scores were significantly higher for the voluntary adopters of IFRS. However, Hassaan (2012) built a mandatory disclosure index to test the relationship between corporate governance and the compliance with IFRS disclosure requirements using a sample of Egyptian companies in the year 2007; the author found no relation between corporate governance and corporate mandatory disclosure. Following is a discussion of the results of the previous studies that examined the effect of both internal and external corporate governance mechanisms on the level of disclosure and the level of IFRS compliance in the Middle East.

Board Independence

The results of the prior studies that examined the effect of board interdependence on the extent of disclosure practices in the Middle East context are mixed; some scholars have asserted a positive relation between the two variables. For example, Ezat and El-Masry (2008) reported that the higher the proportion of independent directors the higher the commitment of timely disclosing. Samaha and Dahawy (2010) investigated the factors that influence the level of voluntary disclosure of the listed companies in Egypt; they found that the number of independent members in the board plays an important role in determining the level of disclosure. Moreover, Al-Janadi et al. (2013) pointed out that good corporate governance requires the increase in the number of non-executive directors; the authors reported that the number of non-executive directors enhances the quality of financial reporting since they are more independent in making decisions and monitoring management, which also helps to protect the interests of shareholders. Boshnak (2017) and Juhmani (2017) found a positive relationship between board independence and the level of compliance with IFRS. Meanwhile, some researchers revealed that there is a negative relationship between board independence and the compliance with IFRS; for instance, using a sample of 97 financial reports of Saudi listed companies for the years 2006 and 2007, Al-Moataz and Hussainey (2012) reported that there is a negative association between board independence and corporate disclosure practices, and this negative relationship may indicate, in developing countries, that outside directors are not really independent. Thus, according to their findings, the higher the number of independent members, the less effective board monitoring and the lower corporate transparency.

However, an insignificant relationship was also detected by scholars between the number of non-executive directors and the extent of disclosure practices. In this respect, Hassaan (2012) reported that board independence is not an effective mechanism in improving the level of compliance with IFRS in both Egypt and Jordan. Despite the fact that the average proportion of non-executive directors among their sampled companies is 82%, Al-Shammari and Al-Sultan (2010) did not detect a significant relationship between the number of non-executive directors and the level of voluntary disclosure in Kuwaiti listed companies. They concluded that non-executive directors in Kuwait context do not seem to have a contribution in the independent monitoring and the reduction of the agency conflict. As well, Al-Akra et al. (2010a) asserted that the number of non-executive directors in the boards has decreased between the years of 1996 and 2004, and they justified this reduction standing on the weak enforcement of corporate governance rules. Additionally, they found an insignificant relationship between the percentage of non-executive directors in the board and the adoption of the mandatory disclosure requirements in Jordan. In another work, Alhazaimeh et al. (2014) revealed an insignificant relationship between non-executive directors and the extent of voluntary disclosure in Jordan, and they recommended that managers and policy makers should implement strategies that facilitate the disclosure process.

Board size

Ezat and El-Masry (2008) conducted a study in Egypt to examine the effect of some firm characteristics on the level of disclosure; they reported that board size has a significant effect on the extent of disclosure. Using a sample of 87 listed companies in Saudi Arabia for the years 2006 and 2007, Al-Janadi et al. (2013) have examined the relationship between board size and the level of voluntary disclosure assuming that there is a positive association between small board size and the extent of voluntary disclosure; they found that the average number of board members among the sampled companies is 8. However, their results showed that firms with larger board size experienced a higher level of disclosure and higher reporting quality relying on the fact that the larger the number of board members the higher the ability of the company to manage its capital resources as there is a variety of experts and qualified directors in the board. Al-Akra et al. (2010b) conducted a study to examine the effect of some corporate governance mechanisms on the level of mandatory disclosure compliance in Jordan using a sample of 80 non-financial companies for the years 1996 and 2004; they found that, as a result of privatization, companies moved from public to private, which has led to a reduction in resources and board size. They concluded that board size has a significant influence on the compliance with the mandatory disclosure requirements of accounting standards. Boshnak (2017) indicated that there is a negative relationship between board size and the level of compliance with IFRS. Nevertheless, Samaha et al. (2012) examined the effect of having large board size on the level of disclosure in the Egyptian context, they found that the average board size is 11 among the sampled companies, and they did not detect a significant relationship between board size and the level of disclosure. Hassaan (2012) reported that the average board size in Egypt is five members and seven members in Jordan, and there is no significant association between board size and the level of compliance with IFRS in both countries. Juhmani (2017) reported that board size is not associated with the level of compliance with IFRS in Bahrain.

Chief Executive Officer Duality

Using a sample of 100 Egyptian companies, Samaha et al. (2012) examined the effect of some corporate governance mechanisms on the level of disclosure; they found that CEO duality is associated with a low level of voluntary disclosure. While Al-Janadi et al. (2013) stated that in Saudi Arabia, the separation between the CEO role and the chairman of the board has a negative influence on the level of voluntary disclosure, and they supported that holding both positions by one person is more effective for companies in achieving their goals and objectives due to the elimination of intervention and contradiction between these two positions. Moreover, a number of studies reported an insignificant relationship between CEO duality and the degree of disclosed information. For example, Al-Shammari and Al-Sultan (2010) examined the relationship between corporate governance mechanisms and voluntary disclosure using 170 companies listed in Kuwait stock exchange for the year 2007; they revealed that 57% of the sampled companies have the chairman of the board of directors acting as the CEO, and there is no significant relation between CEO duality and the level of voluntary disclosure. Similarly, Ezat and El-Masry (2008) and Juhmani (2017) reported that there is a non-significant relationship between CEO duality and the level of voluntary disclosure. Hassaan (2012) conducted a study to examine the effect of some corporate governance mechanisms on the compliance with IFRS in Egypt and Jordan; the author reported that 51% of the sampled companies in Egypt separate between the board chairman and the CEO, and in Jordan 81% of the sampled companies have the CEO and the chair positions held by two different persons. She demonstrated that the separation between the chair position and CEO position is not necessarily enhancing the level of compliance with IFRS.

Ownership Structure

Sarea and Al Nesuf (2013) examined the level of compliance with international accounting standards (IAS) 21 in Bahrain; they reported that foreign ownership and institutional ownership have a significant positive influence on the level of the adoption of IFRS. Samaha and Dahawy (2010) asserted that the lower the managerial ownership the higher the level of voluntary disclosure. In the same context, Samaha et al. (2012) found that the higher the concentrated ownership the lower the level of voluntary disclosure. While in examining the effect of governmental ownership on the level of disclosure in Saudi companies, Al-Janadi et al. (2013) reported that it has a negative effect on determining the level of voluntary disclosure. Alhazaimeh et al. (2014) examined the effect of ownership structure on the level of voluntary disclosure using a sample of 73 non-financial companies listed in Amman stock exchange; they stressed that there is a significant negative relationship between block holders ownership and the level of voluntary disclosure; additionally, they found that foreign ownership has a positive effect on the level of information voluntarily disclosed. Moreover, Haddad et al. (2015) examined the effect of ownership structure on the extent of voluntary disclosure of 57 industrial and services companies listed in Amman stock exchange for the year 2004; they measured ownership structure by government ownership, outside ownership, and managerial ownership; they concluded that there is a positive relationship between government ownership and the level of voluntary disclosure. They justified this result standing on the fact that companies owned by Jordanian government are more likely to commit with the mandatory disclosure requirements and voluntarily disclose more information in order to be more transparent and compliant with regulations, and to attract local and international investors. Additionally, they found that companies with higher proportion of managerial ownership disclose less information in their annual reports, and a non-significant impact of outside ownership on the level of voluntary disclosure. However, Al-Akra et al. (2010a) did not detect a significant relationship between ownership structure and the level of mandatory disclosure implementation.

Audit Committee

In Kuwait, Al-Shammari and Al-Sultan (2010) inspected the effect of some corporate governance mechanisms on the level of disclosure; they reported that only audit committee has a significant effect on disclosure practices in Kuwaiti companies. In the same context, Alanezi and Albuloushi (2011) conducted a study in Kuwait using a sample of 68 listed companies; they concluded a positive association between the existence of audit committee and the compliance with IFRS mandatory disclosure requirements. Using a sample of 97 financial reports of Saudi listed companies in 2006 and 2007, Al-Moataz and Hussainey (2012) asserted that audit committee is considered an effective control mechanism in Saudi Arabia, which plays an important role in enhancing corporate disclosure and transparency; in addition, they found that the higher the number of audit committee members the higher the level of corporate disclosure practices. Al-Akra et al. (2010a) and Samaha and Dahawy (2010) reported that the existence of audit committee has a significant influence on the adoption of disclosure practices in Jordanian companies and Egyptian companies, respectively. Al-Janadi et al. (2013) examined the effect of audit committee in improving the quality of financial reporting, and they expressed that despite the fact that 94% of the audit committee members of the sampled companies are independent members, they do not have a significant influence on the level of voluntary disclosure, and they stressed that stock market regulators have to issue guidelines to clarify how the practices of the audit committee can be more effective.

External Auditor

The type of the external auditor has been evidenced to have a significant influence on the level of compliance with the mandatory disclosure requirements (see Al-Akra et al., 2010a; Pichler et al., 2018). Al-Shiab (2003) conducted a study to examine the extent of compliance with IAS for the period of 1995–2000; the author found that external auditor quality has the main effect in determining the level of compliance with disclosure requirements. In addition, Omar and Simon (2011) reported that audit firm size affects the level of disclosure in Jordanian companies. They pointed out that companies audited by one of the big three audit firms have better disclosure practices than companies audited by other auditing firms due to the idea that small audit firms do not have the resources and experience that big audit firms have. Furthermore, they recommended that the first-tier listed companies should be audited by one of the big audit firms since they are under the public eyes; consequently, they must have a high disclosure level in order to be able to provide a higher quality of information. Al-Janadi et al. (2013) concluded that audit quality, measured as being one of the big-four audit companies, has a significant influence in improving the quality of financial reporting. Demir and Bahadir (2014) asserted that in Turkey, the size of the external auditor is positively associated with companies' level of disclosure due to the idea that big audit firms encourage their clients to have a higher level of compliance with IFRS in comparison with small audit firms. Hassaan (2012) reported that in the Jordanian context, companies audited by big-four auditing companies experienced a higher level of compliance with IFRS than companies audited by non-big-four audit companies. Nevertheless, Al-Shammari (2005) conducted a study in GCC countries and reported that there is a non-significant relationship between external auditor quality and compliance with IFRS, and the non-compliance with these disclosure requirements in these countries is the result of the ineffective role of audit firms and enforcement bodies.

In conclusion, most of the results of the previous studies in developing countries are consistent with the results of the studies conducted in developed countries. In other words, the review of the previous studies that examined the relationship between corporate governance mechanisms and the level of the adoption of IFRS disclosure requirements in developing countries revealed mixed results. However, the only variation was related to the effect of CEO duality on the extent of disclosure practices; several scholars who examined this relationship in developing countries, particularly in the Middle East, revealed that CEO duality is associated with a high level of disclosure. While in developed countries, several authors have agreed that the separation between CEO and the board chairman positions is linked with a high level of disclosure. This is attributed to the differences in the cultural and regulatory frameworks of these countries. Additionally, most of the previous studies reported that in order to enhance the effectiveness of the positive effect of corporate governance mechanisms on companies' disclosure practices, policy makers and regulatory authorities should improve their enforcement procedures over the implementation of good corporate governance practices.

Literature Gap

It was noticed that prior work has not *comprehensively* examined the level of compliance with IFRS across the entire Gulf region. For instance, Al-Shammari (2005) explored the level of compliance with IFRS disclosure requirements in GCC countries for the year 2003, but did not examine the impact of corporate governance on level of compliance. Further, Boshnak (2017) examined the impact of some corporate governance mechanisms on the level of compliance with IFRS in the GCC context, but the sample was formed by only 20 companies from each GCC country; this makes the generalization of the results limited, and made it difficult to detect the influence of each country's effect on the relationship between corporate governance and IFRS compliance. Therefore, we take a further step by examining the relationship between corporate governance and IFRS compliance on all listed companies in GCC member states in order to ensure the generalizability of the results, and detect the impact of the country level on the extent of IFRS compliance and on the relationship between corporate governance and IFRS compliance.

In addition, there is a scarcity in the studies that used recent data to test the level of compliance with IFRS mandatory disclosure requirements in the Middles East in general and in the GCC region in particular. For instance, Al Mutawaa and Hewaidy (2010) examined the level of compliance in Kuwait for the year 2006; Al-Akra et al. (2010a) tested the disclosure compliance in Jordan for the year 2004; Joshi and Al-Mudhahki (2013) used the data for 1999 to test the level of compliance with only IAS 1 in Bahrain. The most recent study was done by Boshnak (2017), which examined the level of compliance with IFRS in the GCC region using companies' annual reports for the year 2013. Nevertheless, the IFRS environment is highly dynamic and changeable as several standards after 2013 were amended or new standards were issued, such as IAS 1 (Presentation of Financial Statements), IAS 16 (Property, Plant and Equipment), IAS 19 (Employees Benefits), IAS 38 (Intangible Assets), IFRS 7 (Financial Instruments: Disclosure), and IFRS 9 (Financial Instruments). Hence, a further examination of the level of compliance with these standards is needed as they were not tested before among GCC countries.

Moreover, some important standards, namely IAS 19 (Employees Benefits) and IAS 26 (Accounting and Reporting by Retirement Benefits Plans), which are related to employees' benefits and end of service benefits, were intentionally overlooked and excluded from the majority previous studies as for reasons related to the nature of the country's labor laws. In other words, studies have justified the exclusion of these standards standing on the idea that country's labor law determines the amount and the calculation of employees' benefits and retirements. However, the way of determining how employees should be paid is not the concern of IAS 19 and IAS 26. These standards, like all other standards, are concerned with how to calculate the amounts that must be paid to employees, the accounting treatment for these amounts, and what should be disclosed in the financial statements. The latter implies that when it comes to how much the company should pay for employees, the labor law will be the reference, but when it comes to how to record these benefits in the books of the company, the company must follow the accounting standards. Therefore, excluding these standards based on the previous justification is invalid, except for some research contexts such as Jordan and Egypt. In more details, IAS 19 and IAS 26 show the accounting treatment for two types of employees' benefits, the first one is the short-term benefits, such as employees' salaries, annual leave, and sick leave. The second type is the post-employment benefits, which are divided into contribution benefit plans and defined benefit plans. Contribution benefit plans are related to post-employment benefits that paid by a third party, most likely a by a mutual fund or a social security. For this type of benefits plans, the responsibility of the company is limited to the monthly amount that it pays to that third party who is responsible to account and pay such benefits. This type of employees' benefits is being applied in some countries such as Jordan and Egypt, which justifies the exclusion of these standards of the studies that were conducted in these countries. The second form of post-employment benefits is the defined benefit plans, which have a complicated and controversial accounting treatment. Within this regard, the company itself is responsible for the post-employment benefits through setting a plan of payment that is determined either by the internal policy of the company or by the country's company law. Hence, the standards are not related to the way of determining these amounts; they rather more concerned with how to calculate and report the plan's liabilities, assets, actuarial losses and gains, and the current and previous cost of such a plan. Consequently, after the extensive review of these two standards and the labour laws in GCC member states, it was concluded that each company in the Gulf region is concerned with both plans (contribution benefit plans for employees who are the citizens of the country and defined benefit plans for the expats), which makes the exclusion of these standards according to the previous fact invalid for the GCC countries, and hence, these two standards are considered applicable in GCC context and were included in this book.

Finally, the effect of some corporate governance mechanisms on the level of compliance with IFRS were not previously tested within GCC region such as audit committee effectiveness (in terms of the number of members in the committee, the number of meetings held during the year, and the level of concentrated ownership). Hence, we consider these variables and discuss them in detail in this book.

Table 5.1 summarizes the previous studies that have examined the effect of corporate governance mechanisms on financial disclosure and IFRS compliance, including the author(s) and the year of each study, the country where the research was conducted, the sample size, the variables tested, and the main findings of each study.

Summary

This chapter has provided the essential needed background in examining the relationship between corporate governance and the level of compliance with IFRS, and to support the formulation of the propositions that will be presented in the next chapter. This chapter started with a discussion of the main theories related to corporate governance and company's disclosure practices. We adopted multiple-theoretical frameworks to develop our propositions and perform our analysis, relying on the fact that standing on one single theory will not be sufficient to provide a complete interpretation of the association between corporate governance mechanisms and financial disclosure practices (Nicholson and Kiel, 2007; Ntim and Soobaroyen, 2013).

The next section discussed the relationship between corporate governance and the level of the adoption of IFRS disclosure requirements. Due to the lack in the number of studies that examined such a relation, studies that tested the relationship between corporate governance and both the extent of disclosure and quality of financial reporting were also presented. The empirical results of the existing literature, in both developed and developing countries, showed mixed results; there is no conclusive results about the relationship between corporate governance and IFRS compliance.

The next chapter sheds lights on the theoretical aspects of the impact of some internal and external corporate governance mechanisms and firm characteristics on the level of compliance with IFRS to provide the necessary justifications of our propositions and theoretical model.

Table 5.1 A summary of empirical studies related to corporate governance and IFRS compliance

Author(s) Year	*Country*	*Sample*	*Independent Variables (measures)*	*Findings*
Cerf (1961)	United States	527	Listing status Return on assets Firm size Number of shareholders	Listed companies disclose more information than non-listed companies. Firm size, return on assets, number of shareholders have a positive effect on the extent of disclosure.
Singhvi and Desai (1971)	United States	155	Firm size Number of shareholders Listing status External auditor Rate of return Earnings margin	All of the independent variables have a positive effect on the extent of financial disclosure.
Firth (1979)	United Kingdom	180	Firm size Listing status Auditor type	Firm size and listing status have a significant relation with the level of voluntary disclosure. While there is insignificant relation between auditor type and voluntary disclosure.
DeAngelo (1981)	No sample shown		Audit firm size	Audit firm size has a positive effect on the audit quality and the level of disclosure.
Forker (1992)	United Kingdom	182	Proportion of non-executive directors Audit committee	A weak association was detected between board independence and audit committee and the quality of disclosure.
Ahmed and Nicholls (1994)	Bangladesh	63	Audit firm size Firm size Leverage	Firm size, and leverage have no impact on the level of compliance with mandatory disclosure requirements. The size of the external auditor has a positive effect on the level of compliance.

(Continued)

Table 5.1 (Continued)

Author(s) Year	*Country*	*Sample*	*Independent Variables (measures)*	*Findings*
Beasley (1996)	United States	150	Outside members in the board Audit committee	The fraction of outside members and the presence of audit committee in the board affects the financial statements fraud.
Dechow et al. (1996)	United States	92	Board independence CEO duality Audit committee Outside block holders	Board independence, audit committee, outside block holders have a negative effect on earnings management. CEO duality has a positive effect on earnings management.
Haniffa (1999)	Malaysia	167	CEO duality Board composition Family ownership Industry type	Industry type, CEO separation, board composition have a significant influence on the level of disclosure.
Chau and Gray (2002)	Hong Kong and Singapore	60 companies in Hong Kong and 62 in Singapore	Size of auditor Ownership structure Profitability	A positive relation between wider ownership structure and the extent of voluntary disclosure. A negative relation between family owned companies and voluntary disclosure.
Depoers (2000)	France	102	Firm size Ownership structure External auditor size Leverage Foreign activities	Big-sized companies and companies that have foreign activities tend to disclose more information. No significant effect of leverage on the level of disclosure. Ownership structure and auditor size don't affect the extent of disclosure.
Donnelly and Lynch (2002)	United Kingdom	262	Ownership structure	Ownership has a significant effect on the quality of earnings.

Fan and Wong (2002)	7 east Asian economics	977	Ownership structure	The high level of ownership concentration and large separation between control and management reduces the informativeness of earnings.
Haniffa and Cooke (2002)	Malaysia	167	The existence of no-executive chairman Family ownership CEO duality	The existence of non-executive chairman is negatively associated with the level of disclosure. No significant association between the level of disclosure and any of the cultural variables.
Al-Shiab (2003)	Jordan	50	Industry type Firm size External audit size	All the independent variables have a significant effect on the extent of disclosure practices implemented by companies.
Anderson and Daoud (2005)	Sweden	54	Board size Board composition External audit size Number of shareholders Firm size Industry type Audit committee	Firm size, board composition, number of shareholders, the existence of audit committee have a positive effect on the extent of disclosure. Industry type, external auditor size, board size don't have association with the extent of disclosure.
Arcay and Vazquez (2005)	Spain	91	Board size Audit committee CEO Duality Ownership concentration Listing status Industry type Firm size	Firm size, listing status, ownership structure, board independence, the existence of audit committee affect the level of voluntary disclosure. CEO does not have a significant influence on the level of voluntary disclosure.

(Continued)

Table 5.1 (Continued)

Author(s) Year	*Country*	*Sample*	*Independent Variables (measures)*	*Findings*
Vafeas (2005)	United States	252	Audit committee Board size Board independence	Board size became smaller over time. Number of independent members increased. Audit committee became more independent and more active. All independent variables has a negative effect on earnings management.
Ahmed et al. (2006)	New Zealand	615 firm-year observations	Board independence Board size	Board size is negatively related to the quality of accounting information. While there is no relation between number of outside directors.
Barako et al. (2006)	Kenya	43	Board independence Institutional ownership External auditor Firm size Leverage The presence of audit committee	Institutional ownership, the presence of audit committee, firm size, foreign ownership, leverage have a positive relationship with the level of disclosure. The proportion of non-executive directors has a negative relation with the level of financial disclosure.
Bradbury et al. (2006)	Singapore and Kuala Lumpur	139 from Singapore 113 from Malaysia	Board size Audit committee independence Board independence	No relation between board independence and accounting quality. There is a significant relation between both board's size and audit committee and accounting quality.
Firth et al. (2007)	5189 firm-year observations	China	Ownership concentration The presence of foreign shareholders Independent directors Board size	All independent variables have a significant effect on the level of earnings management.

Huafang and Jianguo (2007)	China	559	Block holder ownership Foreign ownership Managerial ownership State ownership Boar independence CEO duality Firm size	Block holder ownership, foreign ownership, firm size, and board independence are positively related to the level of voluntary disclosure. Managerial ownership, state ownership are not related to the level of disclosure. CEO duality is associated with low disclosure.
Petra (2007)	United States	203	Percentage of outside members The absence of CEO duality The independence of audit committee	Percentage of outside member has a positive effect on the informativeness of earnings. No significant relation between CEO duality and audit committee on the earnings informativeness.
Tsamenyi et al. (2007)	Ghana	22	Ownership structure Dispersion of shareholding Firm size Leverage	Ownership structure, dispersion of shareholding, and firm size have a significant effect on disclosure. No significant relation between leverage and disclosure.
Al-Shammari (2005)	GCC countries	137	Auditor type Firm size Industry type Leverage Internationality	Firm size, leverage, internationality, industry type affect the extent of disclosure. No significant relation between external auditor and the level of disclosure.
Donnelly and Mulcahy (2008)	Ireland	51	Board independence CEO duality Ownership structure	Companies with higher number of independent board members, and companies with CEO duality have a higher level of voluntary disclosure. Ownership structure doesn't have an influence on the degree of voluntary disclosure.

(*Continued*)

Table 5.1 (Continued)

Author(s) Year	*Country*	*Sample*	*Independent Variables (measures)*	*Findings*
Ezat and El-Masry (2008)	Egypt	50	Firm size Industry type Liquidity Ownership structure Board composition Board size	All independent variables have a significant positive effect on the company's Internet disclosure
Kent and Stewart (2008)	Australia	965	Frequency of board meeting audit committee size and its frequency meetings External auditor Board size	The extent of disclosure is positively related to the frequency of board and audit committee meetings and board size. The level of disclosure is not related to the independence of the audit committee.
Laidroo (2009)		52	Ownership concentration Foreign ownership Institutional ownership Firm size	All independent variables have a negative effect on the level of disclosure
Al-Akra et al. (2010a)	Jordan	80	Ownership structure Number of non-executive directors Board size Audit committee Firm size Profitability Listing status Industry type Auditor type	Audit committee, board size, auditor type, liquidity, profitability, number of non-executive directors, have a significant effect on the level of disclosure. There is no significant relation between ownership structure and the level of disclosure.

Al-Akra et al. (2010b)	Jordan	27	Privatization Regulatory reforms Ownership structure Company size Leverage Profitability Liquidity	Privatization has a significant positive impact on the level of disclosure. Foreign investment, company size, and industry type have a positive effect on the level of disclosure. Foreign investment accompanying with privatization have a significant influence on the level of disclosure.
Al-Shammari and Al-Sultan (2010)	Kuwait	170	Proportion of non-executive directors Proportion of family members potion in the board CEO duality Audit committee	Only audit committee has a positive significant effect of the level voluntary disclosure. No significant association between other independent variables and voluntary disclosure.
Chau and Gray (2010)	Hong Kong	273	Family ownership CEO duality Board independence	The appointment of an independent chairman is positively related to the level of voluntary disclosure. And the existence of independent chairman will mitigate the effect of family ownership on voluntary disclosure. Board independence and family have ownership have a significant relation with the level of voluntary disclosure.
Dimitropoulos and Asteriou (2010)	97	Greece	Board size Board composition	The portion of independent directors in the board has a positive effect on the quality of annual reports. Board size is not related to the quality of earnings.

(Continued)

Table 5.1 (Continued)

Author(s) Year	*Country*	*Sample*	*Independent Variables (measures)*	*Findings*
Samaha and Dahawy (2010)	Egypt	30	Board independence Ownership structure Firm size Industry type Auditor type Audit committee	Audit committee, management ownership, board independence, auditor type, industry type have a positive effect on the level of disclosure. No relation between firm size and the level of disclosure.
Alanezi and Albuloushi (2011)	Kuwait	68	Audit committee Family members in the board Industry type Leverage	Audit committee has a significant positive relation with IFRS disclosure compliance. No significant relation between other variables and IFRS compliance.
Omar and Simon (2011)	Jordan	121	Firm size Profitability Listing status Industry type Audit firm size Firm age	The average compliance with both mandatory and voluntary disclosure is 69%. All the independent variables have a significant effect in explaining the variations of the level of disclosure.
Rouf and Harun (2011)	Bangladesh	94	Management ownership Institutional ownership	Positive relation between voluntary disclosure and institutional ownership. Negative relation with management ownership.
Samaha and Dahawy (2010)	Egypt	100	Board independence Ownership structure Firm size Auditor type	Higher number of non-executive directors has high level of disclosure. Block holder ownership results low level of disclosure managerial ownership and government ownership don't have an effect on the level of disclosure. Industry type, firm size, liquidity, leverage, don't have an effect on the level of disclosure.

Uyar (2011)	Turkey	96	Auditor size Ownership structure Profitability Firm size	Auditor size and firm size have a positive effect on voluntary disclosure. Ownership structure and firm size don't have a significant influence on voluntary disclosure.
Al-Moataz and Hussainey (2012)	Saudi Arabia	97	Board independence Audit committee Profitability Liquidity Debt ratio Firm size	Board independence, audit committee size, profitability, liquidity are significantly associated with the level of corporate governance disclosure. Firm size doesn't have a significant association with the level of disclosure.
Chakroun and Matoussi (2012)	Tunisia	144 firm year observations	Board independence Ownership structure	Board size and ownership structure have a positive effect on the level of voluntary disclosure.
Gao and Kling (2012)	China	8864 observations	Listing status Firm size State ownership Ownership concentration Size of the audit firm	Cross listing does not influence the level of mandatory disclosure. Larger firms tend to disclose more information. State ownership reduces the compliance with disclosure. Concentrated ownership is associated with higher disclosure. Audit firm size doesn't affect the compliance with disclosure.
Ibadin et al. (2012)	Nigeria	118	Board independence Board size Company size Leverage Profitability Audit firm size	None of the independent variables has an effect on the quality of financial reporting.

(Continued)

Table 5.1 (Continued)

Author(s) Year	*Country*	*Sample*	*Independent Variables (measures)*	*Findings*
Samaha et al. (2012)	Egypt	100	Board composition Board size CEO duality Block holder ownership The existence of audit committee	CEO duality and block holders ownership are negatively associated with corporate governance disclosure. Board composition, board size, positively related to the level of corporate governance disclosure. Audit committee has a little role in improving the financial disclosure.
Al-Janadi et al. (2013)	Saudi Arabia	87	Non-executive directors Board size CEO duality Audit quality Government ownership	All independent variables have a positive effect on the level of voluntary disclosure.
Hasan et al. (2013)	Bangladesh	20	External auditor Board independence Board size Institutional ownership	Only external auditor has a significant effect on the level of disclosure.
Allegrini and Greco (2013)	Italy	177	Firm size Leverage Profitability Listing status Ownership diffusion CEO duality Board composition Lead independent director Board committees Board size Board activity Audit committee activity	Board size and diligence and audit committee have a positive significant effect on voluntary disclosure. Board committees, board composition, the presence of lead independent director have no relationship with voluntary disclosure. CEO duality has a negative effect on the voluntary disclosure.

Hassaan (2012)	Egypt and Jordan	75	Boar independence Board leadership Board size Government ownership Management ownership Private ownership Public ownership Firm size Profitability Liquidity Type of auditor Type of business	No significant association between the corporate governance variables and the level of compliance with IFRS. No significant relation between profitability and IFRS compliance. No significant relation between industry type and IFRS compliance. A positive relation between type of auditor and IFRS compliance in Jordan only.
Sarea and Al Nesuf (2013)	Bahrain	19	Management ownership Institutional ownership Foreign investment Return on investment Return on assets Return on equity	Institutional ownership, foreign investment, return on assets, and return on equity have significant positive effect on the level of IFRS compliance. No significant relation between other independent *t* variables and the level of compliance.
Verriest et al. (2013)	EU countries	223	Board independence Board functioning Audit committee effectiveness	All independent variables have a positive effect on the quality of information.
Alhazaimeh et al. (2014)	Jordan		Board activity Foreign ownership Non-executive directors Block holder ownership	All independent variables have a significant influence on the level of voluntary disclosure.

(*Continued*)

Table 5.1 (Continued)

Author(s) Year	*Country*	*Sample*	*Independent Variables (measures)*	*Findings*
Bouchareb et al. (2014)	France	146	Board size Independent board members CEO duality Existence of audit committee ownership structure External audit quality Control variables: firm size The level of debt Quotation of foreign market	Independent board of directors, the presence of an internal audit committee, the concentration of ownership structure, managerial ownership, the quality of external auditor, firm size, and listing status have significant effect in decreasing the level of earnings management. While family ownership has a negative effect on the level of earnings management.
Demir and Bahadir (2014)	Turkey	168	Big-four audit firms Leverage Profitability Firm size Firm age	The average compliance is 79%. Companies audited by big-four audit firms have a higher level of compliance with IFRS. A negative relation with leverage. No significant relation between other independent variables and compliance with IFRS.
Haddad et al. (2015)	Jordan	57	Government ownership Outside ownership Managerial ownership Family domination of the board	Government ownership positively related to the voluntary disclosure. Management ownership is negatively related to the level of disclosure. Family domination of the board is a significant factors in explaining the variation of disclosure practices. Outside ownership does have a significant relation.

Luthan and Satria (2016)	Indonesia	65	Board independence Audit committee composition Quality of audit Managerial ownership Institutional ownership	Board independence, audit committee composition, and quality of auditor have a negative effect on earnings management. Both managerial and institutional ownership don't have a significant effect on earnings management.
Mnif and Znazen (2020)	Canada	63	Board size Board independence Audit committee Independence CEO duality Audit committee size Audit committee meetings frequency	Board size, board independence, and audit committee independence positively affect the level of compliance with IFRS. CEO duality, audit committee size, audit committee meeting frequency have a non-significant effect on IFRS compliance.

Source: Developed by the authors.

References

Aboagye-Otchere, F., Bedi, I., & Ossei Kwakye, T. (2012). Corporate governance and disclosure practices of Ghanaian listed companies. *Journal of Accounting in Emerging Economies, 2*(2), 140–161.

Aburaya, R. (2012). *The relationship between corporate governance and environmental disclosure: UK evidence* (Doctoral dissertation, Durham University).

Ahmed, K., Hossain, M., & Adams, M.B. (2006). The effects of board composition and board size on the informativeness of annual accounting earnings. *Corporate Governance: An International Review, 14*(5), 418–431.

Ahmed, K., & Nicholls, D. (1994). The impact of non-financial company characteristics on mandatory disclosure compliance in developing countries: The case of Bangladesh. *The International Journal of Accounting, 29*(1), 62–77.

Akhtaruddin, H., & Haron, M. (2010). Board ownership, audit committee effectiveness and corporate voluntary disclosure. *Asian Review of Accounting, 18*(3), 245–259.

Aksu, M., & Espahbodi, H. (2016). The impact of IFRS adoption and corporate governance principles on transparency and disclosure: The case of Borsa Istanbul. *Emerging Markets Finance and Trade, 52*(4), 1013–1028.

Al Mutawaa, A., & Hewaidy, A.M. (2010). Disclosure level and compliance with IFRSs: An empirical investigation of Kuwaiti companies. *The International Business & Economics Research Journal, 9*(5), 33–50.

Al-Akra, M., Eddie, I.A., & Ali, M.J. (2010a). The influence of the introduction of accounting disclosure regulation on mandatory disclosure compliance: Evidence from Jordan. *The British Accounting Review, 42*(3), 170–186.

Al-Akra, M., Eddie, I.A., & Ali, M.J. (2010b). The association between privatisation and voluntary disclosure: Evidence from Jordan. *Accounting and Business Research, 40*(1), 55–74.

Alanezi, F.S., & Albuloushi, S.S. (2011). Does the existence of voluntary audit committees really affect IFRS-required disclosure? The Kuwaiti evidence. *International Journal of Disclosure and Governance, 8*(2), 148–173.

Albassam, W. (2014). *Corporate governance, voluntary disclosure and financial performance: Ban empirical analysis of Saudi listed firms using a mixed-methods research design* (Doctoral dissertation, University of Glasgow).

Albrecht, W.S., Albrecht, C.C., & Albrecht, C.O. (2004). Fraud and corporate executives: Agency, stewardship and broken trust. *Journal of Forensic Accounting, 5*(1), 109–130.

Alhazaimeh, A., Palaniappan, R., & Almsafir, M. (2014). The impact of corporate governance and ownership structure on voluntary disclosure in annual reports among listed Jordanian companies. *Procedia-Social and Behavioral Sciences, 129*, 341–348.

Al-Htaybat, K. (2005). *Financial disclosure practices: Theoretical foundation, and an empirical investigation on Jordanian printed and internet formats* (Doctoral dissertation, University of Southampton).

Al-Janadi, Y., Rahman, R.A., & Omar, N.H. (2013). Corporate governance mechanisms and voluntary disclosure in Saudi Arabia. *Corporate Governance, 4*(4), 25–35.

Allegrini, M., & Greco, G. (2013). Corporate boards, audit committees and voluntary disclosure: Evidence from Italian listed companies. *Journal of Management & Governance, 17*(1), 187–216.

Al-Moataz, E., & Hussainey, K. (2012). Determinants of corporate governance disclosure in Saudi companies. *Journal of Economics and Management, 5*(1), 52–84.

Al-Shammari, B., & Al-Sultan, W. (2010). Corporate governance and voluntary disclosure in Kuwait. *International Journal of Disclosure and Governance*, 7(3), 262–280.

Al-Shammari, B.A. (2005). *Compliance with international accounting standards by listed companies in the Gulf Co-operation Council member states: An empirical study*. University of Western Australia.

Al-Shiab, M. (2003). *Financial consequences of IAS adoption: The case of Jordan* (Doctoral dissertation, Newcastle University).

Alzoubi, E.S.S. (2012). Board characteristics and financial reporting quality among Jordanian listed companies: Proposing conceptual framework. *Asian Journal of Finance & Accounting*, *4*(1), 245–258.

Anderson, M., & Daoud, M. (2005). *Corporate governances disclosure by Swedish listed corporations* (Master thesis, Jonkoping International Business School, Jonkoping University, Sweden).

Ansoff, I. (1965). *Corporate strategy*. New York, NY: McGraw Hill.

Apostolou, A.K., & Nanopoulos, K.A. (2009). Voluntary accounting disclosure and corporate governance: Evidence from Greek listed firms. *International Journal of Accounting and Finance*, *1*(4), 395–414.

Ararat, M., & Ugur, M. (2003). Corporate governance in Turkey: An overview and some policy recommendations. *Corporate Governance: The international Journal of Business in Society*, *3*(1), 58–75.

Arcay, M.R.B., & Vazquez, M.F.M. (2005). Corporate characteristics, governance rules and the extent of voluntary disclosure in Spain. *Advances in Accounting*, *21*, 299–331.

Arnold, B., & De Lange, P. (2004). Enron: An examination of agency problems. *Critical Perspectives on Accounting*, *15*(6-7), 751–765.

Baazaoui, H., & Zaraï, M.A. (2019). The effect of firm characteristics on the disclosure of IAS/IFRS information: The cases of Tunisia, France and Canada. *International Business and Accounting Research Journal*, *3*(2), 124–153.

Barako, D.G. (2007). Determinants of voluntary disclosures in Kenyan companies annual reports. *African Journal of Business Management*, *1*(5), 113–128.

Barako, D.G., Hancock, P., & Izan, H.Y. (2006). Factors influencing voluntary corporate disclosure by Kenyan companies. *Corporate Governance: An International Review*, *14*(2), 107–125.

Beasley, M.S. (1996). An empirical analysis of the relation between the board of director composition and financial statement fraud. *Accounting review*, *71*(4) 443–465.

Becker, C.L., DeFond, M.L., Jiambalvo, J., & Subramanyam, K.R. (1998). The effect of audit quality on earnings management. *Contemporary Accounting Research*, *15*(1), 1–24.

Beekes, W., Pope, P., & Young, S. (2004). The link between earnings timeliness, earnings conservatism and board composition: Evidence from the UK. *Corporate Governance: An International Review*, *12*(1), 47–59.

Biondi, Y., Giannoccolo, P., & Reberioux, A. (2009, October). Financial disclosure and the board: Is independence of directors always efficient? *Forum de La Regulation*. Paris.

Boshnak, H. (2017). *Mandatory and voluntary disclosures in GCC listed firms* (Doctoral dissertation, University of the West of England).

Bouchareb, M., Ajina, A., & Souid, S. (2014). Does the adoption of IAS/IFRS with a strong governance mechanism can deter earnings management? *International Journal of Academic Research in Economics and Management Sciences*, *3*(1), 264–282.

Bradbury, M., Mak, Y.T., & Tan, S.M. (2006). Board characteristics, audit committee characteristics and abnormal accruals. *Pacific Accounting Review*, *18*(2), 47–68.

Brennan, N. (2007). *Corporate governance and financial reporting*. SAGE Publications.
Brown, J.R., Falaschetti, D., & Orlando, M.J. (2010). Auditor independence and the quality of information in financial disclosures: Evidence for market discipline versus Sarbanes–Oxley proscriptions. *American Law and Economics Review, 12*(1), 39–68.
Cerf, A. R. (1961). *Corporate reporting and investment decisions*. Berkeley, CA: University of California Press.
Chakroun, R., & Matoussi, H. (2012). Determinants of the extent of voluntary disclosure in the annual reports of the Tunisian firms. *Accounting and Management Information Systems, 11*(3), 335.
Chalevas, C.G. (2011). The effect of the mandatory adoption of corporate governance mechanisms on executive compensation. *The International Journal of Accounting, 46*(2), 138–174.
Chau, G.K., & Gray, S.J. (2002). Ownership structure and corporate voluntary disclosure in Hong Kong and Singapore. *The International Journal of Accounting, 37*(2), 247–265.
Chau, G., & Gray, S.J. (2010). Family ownership, board independence and voluntary disclosure: Evidence from Hong Kong. *Journal of International Accounting, Auditing and Taxation, 19*(2), 93–109.
Chen, H.L. (2011). Does board independence influence the top management team? Evidence from strategic decisions toward internationalization. *Corporate Governance: An International Review, 19*(4), 334–350.
Chen, J.C., & Roberts, R.W. (2010). Toward a more coherent understanding of the organization–society relationship: A theoretical consideration for social and environmental accounting research. *Journal of Business Ethics, 97*(4), 651–665.
Chung, R., Firth, M., & Kim, J.B. (2003). Auditor conservatism and reported earnings. *Accounting and Business Research, 33*(1), 19–32.
Clarke, T. (1998). The stakeholder corporation: A business philosophy for the information age. *Long Range Planning, 31*(2), 182–194.
Coles, J.L., Daniel, N.D., & Naveen, L. (2008). Boards: Does one size fit all? *Journal of Financial Economics, 87*(2), 329–356.
Conyon, M.J., & He, L. (2011). Executive compensation and corporate governance in China. *Journal of Corporate Finance, 17*(4), 1158–1175.
Coombes, P., & Wong, S.C. (2004). Chairman and CEO: One job or two? *The Mckinsey Quarterly: A New Era in Governance, 2*(1) 43–47.
Cormier, D. (2014). The incidence of corporate governance and IFRS on information asymmetry and the value relevance of earnings: Some Canadian evidence. *Cahier de recherche, 2014–01*.
Cotter, J., & Najah, M.M. (2011). Institutional investor influence on global climate change disclosure practices. *Australian Journal of Management, 37*(2), 169–187.
Crowther, D., & Jatana, R. (2007). Agency theory: A cause of failure in corporate governance. *International dimensions of corporate social responsibility* (vol. 1). ICFAI University Press, pp. 135–115.
Dahya, J., & Travlos, N. (2000). Does the one man show pay? Theory and evidence on the dual CEO revisited. *European Financial Management, 6*(1), 85–98.
Davis, J.H., Schoorman, F.D., & Donaldson, L. (1997). Toward a stewardship theory of management. *Academy of Management Review, 22*(1), 20–47.
DeAngelo, L.E. (1981). Auditor size and audit quality. *Journal of Accounting and Economics, 3*(3), 183–199.

Dechow, P.M., Sloan, R.G., & Sweeney, A.P. (1996). Causes and consequences of earnings manipulation: An analysis of firms subject to enforcement actions by the SEC. *Contemporary Accounting Research, 13*(1), 1–36.

Deegan, C. (2013). *Financial accounting theory*. McGraw-Hill Education Australia.

Demir, V., & Bahadir, O. (2014). An investigation of compliance with International Financial Reporting Standards by listed companies in Turkey. *Accounting and Management Information Systems, 13*(1), 4–34.

Denis, D.K., & McConnell, J.J. (2003). International corporate governance. *Journal of Financial and Quantitative Analysis, 38*(1), 1–36.

Depoers, F. (2000). A cost benefit study of voluntary disclosure: Some empirical evidence from French listed companies. *European Accounting Review, 9*(2), 245–263.

Dharmadasa, P., Gamage, P., & Herath, S.K. (2014). Corporate governance, board characteristics and firm performance: Evidence from Sri Lanka. *South Asian Journal of Management, 21*(1), 7–31.

Dimitropoulos, P.E., & Asteriou, D. (2010). The effect of board composition on the informativeness and quality of annual earnings: Empirical evidence from Greece. *Research in International Business and Finance, 24*(2), 190–205.

Donaldson, L. (1990). The ethereal hand: Organizational economics and management theory. *Academy of Management Review, 15*(3), 369–381.

Donaldson, L., & Davis, J.H. (1991). Stewardship theory or agency theory: CEO governance and shareholder returns. *Australian Journal of Management, 16*(1), 49–64.

Donnelly, R., & Lynch, C. (2002). The ownership structure of UK firms and the informativeness of accounting earnings. *Accounting and Business Research, 32*(4), 245–257.

Donnelly, R., & Mulcahy, M. (2008). Board structure, ownership, and voluntary disclosure in Ireland. *Corporate Governance: An International Review, 16*(5), 416–429.

Eisenhardt, K.M. (1989). Making fast strategic decisions in high-velocity environments. *Academy of Management Journal, 32*(3), 543–576.

Eng, L.L., & Mak, Y.T. (2003). Corporate governance and voluntary disclosure. *Journal of Accounting and Public Policy, 22*(4), 325–345.

Ezat, A., & El-Masry, A. (2008). The impact of corporate governance on the timeliness of corporate internet reporting by Egyptian listed companies. *Managerial Finance, 34*(12), 848–867.

Fama, E.F. (1980). Agency problems and the theory of the firm. *Journal of Political Economy, 88*(2), 288–307.

Fama, E.F., & Jensen, M.C. (1983). Separation of ownership and control. *The Journal of Law & Economics, 26*(2), 301–325.

Fan, J.P., & Wong, T.J. (2002). Corporate ownership structure and the informativeness of accounting earnings in East Asia. *Journal of Accounting and Economics, 33*(3), 401–425.

Fekete, S., Matis, D., & Lukac J. (2008). Factors influencing the extent of corporate compliance with IFRS: The case of Hungarian listed companies. *Annales Universitatis Apulensis Series Oeconomica, 1*(10), 1–12.

Fiedler, T., & Deegan, C. (2002). Environmental collaborations within the building and construction industry: A consideration of the motivations to collaborate. In *Proceedings of the Critical Perspectives on Accounting Conference, New York, April.*

Firth, M. (1979). The impact of size, stock market listing, and auditors on voluntary disclosure in corporate annual reports. *Accounting and Business Research, 9*(36), 273–280.

Firth, M., Fung, P.M., & Rui, O.M. (2007). Ownership, two-tier board structure, and the informativeness of earnings: Evidence from China. *Journal of Accounting and Public Policy, 26*(4), 463–496.

Forker, J.J. (1992). Corporate governance and disclosure quality. *Accounting and Business Research, 22*(86), 111–124.

Foster, D., & Jonker, J. (2005). Stakeholder relationships: The dialogue of engagement. *Corporate Governance: International Journal of Business in Society, 5*(5), 51–57.

Freeman, R.E. (2010). *Strategic management: A stakeholder approach.* Cambridge University Press.

Gao, L., & Kling, G. (2012). The impact of corporate governance and external audit on compliance to mandatory disclosure requirements in China. *Journal of International Accounting, Auditing and Taxation, 21*(1), 17–31.

Gibbins, M., Richardson, A., & Waterhouse, J. (1990). The management of corporate financial disclosure: Opportunism, ritualism, policies, and processes. *Journal of Accounting Research, 28*(1), 121–143.

Gray, R., Owen, D., & Adams, C. (1996). *Accounting & accountability: Changes and challenges in corporate social and environmental reporting.* Prentice Hall.

Haddad, A.E., AlShattarat, W.K., AbuGhazaleh, N.M., & Nobanee, H. (2015). The impact of ownership structure and family board domination on voluntary disclosure for Jordanian listed companies. *Eurasian Business Review, 5*(2), 203–234.

Haniffa, R., & Hudaib, M. (2006). Corporate governance structure and performance of Malaysian listed companies. *Journal of Business Finance & Accounting, 33*(7–8), 1034–1062.

Haniffa, R.M. (1999). *Culture, corporate governance and disclosure in Malaysian corporations* (Doctoral dissertation, University of Exeter).

Haniffa, R.M., & Cooke, T.E. (2002). Culture, corporate governance and disclosure in Malaysian corporations. *Abacus, 38*(3), 317–349.

Hasan, M.S., Hossain, S.Z., & Swieringa, R.J. (2013). Corporate governance and financial disclosures: Bangladesh perspective. *Research Journal of Finance and Accounting, 4*(1), 109–119.

Hashim, A.H., & Devis, S. (2009). Board characteristics, ownership structure and earning quality Malaysian evidence. *Research in Accounting in Emerging Economies, 8*, 97–123.

Hassaan, M. (2012). *Corporate governance and compliance with International Financial Reporting Standards (IFRSs): Evidence from two MENA stock exchanges* (Doctoral dissertation, Aston University).

Hermanson, D.R. (2003). Does corporate governance really matter? What the research tells us. *Internal Auditing, 18*(2), 44–45.

Ho, S.S., & Wong, K.S. (2001). A study of the relationship between corporate governance structures and the extent of voluntary disclosure. *Journal of International Accounting, Auditing and Taxation, 10*(2), 139–156.

Hossain, M., Tan, L.M., & Adams, M.C. (1994). Voluntary disclosure in an emerging capital market: Some empirical evidence from companies listed in the Kuala Lumpur stock exchange. *The International Journal of Accounting. 29*(4), 334–351.

Huafang, X., & Jianguo, Y. (2007). Ownership structure, board composition and corporate voluntary disclosure: Evidence from listed companies in China. *Managerial Auditing Journal, 22*(6), 604–619.

Ibadin, I.M., Izedonmi, F., & Ibadin, P.O. (2012). The association between selected corporate governance attributes, company attributes and timeliness of financial reporting in Nigeria. *Research Journal of Finance and Accounting, 3*(9), 137–145.

Jamali, D. (2008). A stakeholder approach to corporate social responsibility: A fresh perspective into theory and practice. *Journal of Business Ethics, 82*(1), 213–231.

Jensen, M.C. (1993). The modern industrial revolution, exit, and the failure of internal control systems. *The Journal of Finance, 48*(3), 831–880.

Jensen, M.C., & Meckling, W.H. (1976). Theory of the firm: Managerial behavior, agency costs and ownership structure. *Journal of Financial Economics, 3*(4), 305–360.

Joshi, P.L., & Al-Mudhahki, J. (2013). Empirical study of compliance with international accounting standards (IAS-1) by stock exchange listed companies in Bahrain. *Journal of Financial Management & Analysis, 26*(2), 43–54.

Juhmani, O. (2017). Corporate governance and the level of Bahraini corporate compliance with IFRS disclosure. *Journal of Applied Accounting Research, 18*(1), 22–41.

Kao, L., & Chen, A. (2004). The effects of board characteristics on earnings management. *Corporate Ownership & Control, 1*(3), 96–107.

Kelton, A.S., & Yang, Y.W. (2008). The impact of corporate governance on Internet financial reporting. *Journal of accounting and Public Policy, 27*(1), 62–87.

Kent, P., & Stewart, J. (2008). Corporate governance and disclosures on the transition to international financial reporting standards. *Accounting & Finance, 48*(4), 649–671.

Kiel, G.C., & Nicholson, G.J. (2003). Board composition and corporate performance: How the Australian experience informs contrasting theories of corporate governance. *Corporate Governance: An International Review, 11*(3), 189–205.

Klein, A. (2002). Audit committee, board of director characteristics, and earnings management. *Journal of Accounting and Economics, 33*(3), 375–400.

Kothari, S.P. (2000). The role of financial reporting in reducing financial risks in the market. In *Conference Series-Federal Reserve Bank of Boston* (Vol. 44, pp. 89–102). Federal Reserve Bank of Boston.

Laidroo, L. (2009). Association between ownership structure and public announcements' disclosures. *Corporate Governance: An International Review, 17*(1), 13–34.

Laing, D., & Weir, C.M. (1999). Governance structures, size and corporate performance in UK firms. *Management Decision, 37*(5), 457–464.

Lee, T.S., & Yeh, Y.H. (2004). Corporate governance and financial distress: Evidence from Taiwan. *Corporate Governance: An international Review, 12*(3), 378–388.

Letza, S., Sun, X., & Kirkbride, J. (2004). Shareholding versus stakeholding: A critical review of corporate governance. *Corporate Governance: An International Review, 12*(3), 242–262.

Li, H., & Qi, A. (2008). Impact of corporate governance on voluntary disclosure in Chinese listed companies. *Corporate Ownership and Control, 5*(2), 360–366.

Lipton, M., & Lorsch, J.W. (1992). A modest proposal for improved corporate governance. *The Business Lawyer, 48* 59–77.

Luthan, E., & Satria, I. (2016). The effect of good corporate governance mechanism to earnings management before and after IFRS convergence. *Procedia-Social and Behavioral Sciences, 219*, 465–471.

Macdonald, N., & Beattie, A. (1993). The corporate governance jigsaw. *Accounting and Business Research, 23*(1), 304–310.

Maher, M., & Andersson, T. (2000). Corporate governance: Effects on firm performance and economic growth. *OECD Working Papers. Available at SSRN 218490.*

Mallin, C. (2002). The relationship between corporate governance, transparency and financial disclosure. *Corporate Governance: An International Review, 10*(4), 253–255.

Mallin, C., & Ow-Yong, K. (2009). Corporate governance in alternative investment market (AIM) companies: Determinants of corporate governance disclosure. *Third Singapore International Conference on Finance 2009, Available at SSRN 1326627.*

Malone, D., Fries, C., & Jones, T. (1993). An empirical investigation of the extent of corporate financial disclosure in the oil and gas industry. *Journal of Accounting, Auditing & Finance, 8*(3), 249–273.

Marashdeh, Z.M.S. (2014). *The effect of corporate governance on firm performance in Jordan* (Doctoral dissertation, University of Central Lancashire).

Marra, A., & Mazzola, P. (2014). Is corporate board more effective under IFRS or "It's Just an Illusion"? *Journal of Accounting, Auditing & Finance, 29*(1), 31–60.

Matolcsy, Z., Tyler, J., & Wells, P. (2012). Is continuous disclosure associated with board independence? *Australian Journal of Management, 37*(1), 99–124.

McKnight, P.J., & Weir, C. (2009). Agency costs, corporate governance mechanisms and ownership structure in large UK publicly quoted companies: A panel data analysis. *The Quarterly Review of Economics and Finance, 49*(2), 139–158.

Mnif, Y., & Znazen, O. (2020). Corporate governance and compliance with IFRS 7: The case of financial institutions listed in Canada. *Managerial Auditing Journal, 35*(3), 448–474.

Morris, R.D. (1987). Signalling, agency theory and accounting policy choice. *Accounting and Business Research, 18*(69), 47–56.

Muth, M., & Donaldson, L. (1998). Stewardship theory and board structure: A contingency approach. *Corporate Governance: An International Review, 6*(1), 5–28.

Nicholson, G.J., & Kiel, G.C. (2007). Can directors impact performance? A case-based test of three theories of corporate governance. *Corporate Governance: An International Review, 15*(4), 585–608.

Noor, M.A.M., & Fadzil, F.H. (2013). Board characteristics and performance from perspective of governance code in Malaysia. *World Review of Business Research, 3*(3), 191–206.

Ntim, C.G., Opong, K.K., Danbolt, J., & Thomas, D.A. (2012). Voluntary corporate governance disclosures by post-apartheid South African corporations. *Journal of Applied Accounting Research, 13*(2), 122–144.

Ntim, C.G., & Soobaroyen, T. (2013). Black economic empowerment disclosures by South African listed corporations: The influence of ownership and board characteristics. *Journal of Business Ethics, 116*(1), 121–138.

OECD (2015). *Organization for Economic Cooperation and Development. OECD Principles of Corporate Governance.* Ankara: OECD Publications.

Omar, B.F.A. (2007). *Exploring the aggregate, mandatory and voluntary financial disclosure behaviour under a new regulatory environment: The case of Jordan* (Doctoral dissertation, University of Hull).

Omar, B., & Simon, J. (2011). Corporate aggregate disclosure practices in Jordan. *Advances in Accounting, 27*(1), 166–186.

Patton, A., & Baker, J.C. (1987). Why won't directors rock the boat. *Harvard Business Review, 65*(6), 10–12.

Pearce, J.A., & Zahra, S.A. (1992). Board composition from a strategic contingency perspective. *Journal of Management Studies, 29*(4), 411–438.

Pergola, T.M. (2005). Management entrenchment: Can it negate the effectiveness of recently legislated governance reform. *Journal of American Academy of Business, 6*(2), 177–183.

Petra, S.T. (2007). The effects of corporate governance on the informativeness of earnings. *Economics of Governance*, *8*(2), 129–152.

Pfeffer, J. (1973). Size, composition, and function of hospital boards of directors: A study of organization-environment linkage. *Administrative Science Quarterly*, *18*(3), 349–364.

Pichler, S., Cordazzo, M., & Rossi, P. (2018). An analysis of the firms-specific determinants influencing the voluntary IFRS adoption: Evidence from Italian private firms. *International Journal of Accounting, Auditing and Performance Evaluation*, *14*(1), 85–104.

Riccardi, W.N. (2019). Do audit firm tenure and size moderate changes in financial reporting quality due to mandatory IFRS adoption? *Auditing: A Journal of Practice & Theory*, *38*(4), 201–224.

Rouf, A., & Harun, A.A. (2011). Ownership structure and voluntary disclosure in annual reports of Bangladesh. *Pakistan Journal of Commerce & Social Sciences*, *5*(1), 129–139.

Samaha, K., & Dahawy, K. (2010). An empirical analysis of corporate governance structures and voluntary corporate disclosure in volatile capital markets: The Egyptian experience. *International Journal of Accounting, Auditing and Performance Evaluation*, 7(1-2), 61–93.

Samaha, K., Dahawy, K., Hussainey, K., & Stapleton, P. (2012). The extent of corporate governance disclosure and its determinants in a developing market: The case of Egypt. *Advances in Accounting*, *28*(1), 168–178.

Sanan, N., & Yadav, S. (2011). Corporate governance reforms and financial disclosures: A case of Indian companies. *IUP Journal of Corporate Governance*, *10*(2), 62–81.

Sarea, A., & Al Nesuf, H. (2013). The impact of management structure and bank characteristics on the level of compliance with IAS 21: Evidence from Bahrain. *International Journal of Accounting and Taxation*, *1*(1), 58–68.

Sellami, Y.M., & Fendri, H.B. (2017). The effect of audit committee characteristics on compliance with IFRS for related party disclosures: Evidence from South Africa. *Managerial Auditing Journal*, *32*(6), 603–626.

Shamser, M., & Annuar, M.N. (1993). Management versus shareholders' interest: Board composition, market risk and shareholder returns of Malaysian listed firms. *Malaysian Management Review*, *29*, 44–52.

Shehata, N. (2013). *Corporate governance disclosure in the Gulf countries* (Doctoral dissertation, Aston University).

Singhvi, S.S., & Desai, H.B. (1971). An empirical analysis of the quality of corporate financial disclosure. *The Accounting Review*, *46*(1), 129–138.

Sternberg, E. (1997). The defects of stakeholder theory. *Corporate Governance: An International Review*, *5*(1), 3–10.

Tricker, R.I. (1984). *Corporate governance: Practices, procedures, and powers in British companies and their boards of directors*. Gower Pub Co.

Tsalavoutas, I. (2011). Transition to IFRS and compliance with mandatory disclosure requirements: What is the signal? *Advances in Accounting*, *27*(2), 390–405.

Tsamenyi, M., Enninful-Adu, E., & Onumah, J. (2007). Disclosure and corporate governance in developing countries: Evidence from Ghana. *Managerial Auditing Journal*, *22*(3), 319–334.

Uyar, A. (2011). Firm characteristics and voluntary disclosure of graphs in annual reports of Turkish listed companies. *African Journal of Business Management*, *5*(17), 7651–7657.

Vafeas, N. (2005). Audit committees, boards, and the quality of reported earnings. *Contemporary Accounting Research*, *22*(4), 1093–1122.

Verriest, A., Gaeremynck, A., & Thornton, D.B. (2013). The impact of corporate governance on IFRS adoption choices. *European Accounting Review, 22*(1), 39–77.

Wang, Y., & Campbell, M. (2012). Corporate governance, earnings management, and IFRS: Empirical evidence from Chinese domestically listed companies. *Advances in Accounting, 28*(1), 189–192.

Watts, R.L., & Zimmerman, J.L. (1983). Agency problems, auditing, and the theory of the firm: Some evidence. *The Journal of Law and Economics, 26*(3), 613–633.

6 Theoretical Model of Corporate Governance and IFRS Compliance

Introduction

Having reviewed the previous studies that examined the extent of disclosure practices implemented by companies, it can be noticed that disclosure practices are driven by different factors and various firm characteristics. This book aims to explore the level of compliance with IFRS disclosure requirements among GCC member states, interpret some firm characteristics as factors affecting the level of compliance with IFRS, and examine some attributes of corporate governance as determinants of the level of compliance with IFRS disclosure requirements. Based on the prior literature, the current book will focus on some measurable and identifiable firm characteristics and corporate governance mechanisms to interpret the variations in companies' disclosure practices. In this chapter, we discuss the factors that could produce variations in the level of IFRS compliance among countries and we present the theoretical model that incorporates the relationship between corporate governance and the level of IFRS compliance.

Development of Propositions

We used a number of theories to support our propositions. For example, the institutional theory was adopted to support the existence of significant differences in the level of compliance with IFRS among GCC countries, as it suggests that the differences in the national culture of these countries may create differences in the effectiveness of their enforcement mechanisms over applying IFRS disclosure requirements. Additionally, the effect of industry type on the level of compliance with IFRS was based on the same theory as the existence of a dominant company in a specific industry will lead to the disclosure practices of other companies operating in the same industry.

Agency theory is another theory that was used to justify the expected relationships between some independent variables and the level of compliance with IFRS. This theory is concerned with the conflict between managers' interests and shareholders' interests, therefore, the effect of profitability and leverage on the level of compliance with IFRS was based on such

DOI: 10.4324/9781003211556-6

a theory as both variables are considered important indicators of manager's performance that prove that their actions are aligned with owners' benefits. Likewise, the impact of having non-executive directors in the board and a CEO from outside the company on the level of compliance with IFRS was supported by this theory as their existence is expected to reduce the agency cost and improve the efficiency of monitoring board of directors' and managers' performance. Additionally, audit committee is seen as a tool to monitor the flow of information and enhance the effectiveness of the internal control system, which also reduces agency cost. The quality of the external auditor is considered a tool to decrease the opportunities for managers to manipulate earnings and provide a reasonable assurance to shareholders about the quality of the disclosed information.

Moreover, the effect of firm size, profitability, and liquidity on the level of compliance with IFRS was based on the signaling theory. This is attributed to the idea that these variables indicate the performance of the company and signaling theory suggests that companies with good performance tend to signal their good performance to stakeholders in order to differentiate themselves from other companies. Similarly, companies with high leverage are expected to disclose more information to prove for shareholders and creditors their abilities to repay their debts, hence, also the effect of leverage on the level of compliance with IFRS was based on such a theory. Likewise, the quality of the external auditor (being one of the big-four audit companies around the world) is an indication of the reporting quality, therefore, it is expected that companies being audited by one of the big-four audit firms disclose more information and have a higher level of compliance with IFRS.

Furthermore, the existence of outside directors, having large board size, and having an external CEO are considered tools to link the company with the external environment to help it to get the needed resources, hence, the relationship between these variables and IFRS compliance was built based on the resource dependency theory. Finally, the legitimacy theory was implemented to support the effect of firm size on the level of compliance as large firms are subject to a higher level of rules and regulations, and thus, they are expected to have a higher level of disclosure.

Choosing the aforementioned variables was based on the following criteria: first, they are associated with the theoretical aspects of the main theories previously discussed. Second, they can without difficulty be measured with the aim of statistical analysis. Third, they can be used in dividing the sample and classifying the targeted companies without ambiguity. Fourth, the availability of data for these variables. The discussion of each variable starts with a brief presentation of the theoretical aspects. Then, the applicable international empirical results related to each of these variables will also be addressed. Thereafter, the relevant literature relating to the Middle Eastern context for each variable will be discussed. Finally, by the end of each section, the testable proposition will be presented.

The Level of IFRS Compliance

Prior research has demonstrated that the variations in the level of compliance with IFRS are affected by some factors such as cultural factors, education, internationality, and the level of proficiency of accounting profession (see, for example, Zeghal and Mhedhbi, 2006; Daske et al., 2008). Haniffa and Cooke (2002) revealed that the level of compliance with IFRS is affected by five groups of factors, which are economy, capital markets, accounting and regulatory framework, enforcement mechanisms, and culture. Moreover, environmental and institutional factors of each country were evidenced to have an effect on the level of compliance with IFRS (Zeghal and Mhedhbi, 2006).

According to the institutional theory, culture and environment affect the level of the adoption of IFRS, relying on the fact that values, norms, and the structure of the economy form the enforcement procedures over companies to monitor the degree of implementing the disclosure requirements of these standards. Additionally, from a legitimacy theory point of view, the level of the adoption of IFRS is a matter of the extent of the rules and regulations that govern and control such adoption, which will affect the tendency of companies to follow these disclosure requirements. In developing countries, it was evidenced that the cost of non-compliance, in terms of penalties, is lower than the cost of compliance with IFRS (Al-Htaybat, 2005; Dahawy and Conover, 2007).

Empirically, it has been shown that culture affects the level of compliance with IFRS as it is responsible for creating the awareness among financial statements preparers and users about the importance of financial disclosure (Saudagaran and Meek, 1997). Moreover, it was also evidenced that national culture is responsible for forming the laws and regulations that shape the enforcement mechanisms toward monitoring IFRS adoption; the latter implies that the lack of appropriate enforcement actions may lead to high non-compliance with the disclosure requirements of these standards (Rahman, 1999; Nobes, 2006; Mbir et al., 2020). Qu et al. (2012) and Pricope (2016) revealed that the level of financial disclosure positively reacted to the enforcements made by market regulatory authorities. In the Middle Eastern context, Alsaqqa and Sawan (2013) reported that IFRS compliance is influenced by the level of knowledge and education of financial statements users about the international accounting standards. Additionally, the inadequate enforcement mechanisms were evidenced to have an effect on the level of IFRS adoption (see, for example, Samaha et al., 2012; Demir and Bahadir, 2014).

The differences among countries and among GCC member states, in respect to their capabilities to enforce their listed companies to comply with IFRS disclosure requirements, will create variations in the level of adopting these requirements among companies. Prior work that attempted to examine the level of compliance with IFRS revealed that the variations in the level of compliance among companies are the result of the differences in their country of origins (see, for example, Tower et al., 1999; Street and Bryant, 2000; Al-Shammari, 2005).

Furthermore, there are variations among GCC member states in relation to their enforcement and monitoring mechanisms, which create differences in the level of the adoption of these standards among these countries (see Al-Shammari, 2005); Al-Shammari (2005) reported that there are variations in the rules and regulations that govern the auditing profession among these countries in terms of the auditor's qualification required to enter the profession. Finally, he also argued that these states have applied IFRS at different dates and it is expected that early adopter countries will have more experience regarding how to enforce their companies to implement these standards, which will affect the level of compliance with IFRS. His results revealed that the level of compliance in these countries is not the same.

Despite the fact that GCC member states are similar in their cultural and economic contexts, the enforcement levels in these countries are not the same and their experience in implementing IFRS is not the same due to differences regarding the timing of adopting IFRS. Therefore, it is expected that the level of compliance with IFRS among these states will not be the same.

Based on the above-outlined reasoning, the first proposition can be stated as follows:

> *There are significant statistical differences between GCC member states in their levels of compliance with the overall mandatory disclosure requirements of IFRS.*

Firm Characteristics and IFRS Compliance

The review of prior work has shown that the characteristics of companies, such as firm size, firm age, listing status, liquidity, profitability, and industry type play an important role in determining the level of the adoption of IFRS (Hassaan, 2012). Morris and Gray (2007) found that country-level variables and firm-level variables affect the level of the adoption of IFRS. Therefore, this section presents a discussion of the relationship between some firm characteristics, these are firm size, industry type, profitability, leverage, and liquidity, and the level of compliance with IFRS disclosure requirements in GCC member states.

Firm Size

Firm size affects the level of compliance with IFRS from different perspectives. Firstly, large companies are more closely scrutinized by investors and they are subject to greater regulations (Watts and Zimmerman, 1986). Therefore, from a legitimacy theory point of view, large companies usually tend to implement higher level of disclosure to earn legitimacy and social acceptance. Secondly, large companies require more capital; Brown and Martinsson (2014) demonstrated that the high level of IFRS compliance and the high level of transparency decrease the cost of capital. In other words, raising capital from outside resources increases the agency cost, in terms of cost of capital, and disclosing more information to public reduces this cost through decreasing the level of information asymmetry between insiders and outsiders (Diamond and Verrecchia, 1991; Inchausti, 1997). Additionally, as the signaling theory asserts, large firms need to collect larger amounts of capital; hence, it is expected that they will have a higher level of compliance with IFRS disclosure requirements to be well-known by investors, which facilitates the collection of capital when issuing new shares (Baazaoui and Zaraï, 2019). Thirdly, from a cost-benefit analysis perspective, there are some problematic standards under IFRS that require high costs to implement regarding training employees, enhancing their knowledge about IFRS, and gathering and organizing information in the annual reports, thus, it is expected that larger firms can afford these costs easier than smaller firms, accordingly, they are anticipated to have a higher level of compliance with IFRS. Furthermore, larger firms are expected to have the needed resources and expertise to demonstrate the required level of disclosed information. Omar and Simon (2011) suggested that gathering, classifying, and demonstrating information are costly, and large firms can easily afford these costs, hence, they are expected to have a higher level of disclosure.

Mixed results have been presented by scholars regarding the association between firm size and the level of disclosure. Cooke (1992), Depoers (2000), and Arcay and Vazquez (2005) revealed a positive relationship between the size of the firm and the level of disclosure. Likewise, Alves et al. (2012) stressed that firm size is one of the main determinants of the level of disclosure in the annual reports of Portuguese and Spanish-listed firms. However, McNally et al. (1982) concluded that there is no relationship between voluntary disclosure and firm size in New Zealand. In the Middle Eastern context, Omar and Simon (2011), Joshi and Al-Mudhahki (2013), and Demir and Bahadir (2014) reported a positive relationship between firm size and the level of compliance with disclosure requirements. Using a sample of Kuwaiti non-financial companies, Al Mutawaa and Hewaidy (2010) found a significant positive relationship between firm size and the extent of the adoption of IFRS disclosure requirements. In the UAE, Alsaqqa and Sawan (2013) concluded that large companies can afford the cost of implementing IFRS more than small companies. Similarly, Alhazaimeh et al. (2014) stated that large companies have a higher level of disclosure than small companies in Jordan. Nevertheless, Al-Moataz and Hussainey (2012) did not find a significant relationship between firm size and the level of disclosure in Saudi Arabia.

Although the results of the previous studies are mixed in relation to the association between firm size and the level of disclosure, large GCC listed firms are more likely motivated to disclose more information than small firms to derive the potential benefits of the disclosure.

Therefore, standing on the previous discussion, firm size will be considered an independent variable to explore its effect on the level of compliance with IFRS, and a control variable when exploring the relationship between corporate governance and IFRS compliance.

Based on the above discussion, the second proposition can be stated as follows:

> *There is a significant relationship between firm size and the extent of compliance with IFRS disclosure requirements in GCC member states.*

Industry Type

According to Suwaidan (1997), the level of disclosure varies among different sectors of operations as a result of four justifications. First, competition plays an important role in determining the level of disclosure as in some cases companies may be reluctant to reveal information about their activities to competitors. Depoers (2000) reported that companies tend to hide information if it will affect their competitive advantages. Second, other companies may imitate the disclosure practices of the dominant companies in a specific industry since the former may consider these dominant companies' disclosure practices as the most appropriate to be implemented (Omar and Simon, 2011). Third, accounting policies and systems that govern the industry may determine the trend of the disclosure practices in these industries; for example, banking sector lies under a greater regulatory pressure than other sectors, and hence, they disclose more information (Craig and Diga, 1998). Fourth, the extent of social responsibility of an industry also determines the level of disclosure implemented in such industry; the latter implies that some sectors are a matter of higher social responsibility than others, for instance, manufacturing companies are more concerned with pollution than other types of companies; therefore, they are expected to have a higher level of disclosure.

Empirical results regarding the effect of industry type on the level of disclosure were general. Cooke (1991) reported that the type of the industry in which the company is operating affects its level of disclosure in Japan. As well, Cooke (1992) concluded that manufacturing companies significantly disclose more information than other types of industries. Street and Gray (2002) stated that companies operating in the commerce industry disclose more information than transportation industry. However, Anderson and Daoud (2005) found no evidence on the association between industry type and disclosure in Swedish-listed firms. The same results were reported by Glaum and Street (2003) in Germany. In the Middle Eastern context, Al-Shammari (2005), Haddad et al. (2015), and Boshnak (2017) pointed out that the type of the industry affects the degree of companies' disclosure practices. Additionally, Al Mutawaa and Hewaidy (2010) concluded that Kuwaiti companies listed in the investment sector have a higher level of disclosure than other industry sectors. Likewise, Omar and Simon (2011) found that industrial companies disclose more information than services companies as their activities' nature and complexity are different; they further argued that there are some standards applicable only for manufacturing companies, as a consequence, they will have higher level of disclosure.

In alignment with the results reported by previous studies considering the relationship between industry type and the level of disclosure, and standing on the fact that some accounting standards are applicable only for certain industries, it is expected that the level of compliance with IFRS will be different among the different sectors of operations.

In this book, industry type will be considered an independent variable to explore its effect on the level of compliance with IFRS, and a control variable when exploring the relationship between corporate governance and IFRS compliance.

Based on the previous discussion, the third proposition can be presented as follows:

> *There is a significant relationship between industry type and the extent of compliance with IFRS disclosure requirements in GCC member states.*

Profitability

From the agency theory point of view, profitability plays a significant role in determining the level of financial disclosure as it is considered a significant indication of managers' performance which affects their continuation and compensation arrangements (Omar and Simon, 2011). Singhvi and Desai (1971) and Inchausti (1997) argued that managers tend to disclose more information in case of high performance to justify their compensations, improve shareholders' confidence, and assure their managerial positions. As the signaling theory alerts us, high profitability of the company is considered a good signal for the company, which gives it an incentive to demonstrate this information in order to avoid the undervaluation of its shares. In other words, high performance companies tend to disclose more information in order to differentiate themselves from other companies and enhance their images in the investors' minds. Compliance with IFRS disclosure requirements could be considered a signal of high performance (Omar and Simon, 2011). Moreover, scholars have suggested that highly profitable companies tend to signal their good performance through disclosing more information (Wallace and Naser, 1995; Abd-Elsalam, 1999).

Empirically, Inchausti (1997) and Apostolou and Nanopoulos (2009) reported a positive association between profitability and the extent of disclosure. Using a sample of Italian firms, Pichler et al. (2018) concluded that companies with greater profitability are more likely to adopt IFRS. However, Wallace and Naser (1995) reported a negative relationship between profitability and disclosure for firms listed in Hong Kong stock exchange. In another work, Chau and Gray (2002) did not detect a significant relationship between the two variables in Hong Kong and Singapore. Similarly, Street and Bryant (2000) and Glaum and Street (2003) reported no association between profitability and the level of disclosure in the United States and Germany respectively. Looking more specifically at the case of the Middle East, Al-Moataz and Hussainey (2012), Al-Janadi et al. (2013), and Alturki (2014) revealed a positive relationship between profitability and the level of disclosure. Likewise, Al-Akra et al. (2010) concluded a positive relationship between profitability and the level of mandatory disclosure requirements, and they reported that managers of profitable firms tend to disclose more information to enhance investors' confidence and signal their superior performance. In contrast, Al Mutawaa and Hewaidy (2010) did not find a significant relationship between profitability and IFRS compliance in Kuwait. As well, Demir and Bahadir (2014) reported that there is a non-significant statistical relationship between profitability and the level of disclosure. Also, Haddad et al. (2015) did not find a significant relationship between profitability and the level of disclosure in Jordan.

The above results are somewhat mixed. However, it is expected that IFRS compliance produces more information; therefore, GCC listed firms with high profitability are anticipated to comply with IFRS more than low profitability firms.

In our analysis, profitability will be considered an independent variable to explore its effect on the level of compliance with IFRS, and a control variable when exploring the relationship between corporate governance and IFRS compliance.

Based on the previous outlined discussion, the fourth proposition can be stated as follows:

> *There is a significant relationship between profitability and the extent of compliance with IFRS disclosure requirements in GCC member states.*

Leverage

Leverage refers to the ability of the company to utilize its financing resources such as debts and borrowed funds to improve the return on equity (Ezat and El-Masry, 2008). Agency theory suggests that there is a conflict of interests between managers and owners about the efficiency of the former in managing the company's resources, therefore, companies with higher leverage are expected to disclose more information in order to prove to shareholders their ability to repay debts (Ahmed and Courtis, 1999).

Lopes and Rodrigues (2007) and Hassan (2009) stated that having a high level of leverage will increase agency cost, thus, companies with high amount of debt tend to disclose more information to mitigate such cost. Moreover, as the level of leverage increases for a company, the monitoring and controlling cost will increase, and hence, it is expected to disclose more information (Jensen and Meckling, 1976). From a signaling theory point of view, companies with high leverage tend to prove to creditors that they are capable of paying their debts (Ezat and El-Masry, 2008). When the company increases its level of debts, owners and creditors need more information to assess the company's ability to meet its obligations (Jensen and Meckling, 1976; Bradbury, 1992; Wallace et al., 1994).

Empirically, mixed results were provided by previous studies regarding the effect of leverage on the level of disclosure. For example, Robbins and Austin (1986) reported a positive relationship between debt and disclosure in the United States. In Malaysia, Haji and Ghazali (2013) asserted that there is a significant effect of leverage on the level of disclosure. However, Hodgdon and Hughes (2016) found a negative relationship between leverage and the level of disclosure. Whereas Ho and Wong (2001) concluded that there is a non-significant relationship between the two variables in Hong Kong. Moreover, Klein (2002) stated that there is a positive relationship between leverage and earnings management in the United States. In the Middle Eastern context, Al-Akra et al. (2010) indicated that leverage has a significant influence on the level of disclosure implemented by Jordanian companies. Likewise, Al-Shammari (2005) stated that leverage has a significant positive relationship with the level of compliance with IFRS in some GCC member states. Similarly, Alfaraih (2009) found a positive significant relationship between leverage and the level of compliance with IFRS in Kuwait. In contrast, Haddad et al. (2015) did not find a significant relationship between leverage and disclosure in Jordan. Hassaan (2012) stated that there is no association between leverage and the level of compliance with IFRS in Egypt.

In spite of the mixed results reported by previous studies regarding the relationship between leverage and the level of compliance with IFRS, firms with high leverage are expected to disclose more information to prove to regulators, creditors, and shareholders their ability to meet their debts.

In this book, leverage will be considered an independent variable to explore its effect on the level of compliance with IFRS, and a control variable when exploring the relationship between corporate governance and IFRS compliance.

Based on the discussion demonstrated above, the fifth proposition can be presented as:

> *There is a significant relationship between leverage and extent of compliance with IFRS disclosure requirements in GCC member states.*

Liquidity

Liquidity refers to the company's capability of converting assets into cash without losing much of their value (Ezat and El-Masry, 2008). Hassaan (2012) defined liquidity as the ability of the company to pay its short-term debts without selling long-term assets. Liquidity could be used as an indication of the going concern assumption for the company (Omar, 2007). Based on signaling theory, Abd-Elsalam (1999) and Barako et al. (2006) pointed out that companies with high level of liquidity disclose more information to signal themselves from other companies with lower liquidity. On the other hand, Agency theory supports the idea that firms with low level of liquidity disclose more information to minimize the conflict between owners and managers (Abd-Elsalam, 1999). In addition, companies with low liquidity will have a high level of disclosure to meet the needs of shareholders and lenders for affirmation of the ability of the company to pay its short-term debts (Wallace and Naser, 1995).

The empirical results regarding the relationship between liquidity and the level of disclosure are inconclusive. Camfferman and Cooke (2002) found a significant positive relationship between the two variables for a sample of UK and Dutch companies. Nevertheless, Wallace et al. (1994) and Gul and Leung (2004) indicated a negative relationship between the level of disclosure and liquidity in Spain and Hong Kong respectively. While Barako et al. (2006) did not find a significant relationship between liquidity and voluntary disclosure. Similarly, using a sample of 229 UK companies, Aburaya (2012) did not detect a significant relationship. In the Middle East, Hassaan (2012) stated that a significant relationship exists between liquidity and the level of compliance with IFRS disclosure requirements in the Jordanian and Egyptian contexts. In Saudi Arabia context, Al-Moataz and Hussainey (2012) reported that liquidity is one of the main determinants of level of disclosure. However, Al-Shammari (2005) expressed that liquidity is not a significant explanatory variable of the level of compliance with IFRS in GCC countries. As well, Alfaraih (2009) and Haddad et al. (2015) concluded that the relationship between liquidity and the level of compliance with IFRS is statistically not significant in Kuwait and Jordan respectively. In the GCC context, Boshnak (2017) did not find any significant relation between liquidity and the level of disclosure.

Despite the mixed results of the previous studies regarding the relationship between liquidity and the level of compliance with IFRS disclosure requirements, it is expected that companies with high level of liquidity will disclose more information as they do not have to hide information about their financial situation from the users of the financial statements.

Liquidity will be considered an independent variable to explore its effect on the level of compliance with IFRS, and a control variable when exploring the relationship between corporate governance and IFRS compliance.

Based on the above discussion, the sixth proposition can be presented as:

> *There is a significant relationship between liquidity and extent of compliance with IFRS disclosure requirements in GCC member states.*

Corporate Governance and IFRS Compliance

The main aim of this book is to investigate some mechanisms of corporate governance as determinants of the level of compliance with IFRS. Based on prior work, we primarily focus on some identifiable and measurable corporate governance mechanisms to explain their relationships with the level of compliance with IFRS. As discussed previously, several researchers have suggested that improving corporate governance will enhance the company's financial disclosure practices since it is considered an effective mechanism in controlling the performance of companies' managers (Petra, 2007; Firth et al., 2007). Additionally, scholars reported that weak internal control over opportunistic managers leads to a failure in financial reporting (Bouchareb et al., 2014), and improving corporate governance helps in monitoring the performance of managers, which enhances companies' financial disclosure practices (Firth et al., 2007; Petra, 2007).

The following subsections review the theoretical aspects and relevant literature of the chosen corporate governance mechanisms, which are board independence, board size, CEO duality, ownership structure, audit committee, and external auditor, and their relationships with the level of compliance with IFRS. By the end of each section, the appropriate proposition will be proposed.

Board Independence

Board independence is defined as the proportion of non-executive directors to the total number of board members (Shamser and Annuar, 1993; Laing and Weir, 1999). The corporate governance codes issued by OECD recommended the existence of non-executive members to improve the independence of the board. However, reviewing the results of the previous studies showed that there are two points of views; some researchers recommended the existence of high proportion of outside members, while some others argued having more executive members.

Proponents of non-executive directors have built their assumptions based on the agency theory and resource dependency theory. As discussed earlier, both theories support the existence of outside members; particularly, agency theory suggests that the existence of non-executive directors enhances the control function of the board of directors and efficiently improves its performance as non-executive directors can monitor and control the activities of other board members, which reduces the agency cost. Agency cost appears because the benefits of shareholders are different from the benefits of managers and this may create a conflict of interests where both principals and agents always aim to maximize their benefits at the same time. Outside members can help in resolving this conflict of interests as they will improve the supervision over the activities of opportunistic managers. Moreover, agency theory supports that non-executive directors will detect the expropriation of company's resources, which will align with the benefits of both owners and managers. Additionally, it supports the idea that in order to decrease agency cost, the level of information asymmetry should be decreased. Prior work supported the argument that in order to reduce information asymmetry, the level of the disclosed information should be increased and the latter is easier with the existence of outside directors as they will monitor the flow of disclosed information (Biondi et al., 2009). For resource dependency theory, outside directors are seen as a channel to link the company with outside environment since they are working outside the company and they are expected to have more relations, which will assist the company to get its needed resources. Furthermore, those members have more knowledge and experience as they may be working in different industries. In contrast, opponents of more non-executive members in the board argued that the lack of knowledge that outside members have about the usual performance of the company will mitigate the effectiveness of the control function of the board of directors since executive directors can understand the company's operations easier than non-executive directors (Jensen, 1993).

Empirical studies that examined the relationship between board independence and the quality of financial reporting revealed mixed results. Scholars have demonstrated that the quality of financial reporting is positively related to the proportion of independent directors. For example, Verriest et al. (2013), Agyei-Mensah (2017), and Mnif and Znazen (2020) reported that the more the number of non-executive directors the higher the level of disclosure. Similarly, Kelton and Yang (2008) revealed that the level of internet financial reporting is positively related to the number of outside members in the board in the United States. Additionally, Bouchareb et al. (2014) expressed that board independence has a significant effect in reducing the level of earnings management. However, Eng and Mak (2003) and Huafang and Jianguo (2007) indicated a negative relationship between board independence and the level of corporate disclosure. Whereas Ibadin et al. (2012), Matolcsy et al. (2012), and Hasan et al. (2013) found that there is a non-significant relationship between board independence and the level of disclosure. In the Middle Eastern context, Ezat and El-Masry (2008) and Samaha and Dahawy (2010) asserted that there is a positive relationship between board independence and the level of disclosure in Egypt. Likewise, Al-Janadi et al. (2013) revealed that the existence of non-executive directors enhances the monitoring function of the board of directors, the protection of shareholders' interests, and the quality of financial reporting. Moreover, Juhmani (2017) reported a positive relationship between board independence and the level of compliance with IFRS in Bahrain. In contrast, Al-Moataz and Hussainey (2012) concluded a negative relationship between board independence and corporate disclosure practices in Saudi Arabia. While Al-Shammari and Al-Sultan (2010) and Hassaan (2012) did not find a significant relationship between board independence and extent of disclosure.

Overall, it could be concluded that the existence of non-executive directors in the board plays an important role in enhancing monitoring management's activities, which will affect the level of compliance with IFRS disclosure requirements.

Based on the justifications outlined above, the seventh proposition can be stated as follows:

> *There is a significant relationship between board independence and the extent of compliance with IFRS disclosure requirements in GCC member states.*

Board Size

Board size is considered an essential perspective in determining board composition, and the size of the board should be aligned with the company's needs and goals (Noor and Fadzil, 2013). In broad terms, there are two streams expressed by scholars regarding the optimal size of the board. Proponents of small board recommended that the smaller the size of the board the more effective the monitoring function of such a board; this contributes to the easiness of coordination and communication between managers and the board as in large boards there is an inefficient communication between board members (Lipton and Lorsch, 1992; Kao and Chen, 2004). However, the other stream supported that having more members in the board enhances the effectiveness of the board, especially, for large companies where large boards achieve their desired functions (Coles et al., 2008). From the agency theory point of view, large board size has a major role in enhancing the monitoring function of the board and making strategic decisions, and it suggests that there is a lower possibility for large boards to be dominated by managers (Samaha et al., 2012). Additionally, from the resource dependency theory point of view, large boards may bring to the company high expertise diversity (Yermack, 1996; Laksmana, 2008). In this respect, Klein (2002) and Haniffa and Cooke (2002) asserted that large boards provide the company with more experience and knowledge, which is considered an enhancement in monitoring and controlling functions of the board.

Different studies have examined the association between board size and the quality of disclosure. Agyei-Mensah (2017) and Mnif and Znazen (2020) found a positive relationship between the size of the board and the level of disclosure. Ahmed et al. (2006) and Bradbury et al. (2006), on the other hand, expressed that board size is negatively related to the quality of financial reporting. As well, Beasley (1996) confirmed that as the number of board members decreases the possibility of financial statement fraud also decreases. Additionally, Arcay and Vazquez (2005) and Hasan et al. (2013) pointed out that board size is not associated with the provision of voluntary disclosure. Also, Bouchareb et al. (2014) reported that board size does not have an effect on the level of fraud practices in companies in France. In the Middle Eastern context, Ezat and El-Masry (2008) and Al-Janadi et al. (2013) reported a positive relationship between board size and degree of disclosure in Egypt and Saudi Arabia respectively. However, Samaha et al. (2012) did not find a significant relationship between board size and the extent of disclosure in Egypt. As well, Hassaan (2012) stated that board size is not significantly related to the level of compliance with IFRS in both Egypt and Jordan. Using a sample of Bahraini companies, Juhmani (2017) stated that board size is not associated with the level of compliance with IFRS.

In spite of the mixed results regarding the relationship between board size and the level of disclosure, it is expected that the more the number of the board members the higher the effectiveness of the monitoring function of the board and the higher the level of compliance with IFRS disclosure requirements.

Based on the above-outlined discussion, the eighth proposition can be stated as follows:

> *There is a significant relationship between board size and the extent of compliance with IFRS disclosure requirements in GCC member states.*

CEO Duality

The separation between the chairman of the board and the CEO positions is considered an indication of good corporate governance (OECD, 2015). From the agency theory point of view, the separation between the two positions is crucial to avoid the concentration of authority in the hands of one person (Hashim and Devis, 2009). This helps in eliminating the conflict of interests between managers and owners and improving the independence of the board, which will increase its monitoring and controlling effectiveness (Jensen, 1993). Additionally, the agency theory supports the separation between CEO and chairman of the board as this enhances the latter's independence, where the independent chairman will efficiently oversee and monitor management activities (Al-Janadi et al., 2013). From the resource dependency theory point of view, having a CEO from outside the company links the company with the resources needed from the external environment and bringing external prospects to the company helps in achieving its goals and objectives (Dahya and Travlos, 2000). On the other hand, the stewardship theory recommends combining both positions as this will help to focus on achieving the objectives of the company through enhancing the decision-making process (Eisenhardt, 1989).

Empirically, the results of the previous studies that examined the relationship between CEO duality and the level of disclosure are mixed.

Forker (1992) and Jensen (1993) concluded that the separation between the two positions improves the desired functions of the board of directors and increases the quality of financial reporting. Moreover, Chau and Gray (2010), and Marra and Mazzola (2014) reported that holding these two positions by two different persons is associated with high level of disclosure. Further, Beekes et al. (2004) and Firth et al. (2007) found that accounting information is more relevant for companies that separate between CEO and chairman of board of directors. Nevertheless, Arcay and Vazquez (2005), Ahmed et al. (2006), and Petra (2007) expressed that CEO duality is not significantly associated with the level of disclosure and financial reporting quality. Additionally, looking at a number of studies from the Middle East, Samaha et al. (2012) expressed a positive relationship between CEO duality and the level of disclosure in Egypt. In contrast, Al-Janadi et al. (2013) supported the idea that the separation between CEO and the chairman of the board is negatively related to the level of disclosure; they justified their results based on the fact that holding both positions by one person enhances the coordination and eliminates the interventions between the two positions. However, Ezat and El-Masry (2008) and Al-Shammari and Al-Sultan (2010) did not find a significant relation between CEO duality and the level of disclosure in Egypt and Kuwait respectively. As well, Juhmani (2017) concluded that CEO duality is not linked with the level of compliance with IFRS in Bahrain. Hassaan (2012) showed that the separation between CEO and chairman of the board does not necessarily enhance the level of compliance with IFRS disclosure requirements in both Jordan and Egypt.

The results regarding the relationship between CEO duality and the level of disclosure do not reach at definite conclusions; however, it is anticipated that holding the position of chairman of the board and the position of CEO by the same person will limit the efficiency and independence of the role of CEO position in monitoring and controlling the activities of the company's managers, which will limit the extent of compliance with IFRS disclosure requirements.

Based on the above discussion, the ninth proposition is proposed as follows:

> *There is a significant relationship between CEO duality and the extent of compliance with IFRS disclosure requirements in GCC member states.*

Ownership Structure

The number of shares owned by one individual investor affects the structure of the ownership in the company (Denis and McConnell, 2003). In our book, based on the availability of the data, two main types of ownership structures were examined to test the existence of significant effects of these structures on the level of compliance with IFRS, these are concentrated ownership and institutional ownership. According to the existing literature, high level of ownership concentration is expected to enhance the monitoring power of shareholders over the company's management as shareholders with large ownership percentages have more incentives to track the company's performance and its strategic decisions. Maher and Andersson (2000) and Lee and Yeh (2004) suggested that the probability that managers will utilize company's resources into their own interests is higher in companies with dispersed ownership. Therefore, it is expected that companies with concentrated ownership will have better corporate governance (Arcay and Vazquez, 2005).

According to the agency theory, the separation between ownership and control has created the agency cost, and compliance with IFRS is considered a tool to reduce such cost. In other words, Dumontier and Raffournier (1998) suggested that IFRS compliance may be considered a monitoring activity for shareholders and bonding activity for managers. It is anticipated that companies with dispersed ownership will have higher disclosure levels than concentrated ownership companies, as the separation between ownership and control is greater in dispersed companies (Jensen and Meckling, 1976; Hossain et al., 1994). Companies with dispersed ownership will have a higher level of agency cost as they are subject to more conflict of interests, and widely held companies are expected to disclose more information to signal that they are acting in line with the interests of owners and the opposite will happen in concentrated companies. Additionally, institutional ownership is expected to have an effect on the level of disclosure implemented by companies as it may have an effect on controlling the disclosure practices of the company; particularly, companies with institutional ownership may voluntarily disclose higher level of information to meet shareholders' expectations (Barako et al., 2006).

Empirically, the results of the previous studies that examined the relationship between both types of ownership structures and the level of disclosure are mixed. For example, Beekes et al. (2004) and Bouchareb et al. (2014) reported a negative relationship between concentrated ownership and the level of earnings management. In addition, Ballas et al. (2018) concluded a positive relationship between concentrated ownership and the level of compliance with IFRS in Greece. However, Donnelly and Lynch (2002) and Fan and Wong (2002) revealed that the quality of financial reporting is lower for companies with concentrated ownership. As well, Laidroo (2009) expressed a negative relationship between concentrated ownership and the level of disclosure. Using a sample of Italian firms, Pichler et al. (2018) concluded a negative relationship between concentrated ownership and the level of compliance with IFRS. Additionally, in widely held companies, the level of information asymmetry between managers and owners is high, and disclosing more information is considered an effective mechanism to reduce this asymmetry (Hossain et al., 1994; Abad et al., 2018). Further, Apostolou and Nanopoulos (2009) and Hasan et al. (2013) stated a positive relationship between dispersed ownership and the level of disclosure in Greece and Bangladesh respectively. Nevertheless, Depoers (2000), Anderson and Daoud (2005), and Uyar (2011) concluded that there is a non-significant relationship between ownership structure and the level of disclosure. Regarding the institutional ownership, Laidroo (2009) and Gao and Kling (2012) found a positive relationship between institutional ownership and the level of disclosure. Likewise, Barako et al. (2006) asserted that the existence of institutional ownership plays a significant role in determining the effectiveness of disclosure practices implemented by companies. In the context of the Middle East, Samaha et al. (2012) and Alhazaimeh et al. (2014) revealed a negative relationship between concentrated ownership and the level of disclosure in Egypt and Jordan respectively. In Bahrain, Sarea and Al Nesuf (2013) found a positive effect of institutional ownership on the level of disclosure. Moreover, Haddad et al. (2015) reported that governmental ownership has a positive effect on the level of disclosure in Jordanian companies, and this is contributed to the idea that these companies tend to show more compliance with rules and regulations than other companies.

Despite the mixed results regarding the relationship between ownership structure and the level of disclosure, the incentives of shareholders to monitor and oversee managers' activities depend on the number of shares they own. Therefore, it is expected that the structure of the ownership will have an effect on the degree of compliance with IFRS disclosure requirements.

Based on the previous discussion, the tenth proposition can be stated as follows:

> *There is a significant relationship between ownership structure and the extent of compliance with IFRS disclosure requirements in GCC member states.*

This proposition can be divided into the following two propositions:

a *There is a significant relationship between concentrated ownership and the extent of compliance with IFRS disclosure requirements in GCC member states.*
b *There is a significant relationship between institutional ownership and the extent of compliance with IFRS disclosure requirements in GCC member states.*

Audit Committee

Audit committee is one of the most important committees formed by the board of directors in helping the company to achieve its strategic goals, as it is considered a monitoring tool over managers' activities (Fama and Jensen, 1983). From an agency theory perspective, the effectiveness of audit committee is considered a major factor in decreasing the agency cost through improving the quality of information flow between managers and owners (Bradbury, 1990). This contributes to the role of this committee in supporting and advising the board of directors about major accounting issues, the preparation of financial statements, and in ensuring that these statements were prepared in accordance with accounting rules and regulations (Brennan, 2007). Additionally, audit committee is considered a formal communication channel between board members, internal control system, and external auditor (Bradbury et al., 2006). Agency theory suggests that the existence of audit committee enhances the effectiveness of the internal control and this improves disclosure quality (Forker, 1992). In addition, it proposes that audit committee decreases agency cost if it includes non-executive directors (Samaha et al., 2012). From the resource dependency theory perspective, the existence of non-executive directors in this committee will bring to the company the needed financial expertise to monitor the financial decisions of managers.

Several studies have examined how the effectiveness of the audit committee affects the level of disclosure; most of them reported a positive relationship between the two variables. For example, Arcay and Vazquez (2005) revealed that the existence of an effective audit committee prevents companies from hiding information that may be beneficial for financial statements users. In Italy, Allegrini and Greco (2013) asserted that the higher the effectiveness of audit committee the higher the level of disclosure. Additionally, Verriest et al. (2013) and Bouchareb et al. (2014) stated a negative relationship between the effectiveness of audit committee and the level of earnings management. As well, Kelton and Yang (2008) found that the higher the number of audit committee members the greater the tendency for companies to implement high level of internet financial reporting. Regarding the number of audit committee meetings, Allegrini and Greco (2013) reported that the number of audit committee meetings has a positive effect on the level of information disclosed by a company. Similarly, Kent and Stewart (2008) reported that the number of meetings held by the audit committee is positively related to the level of disclosure of Australian international financial reporting standards. Nevertheless, Sellami and Fendri (2017) stated that audit committee size and the number of audit committee meetings held during the year do not affect the level of disclosure in South Africa. In the Middle Eastern context, Al-Akra et al. (2010), Samaha and Dahawy (2010), and Alanezi and Albuloushi (2011) concluded that audit committee positively affects the level of disclosure and the level of compliance with IFRS mandatory disclosure requirements. Al-Moataz and Hussainey (2012) stressed that audit committee is an effective mechanism in governing corporates' disclosure and transparency, and they reported that the higher the number of audit committee members the higher the level of corporate disclosure practices. However, Al-Janadi et al. (2013) did not find a significant influence of audit committee on the level of voluntary disclosure.

Overall, it could be concluded that the effectiveness of the audit committee has a significant role in determining the level of compliance with IFRS, as the existence of such a committee enhances the internal control system of the firm, and it is considered the official linkage between the company and the external auditor.

Based on the discussion above, the eleventh proposition can be stated as follows:

> *There is a significant relationship between the effectiveness of audit committee and the extent of compliance with IFRS disclosure requirements in GCC member states.*

This proposition can be divided into the following two propositions:

a *There is a significant relationship between the number of audit committee members and the extent of compliance with IFRS disclosure requirements in GCC member states.*
b *There is a significant relationship between the number of audit committee meetings held during the year and the extent of compliance with IFRS disclosure requirements in GCC member states.*

External Auditor

According to the agency theory, the separation between ownership and control has created a conflict of interests between managers and owners, which is referred to as the agency cost, and the existence of the external auditor may be considered a tool to minimize such cost through reducing the level of information asymmetry between insiders and outsiders (Anderson and Daoud 2005; Barako et al., 2006). Additionally, agency theory suggests that the independence of the external auditor mitigates managers' opportunities to manipulate earnings and helps in monitoring managers' actions to ensure the integrity of financial reporting (Chung et al., 2003; Hasan et al., 2013). This stands on the idea that the quality of the external auditor plays an important role in determining the level of disclosure and providing a reasonable assurance to shareholders that the financial statements were prepared in accordance with accounting rules and regulations (Brennan, 2007). Moreover, the agency theory considers the external auditor a tool to decrease the agency cost through enhancing the level of information provided to public, which helps in decreasing the level of information asymmetry (Jensen and Meckling, 1976). Moreover, the ability of the external auditor in detecting material errors in the financial statements affects the extent of the disclosed information (DeAngelo, 1981; Gao and Kling, 2012). Therefore, the quality of the external auditor has a positive effect on financial disclosure (Chung et al., 2003; Bouchareb et al., 2014). In addition, as the signaling theory reminds us, the quality of the external auditor is considered an indication of the firm value (Hossain et al., 1995).

In broad terms, audit quality refers to the ability of the auditor to detect material financial errors (DeAngelo, 1981). However, previous studies have expressed audit quality from two different perspectives. First, the size of the audit firm was applied as an indication of the quality of external auditing standing on the fact that big audit firms are usually linked with clients who have better disclosure practices (Ahmed and Nicholls, 1994). Additionally, small audit firms may be affected by their clients' needs due to their low market share, which may affect the level of disclosure implemented by these companies (Malone et al., 1993). Furthermore, Kent and Stewart (2008) reported a positive relationship between the size of the audit firm and the level of mandatory disclosure requirements. Second, being one of the big-four audit companies in the world was also presented as an indication of the quality of the external auditor (Brown et al., 2010). Scholars concluded that companies audited by one of the big-four auditors experienced a higher level of disclosure and higher level of compliance with IFRS (Pichler et al., 2018; Riccardi, 2019). However, Depoers (2000), Anderson and Daoud (2005), and Barako et al. (2006) did not find a significant relationship between the quality of the external auditor and the level of disclosure.

In relation to studies conducted in Middle East, Al-Akra et al. (2010) revealed that the type of the external auditor plays a significant role in determining the extent of compliance with mandatory disclosure requirements in Jordan. Furthermore, Omar and Simon (2011) and Demir and Bahadir (2014) expressed that the size of external auditor firm influences the level of disclosure implemented by companies; the latter contributed to the idea that big audit firms have more resources and experience that needed to encourage their clients to have a higher level of compliance with IFRS in comparison with small audit firms. As well, Al-Shiab (2003) confirmed that the quality of the external auditor has a major effect on the level of compliance with IAS disclosure requirements. However, Al-Shammari (2005) did not find a significant relationship between external auditor quality and compliance with IFRS in the GCC context.

The above review has revealed some mixed results regarding the relationship between external auditor quality and the level of disclosure; however, it is expected that the existence of a high-quality external auditor will enhance the assurance about financial statements, as such an auditor has to express an opinion about the adoption of the international accounting standards in preparing these statements. Therefore, having a third-party opinion about the preparation of financial statements will enhance the level of compliance with IFRS.

Based on the discussion outlined above, the twelfth proposition can be stated as follows:

> *There is a significant relationship between the quality of external auditor and the extent of compliance with IFRS disclosure requirements in GCC member states.*

Theoretical Framework of Corporate Governance and IFRS Compliance

Based on our propositions addressed in this chapter, the theoretical framework model regarding the relationship between both firm characteristics

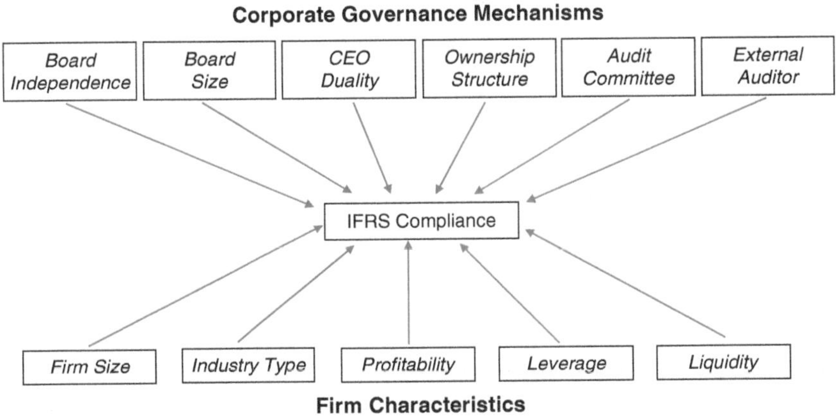

Figure 6.1 Theoretical framework of corporate governance and IFRS compliance.

Notes:

1 All firm characteristics are also treated as control variables in the regression model.
2 Ownership structure is measured by concentrated ownership and institutional ownership.
3 Audit committee is measured by the number of audit committee members and the number of audit committee meetings held during the year.

and corporate governance and IFRS compliance is schematically demonstrated in figure 6.1.

Summary

This chapter demonstrated the theoretical framework and propositions development to address our objectives and questions. The extent of the enforcement mechanisms implemented by countries is expected to influence the level of compliance with IFRS disclosure requirements. Therefore, in assessing the variations in the level of compliance among GCC member states, the differences in the enforcement actions over the extent of compliance are considered a factor in creating the variations in the level of compliance among these countries.

Twelve propositions were presented in this chapter. The first proposition addresses the existence of variations in the level of compliance with IFRS among GCC member states. Five propositions address the effect of a number of firm characteristics on the level of compliance with IFRS; which are firm size, industry type, profitability, leverage, and liquidity. The remaining six propositions address the relationship between a number of corporate governance mechanisms and the level of compliance with IFRS; these include board independence, board size, CEO duality, ownership structure, audit committee, and external auditor.

The next chapter presents the variables measurement that were used in this book to accomplish our objectives and test our propositions.

References

Abad, D., Cutillas-Gomariz, M.F., Sánchez-Ballesta, J.P., & Yagüe, J. (2018). Does IFRS mandatory adoption affect information asymmetry in the stock market? *Australian Accounting Review*, *28*(1), 61–78.

Abd-Elsalam, O.H. (1999). *The introduction and application of international accounting standards to accounting disclosure regulations of a capital market in a developing country: The case of Egypt* (Doctoral dissertation, Heriot-Watt University).

Aburaya, R. (2012). *The relationship between corporate governance and environmental disclosure: UK evidence* (Doctoral dissertation, Durham University).

Agyei-Mensah, B.K. (2017). The relationship between corporate governance mechanisms and IFRS 7 compliance: Evidence from an emerging market. *Corporate Governance: The International Journal of Business in Society*, *17*(3), 446–465.

Ahmed, K., & Courtis, J.K. (1999). Associations between corporate characteristics and disclosure levels in annual reports: A meta-analysis. *The British Accounting Review*, *31*(1), 35–61.

Ahmed, K., & Nicholls, D. (1994). The impact of non-financial company characteristics on mandatory disclosure compliance in developing countries: The case of Bangladesh. *The International Journal of Accounting*, *29*(1), 62–77.

Ahmed, K., Hossain, M., & Adams, M.B. (2006). The effects of board composition and board size on the informativeness of annual accounting earnings. *Corporate Governance: An International Review*, *14*(5), 418–431.

Al Mutawaa, A., & Hewaidy, A.M. (2010). Disclosure level and compliance with IFRSs: An empirical investigation of Kuwaiti companies. *The International Business & Economics Research Journal*, *9*(5), 33–50.

Al-Akra, M., Eddie, I.A., & Ali, M.J. (2010). The influence of the introduction of accounting disclosure regulation on mandatory disclosure compliance: Evidence from Jordan. *The British Accounting Review*, *42*(3), 170–186.

Alanezi, F.S., & Albuloushi, S.S. (2011). Does the existence of voluntary audit committees really affect IFRS-required disclosure? The Kuwaiti evidence. *International Journal of Disclosure and Governance*, *8*(2), 148–173.

Alfaraih, M. (2009). *Compliance with international financial reporting standards (IFRS) and the value relevance of accounting information in emerging stock markets: Evidence from Kuwait* (Doctoral dissertation, Queensland University of Technology).

Alhazaimeh, A., Palaniappan, R., & Almsafir, M. (2014). The impact of corporate governance and ownership structure on voluntary disclosure in annual reports among listed Jordanian companies. *Procedia-Social and Behavioral Sciences*, *129*, 341–348.

Al-Htaybat, K. (2005). *Financial disclosure practices: Theoretical foundation, and an empirical investigation on Jordanian printed and internet formats* (Doctoral dissertation, University of Southampton).

Al-Janadi, Y., Rahman, R.A., & Omar, N.H. (2013). Corporate governance mechanisms and voluntary disclosure in Saudi Arabia. *Corporate Governance*, *4*(4), 25–35.

Allegrini, M., & Greco, G. (2013). Corporate boards, audit committees and voluntary disclosure: Evidence from Italian listed companies. *Journal of Management & Governance*, *17*(1), 187–216.

Al-Moataz, E., & Hussainey, K. (2012). Determinants of corporate governance disclosure in Saudi companies. *Journal of Economics and Management*, *5*(1), 52–84.

Alsaqqa, I., & Sawan, N. (2013). The advantages and the challenges of adopting IFRS into UAE stock market. *International Journal of Business and Management*, *8*(19), 1–23.

Al-Shammari, B.A. (2005). *Compliance with international accounting standards by listed companies in the Gulf Co-operation Council member states: An empirical study*. (Doctoral dissertation, University of Western Australia).

Al-Shammari, B., & Al-Sultan, W. (2010). Corporate governance and voluntary disclosure in Kuwait. *International Journal of Disclosure and Governance*, 7(3), 262–280.

Al-Shiab, M. (2003). *Financial consequences of IAS adoption: The case of Jordan* (Doctoral dissertation, Newcastle University).

Alturki, K. (2014). Voluntary disclosure by Saudi companies. *Research Journal of Finance and Accounting*, *5*(20), 77–94.

Alves, H.R.A.M., Rodrigues, A.M., & Canadas, N. (2012). Factors influencing the different categories of voluntary disclosure in annual reports: An analysis for Iberian Peninsula listed companies. *Tékhne*, *10*(1), 15–26.

Anderson, M. and Daoud, M. (2005), '*Corporate governances disclosure by Swedish listed corporations*', Master Thesis, Jonkoping International Business School, Jonkoping University, Sweden.

Apostolou, A.K., & Nanopoulos, K.A. (2009). Voluntary accounting disclosure and corporate governance: Evidence from Greek listed firms. *International Journal of Accounting and Finance*, *1*(4), 395–414.

Arcay, M.R.B., & Vazquez, M.F.M. (2005). Corporate characteristics, governance rules and the extent of voluntary disclosure in Spain. *Advances in Accounting*, *21*, 299–331.

Baazaoui, H., & Zaraï, M.A. (2019). The effect of firm characteristics on the disclosure of IAS/IFRS information: The cases of Tunisia, France and Canada. *International Business and Accounting Research Journal*, *3*(2), 124–153.

Ballas, A., Sykianakis, N., Tzovas, C., & Vassilakopoulos, C. (2018). Measuring compliance with IFRS mandatory disclosure requirements: Some evidence from Greece. In *Perspectives, Trends, and Applications in Corporate Finance and Accounting* (pp. 273–300). IGI Global.

Barako, D.G., Hancock, P., & Izan, H.Y. (2006). Factors influencing voluntary corporate disclosure by Kenyan companies. *Corporate Governance: An International Review*, *14*(2), 107–125.

Beasley, M.S. (1996). An empirical analysis of the relation between the board of director composition and financial statement fraud. *Accounting Review*, *71*(4) 443–465.

Beekes, W., Pope, P., & Young, S. (2004). The link between earnings timeliness, earnings conservatism and board composition: Evidence from the UK. *Corporate Governance: An International Review*, *12*(1), 47–59.

Biondi, Y., Giannoccolo, P. & Reberioux, A. (2009). 'Financial disclosure and the board: Is independence of directors always efficient?' *Forum de La Regulation*. Paris. October.

Boshnak, H. (2017). *Mandatory and voluntary disclosures in GCC listed firms* (Doctoral dissertation, University of the West of England).

Bouchareb, M., Ajina, A., & Souid, S. (2014). Does the adoption of IAS/IFRS with a strong governance mechanism can deter earnings management? *International Journal of Academic Research in Economics and Management Sciences*, *3*(1), 264–282.

Bradbury, M.E. (1990). The incentives for voluntary audit committee formation. *Journal of Accounting and Public Policy*, *9*(1), 19–36.

Bradbury, M.E. (1992). Voluntary disclosure of financial segment data: New Zealand evidence. *Accounting & Finance*, *32*(1), 15–26.

Bradbury, M., Mak, Y.T., & Tan, S.M. (2006). Board characteristics, audit committee characteristics and abnormal accruals. *Pacific Accounting Review*, *18*(2), 47–68.

Brennan, N. (2007). *Corporate governance and financial reporting.* Sage Publications.

Brown, J.R., & Martinsson, G. (2014). *Financial Disclosure, Corporate Transparency,* and Innovation. Working paper, Iowa State University, January 14.

Brown, J.R., Falaschetti, D., & Orlando, M.J. (2010). Auditor independence and the quality of information in financial disclosures: Evidence for market discipline versus Sarbanes–Oxley proscriptions. *American Law and Economics Review, 12*(1), 39–68.

Camfferman, K., & Cooke, T.E. (2002). An analysis of disclosure in the annual reports of UK and Dutch companies. *Journal of International Accounting Research, 1*(1), 3–30.

Chau, G.K., & Gray, S.J. (2002). Ownership structure and corporate voluntary disclosure in Hong Kong and Singapore. *The International Journal of Accounting, 37*(2), 247–265.

Chau, G., & Gray, S.J. (2010). Family ownership, board independence and voluntary disclosure: Evidence from Hong Kong. *Journal of International Accounting, Auditing and Taxation, 19*(2), 93–109.

Chung, R., Firth, M., & Kim, J.B. (2003). Auditor conservatism and reported earnings. *Accounting and Business Research, 33*(1), 19–32.

Coles, J.L., Daniel, N.D., & Naveen, L. (2008). Boards: Does one size fit all? *Journal of Financial Economics, 87*(2), 329–356.

Cooke, T.E. (1991). An assessment of voluntary disclosure in the annual reports of Japanese corporations. *The International Journal of Accounting, 26*(3), 174–189.

Cooke, T.E. (1992). The impact of size, stock market listing and industry type on disclosure in the annual reports of Japanese listed corporations. *Accounting and Business Research, 22*(87), 229–237.

Craig, R., & Diga, J. (1998). Corporate accounting disclosure in ASEAN. *Journal of International Financial Management & Accounting, 9*(3), 246–274.

Dahawy, K., & Conover, T. (2007). Accounting disclosure in companies listed on the Egyptian stock exchange. *Middle Eastern Finance and Economics, 1*(1), 5–20.

Dahya, J., & Travlos, N. (2000). Does the one man show pay? Theory and evidence on the dual CEO revisited. *European Financial Management, 6*(1), 85–98.

Daske, H., Hail, L., Leuz, C., & Verdi, R. (2008). Mandatory IFRS reporting around the world: Early evidence on the economic consequences. *Journal of Accounting Research, 46*(5), 1085–1142.

DeAngelo, L.E. (1981). Auditor size and audit quality. *Journal of Accounting and Economics, 3*(3), 183–199.

Demir, V., & Bahadir, O. (2014). An investigation of compliance with International Financial Reporting Standards by listed companies in Turkey. *Accounting and Management Information Systems, 13*(1), 4–34.

Denis, D.K., & McConnell, J.J. (2003). International corporate governance. *Journal of Financial and Quantitative Analysis, 38*(1), 1–36.

Depoers, F. (2000). A cost benefit study of voluntary disclosure: Some empirical evidence from French listed companies. *European Accounting Review, 9*(2), 245–263.

Diamond, D.W., & Verrecchia, R.E. (1991). Disclosure, liquidity, and the cost of capital. *The Journal of Finance, 46*(4), 1325–1359.

Donnelly, R., & Lynch, C. (2002). The ownership structure of UK firms and the informativeness of accounting earnings. *Accounting and Business Research, 32*(4), 245–257.

Dumontier, P., & Raffournier, B. (1998). Why firms comply voluntarily with IAS: An empirical analysis with Swiss data. *Journal of International Financial Management & Accounting*, *9*(3), 216–245.

Eisenhardt, K.M. (1989). Making fast strategic decisions in high-velocity environments. *Academy of Management Journal*, *32*(3), 543–576.

Eng, L.L., & Mak, Y.T. (2003). Corporate governance and voluntary disclosure. *Journal of Accounting and Public Policy*, *22*(4), 325–345.

Ezat, A., & El-Masry, A. (2008). The impact of corporate governance on the timeliness of corporate internet reporting by Egyptian listed companies. *Managerial Finance*, *34*(12), 848–867.

Fama, E.F., & Jensen, M.C. (1983). Separation of ownership and control. *The Journal of Law & Economics*, *26*(2), 301–325.

Fan, J.P., & Wong, T.J. (2002). Corporate ownership structure and the informativeness of accounting earnings in East Asia. *Journal of Accounting and Economics*, *33*(3), 401–425.

Firth, M., Fung, P.M., & Rui, O.M. (2007). Ownership, two-tier board structure, and the informativeness of earnings – Evidence from China. *Journal of Accounting and Public Policy*, *26*(4), 463–496.

Forker, J.J. (1992). Corporate governance and disclosure quality. *Accounting and Business Research*, *22*(86), 111–124.

Gao, L., & Kling, G. (2012). The impact of corporate governance and external audit on compliance to mandatory disclosure requirements in China. *Journal of International Accounting, Auditing and Taxation*, *21*(1), 17–31.

Glaum, M., & Street, D.L. (2003). Compliance with the disclosure requirements of Germany's new market: IAS versus US GAAP. *Journal of International Financial Management & Accounting*, *14*(1), 64–100.

Gul, F.A., & Leung, S. (2004). Board leadership, outside directors' expertise and voluntary corporate disclosures. *Journal of Accounting and Public Policy*, *23*(5), 351–379.

Haddad, A.E., AlShattarat, W.K., AbuGhazaleh, N.M., & Nobanee, H. (2015). The impact of ownership structure and family board domination on voluntary disclosure for Jordanian listed companies. *Eurasian Business Review*, *5*(2), 203–234.

Haji, A.A., & Ghazali, N.A.M. (2013). The quality and determinants of voluntary disclosures in annual reports of Shari'ah compliant companies in Malaysia. *Humanomics*, *29*(1), 24–42.

Haniffa, R.M., & Cooke, T.E. (2002). Culture, corporate governance and disclosure in Malaysian corporations. *Abacus*, *38*(3), 317–349.

Hasan, M.S., Hossain, S.Z., & Swieringa, R.J. (2013). Corporate governance and financial disclosures: Bangladesh perspective. *Research Journal of Finance and Accounting*, *4*(1), 109–119.

Hashim A.H., and Devis, S. (2009). Board characteristics, ownership structure and earning quality Malaysian evidence, *Research in Accounting in Emerging Economies*, *8*, 97–123.

Hassaan, M. (2012). *Corporate governance and compliance with International Financial Reporting Standards (IFRSs): Evidence from two MENA stock exchanges* (Doctoral dissertation, Aston University).

Hassan, M. (2009). UAE corporations-specific characteristics and level of risk disclosure. *Managerial Auditing Journal*, *24*(7), 668–687.

Ho, S.S., & Wong, K.S. (2001). A study of the relationship between corporate governance structures and the extent of voluntary disclosure. *Journal of International Accounting, Auditing and Taxation, 10*(2), 139–156.

Hodgdon, C., & Hughes, S.B. (2016). The effect of corporate governance, auditor choice and global activities on EU company disclosures of estimates and judgments. *Journal of International Accounting, Auditing and Taxation, 26*(*C*), 28–46.

Hossain, M., Perera, M.H.B., & Rahman, A.R. (1995). Voluntary disclosure in the annual reports of New Zealand companies. *Journal of International Financial Management & Accounting, 6*(1), 69–87.

Hossain, M., Tan, L.M., & Adams, M.C. (1994). Voluntary disclosure in an emerging capital market: Some empirical evidence from companies listed in the Kuala Lumpur stock exchange. *The International Journal of Accounting, 29*(4), 334–351.

Huafang, X., & Jianguo, Y. (2007). Ownership structure, board composition and corporate voluntary disclosure: Evidence from listed companies in China. *Managerial Auditing Journal, 22*(6), 604–619.

Ibadin, I.M., Izedonmi, F., & Ibadin, P.O. (2012). The association between selected corporate governance attributes, company attributes and timeliness of financial reporting in Nigeria. *Research Journal of Finance and Accounting, 3*(9), 137–145.

Inchausti, B.G. (1997). The influence of company characteristics and accounting regulation on information disclosed by Spanish firms. *European Accounting Review, 6*(1), 45–68.

Jensen, M.C. (1993). The modern industrial revolution, exit, and the failure of internal control systems. *The Journal of Finance, 48*(3), 831–880.

Jensen, M.C., & Meckling, W.H. (1976). Theory of the firm: Managerial behavior, agency costs and ownership structure. *Journal of Financial Economics, 3*(4), 305–360.

Joshi, P.L., & Al-Mudhahki, J. (2013). Empirical study of compliance with international accounting standards (IAS-1) by stock exchange listed companies in Bahrain. *Journal of Financial Management & Analysis, 26*(2), 43–54.

Juhmani, O. (2017). Corporate governance and the level of Bahraini corporate compliance with IFRS disclosure. *Journal of Applied Accounting Research, 18*(1), 22–41.

Kao, L., & Chen, A. (2004). The effects of board characteristics on earnings management. *Corporate Ownership & Control, 1*(3), 96–107.

Kelton, A.S., & Yang, Y.W. (2008). The impact of corporate governance on Internet financial reporting. *Journal of Accounting and Public Policy, 27*(1), 62–87.

Kent, P., & Stewart, J. (2008). Corporate governance and disclosures on the transition to international financial reporting standards. *Accounting & Finance, 48*(4), 649–671.

Klein, A. (2002). Audit committee, board of director characteristics, and earnings management. *Journal of Accounting and Economics, 33*(3), 375–400.

Laidroo, L. (2009). Association between ownership structure and public announcements' disclosures. *Corporate Governance: An International Review, 17*(1), 13–34.

Laing, D., & Weir, C.M. (1999). Governance structures, size and corporate performance in UK firms. *Management Decision, 37*(5), 457–464.

Laksmana, I. (2008). Corporate board governance and voluntary disclosure of executive compensation practices. *Contemporary Accounting Research, 25*(4), 1147–1182.

Lee, T.S., & Yeh, Y.H. (2004). Corporate governance and financial distress: Evidence from Taiwan. *Corporate Governance: An International Review, 12*(3), 378–388.

Lipton, M., & Lorsch, J.W. (1992). A modest proposal for improved corporate governance. *The Business Lawyer, 48* 59–77.

Lopes, P.T., & Rodrigues, L.L. (2007). Accounting for financial instruments: An analysis of the determinants of disclosure in the Portuguese stock exchange. *The International Journal of Accounting*, *42*(1), 25–56.

Maher, M., & Andersson, T. (2000). Corporate governance: Effects on firm performance and economic growth. *OECD Working Papers. Available at SSRN 218490.*

Malone, D., Fries, C., & Jones, T. (1993). An empirical investigation of the extent of corporate financial disclosure in the oil and gas industry. *Journal of Accounting, Auditing & Finance*, *8*(3), 249–273.

Marra, A., & Mazzola, P. (2014). Is corporate board more effective under IFRS or 'it's just an illusion'? *Journal of Accounting, Auditing & Finance*, *29*(1), 31–60.

Matolcsy, Z., Tyler, J., & Wells, P. (2012). Is continuous disclosure associated with board independence? *Australian Journal of Management*, *37*(1), 99–124.

Mbir, D.E.G., Agyemang, O.S., Tackie, G., & Abeka, M.J. (2020). IFRS compliance, corporate governance and financial reporting quality of GSE-listed non-financial firms. *Cogent Business & Management*, 7(1), 1–18.

McNally, G.M., Eng, L.H., & Hasseldine, C.R. (1982). Corporate financial reporting in New Zealand: An analysis of user preferences, corporate characteristics and disclosure practices for discretionary information. *Accounting and Business Research*, *13*(49), 11–20.

Mnif, Y., & Znazen, O. (2020). Corporate governance and compliance with IFRS 7: The case of financial institutions listed in Canada. *Managerial Auditing Journal*, *35*(3), 448–474.

Morris, R.D., & Gray, S.J. (2007). Corporate transparency differences in the Asian region: The feasibility of global standardization in practice. In *AFAANZ Conference, Gold Coast, July*.

Nobes, C. (2006). The survival of international differences under IFRS: Towards a research agenda. *Accounting and Business Research*, *36*(3), 233–245.

Noor, M.A.M., & Fadzil, F.H. (2013). Board characteristics and performance from perspective of governance code in Malaysia. *World Review of Business Research*, *3*(3), 191–206.

OECD (2015). *Organization for Economic Cooperation and Development. OECD Principles of Corporate Governance.* Ankara: OECD Publications.

Omar, B.F.A. (2007). *Exploring the aggregate, mandatory and voluntary financial disclosure behaviour under a new regulatory environment: the case of Jordan* (Doctoral dissertation, University of Hull).

Omar, B., & Simon, J. (2011). Corporate aggregate disclosure practices in Jordan. *Advances in Accounting*, *27*(1), 166–186.

Petra, S.T. (2007). The effects of corporate governance on the informativeness of earnings. *Economics of Governance*, *8*(2), 129–152.

Pichler, S., Cordazzo, M., & Rossi, P. (2018). An analysis of the firms-specific determinants influencing the voluntary IFRS adoption: Evidence from Italian private firms. *International Journal of Accounting, Auditing and Performance Evaluation*, *14*(1), 85–104.

Pricope, C.F. (2016). The role of institutional pressures in developing countries. Implications for IFRS. *Theoretical and Applied Economics*, *22*(2), 27–40.

Qu, W., Cooper, B.J., Wise, V., & Leung, P. (2012). Voluntary disclosure in a changing regulatory environment – evidence from Chinese stock market. *International Journal of Economics and Finance*, *4*(4), 30.

Rahman, M.Z. (1999). *The role of accounting disclosure in the East Asian financial crisis: Lessons learned?* Geneva: United Nations Conference on Trade and Development, 1999.

Riccardi, W.N. (2019). Do audit firm tenure and size moderate changes in financial reporting quality due to mandatory IFRS adoption? *Auditing: A Journal of Practice & Theory*, *38*(4), 201–224.

Robbins, W.A., & Austin, K.R. (1986). Disclosure quality in governmental financial reports: An assessment of the appropriateness of a compound measure. *Journal of Accounting Research*, *24*(2) 412–421.

Samaha, K., & Dahawy, K. (2010). An empirical analysis of corporate governance structures and voluntary corporate disclosure in volatile capital markets: The Egyptian experience. *International Journal of Accounting, Auditing and Performance Evaluation*, 7(1–2), 61–93.

Samaha, K., Dahawy, K., Hussainey, K., & Stapleton, P. (2012). The extent of corporate governance disclosure and its determinants in a developing market: The case of Egypt. *Advances in Accounting*, *28*(1), 168–178.

Sarea, A., & Al Nesuf, H. (2013). The impact of management structure and bank characteristics on the level of compliance with IAS 21: Evidence from Bahrain. *International Journal of Accounting and Taxation*, *1*(1), 58–68.

Saudagaran, S.M., & Meek, G.K. (1997). A review of research on the relationship between international capital markets and financial reporting by multinational firms. *Journal of Accounting Literature*, *16*, 127–159.

Sellami, Y.M., & Fendri, H.B. (2017). The effect of audit committee characteristics on compliance with IFRS for related party disclosures: Evidence from South Africa. *Managerial Auditing Journal*, *32*(6), 603–626.

Shamser, M., & Annuar, M.N. (1993). Management versus shareholders' interest: Board composition, market risk and shareholder returns of Malaysian listed firms. *Malaysian Management Review*, *29*, 44–52.

Singhvi, S.S., & Desai, H.B. (1971). An empirical analysis of the quality of corporate financial disclosure. *The Accounting Review*, *46*(1), 129–138.

Street, D.L., & Bryant, S.M. (2000). Disclosure level and compliance with IASs: A comparison of companies with and without US listings and filings. *The International Journal of Accounting*, *35*(3), 305–329.

Street, D.L., & Gray, S.J. (2002). Factors influencing the extent of corporate compliance with International Accounting Standards: Summary of a research monograph. *Journal of International Accounting, Auditing and Taxation*, *11*(1), 51–76.

Suwaidan, M.S. (1997). *Voluntary disclosure of accounting information: The case of Jordan* (Doctoral dissertation, University of Aberdeen).

Tower, G., Hancock, P., & Taplin, R.H. (1999). A regional study of listed companies' compliance with international accounting standards. *In Accounting Forum*, *23*(3), 293–305.

Uyar, A. (2011). Firm characteristics and voluntary disclosure of graphs in annual reports of Turkish listed companies. *African Journal of Business Management*, *5*(17), 7651–7657.

Verriest, A., Gaeremynck, A., & Thornton, D.B. (2013). The impact of corporate governance on IFRS adoption choices. *European Accounting Review*, *22*(1), 39–77.

Wallace, R.O., & Naser, K. (1995). Firm-specific determinants of the comprehensiveness of mandatory disclosure in the corporate annual reports of firms listed on the stock exchange of Hong Kong. *Journal of Accounting and Public policy*, *14*(4), 311–368.

Wallace, R.O., Naser, K., & Mora, A. (1994). The relationship between the comprehensiveness of corporate annual reports and firm characteristics in Spain. *Accounting and Business Research*, *25*(97), 41–53.

Watts, R.L., & Zimmerman, J.L. (1983). Agency problems, auditing, and the theory of the firm: Some evidence. *The Journal of Law and Economics*, *26*(3), 613–633.

Watts, R.L., & Zimmerman, J.L. (1986). *Positive accounting theory*. Prentice-Hall:Englewood Cliffs, NJ.

Yermack, D. (1996). Higher market valuation of companies with a small board of directors. *Journal of Financial Economics*, *40*(2), 185–211.

Zeghal, D., & Mhedhbi, K. (2006). An analysis of the factors affecting the adoption of international accounting standards by developing countries. *The International Journal of Accounting*, *41*(4), 373–386.

7 Measurement, IFRS Disclosure Index, and Data

Introduction

The aim of this book is to examine the level of compliance with International Financial Reporting Standards (IFRS) and the effect of corporate governance and firm characteristics on such a compliance. Therefore, to measure the company's level of compliance with IFRS, we used a self-built disclosure index, this index includes all the mandatory disclosure requirements of the applicable standards to the Gulf Cooperation Council (GCC) context and our focus. Further, the independent variables include some firm characteristics and corporate governance mechanisms. However, firm characteristics were also treated as control variables when examining the relationship between corporate governance and IFRS compliance.

Measurement of Variables

This section is divided into two parts, the first one demonstrates corporate governance mechanisms, and the other part presents the selected firm characteristics. This section discusses the operationalization and measurements of these variables, and the research model required to achieve the objectives of this book.

Corporate Governance Mechanisms

Corporate governance is defined as a "set of principles that concerning governing companies and how these principles are disclosed or communicated externally" (Parum, 2005: p. 702). Furthermore, corporate governance deals with the relationships between company's management, its board, its shareholders, and other stakeholders (OECD, 2015). Corporate governance mechanisms included in this book are board independence, board size, chief executive officer (CEO) duality, ownership structure, audit committee, and external auditor.

DOI: 10.4324/9781003211556-7

Board Independence

Board independence could be defined as the percentage of outside directors to the total number of directors (Shamser and Annuar, 1993; Laing and Weir, 1999). Within the agency theory framework, independent non-executive directors are seen useful because they can monitor and control the actions of opportunistic executive directors, which helps in resolving agency problems and reducing the agency cost (Jensen and Meckling, 1976; Fama and Jensen, 1983). Moreover, the presence of outside directors enhances board independence and this improves the efficiency of the company's performance (Beekes et al., 2004; Dharmadasa et al., 2014). However, the existence of nonexecutive directors may reduce the effectiveness of the board's function in monitoring the firm, due to their limited level of knowledge about the day-to-day activities compared with the executive directors' knowledge as the latter have more access to the company's operations (Patton and Baker, 1987; Muth and Donaldson, 1998). In this book, board independence was measured by computing the percentage of the independent outside directors from the total number of directors; this was done by dividing the number of independent directors by the total number of board members.

Board Size

Mixed results were reported by the prior work regarding the optimal size of the board of directors that the company must have. In more detail, some scholars suggested that small boards are more effective than large boards as the former have a higher degree of coordination and less communication difficulties (see, for example, Lipton and Lorsch, 1992; Jensen, 1993). Arcay and Vazquez (2005) stated that the smaller the size of the board the better the corporate governance. However, some scholars found that large board size is more beneficial for companies, for instance, Haniffa and Cooke (2002) and Klein (2002) suggested that having more members in the board provides companies with more experience and knowledge, which enhances the board's monitoring and controlling functions. Noor and Fadzil (2013) suggested that board size must meet the needs and the objectives of the company; large firms tend to have large board size in order to improve its desired functions (Coles et al., 2008). The most common practice in measuring board size is to use the total number of board members, thus, the number of board members was obtained from the annual report of each company.

CEO Duality

According to OECD (2015), the separation between CEO and board chairman positions is required in order to have a good corporate governance. Both theorists and regulators have argued that the separation between the CEO and board chairman roles is an important determinant of board effectiveness (Fama and Jensen, 1983; Yermack, 1996). The agency theory supports the idea that CEO duality leads to narrow the authority in the hands of one person (Hashim and Devis, 2009). Acting as the CEO and the chairman of the board of directors at the same time produces a conflict of interests and reduces the efficiency of the board of directors as an internal control tool (Coombes and Wong, 2004). Moreover, having the chairman from outside the company connects it with the external environment, which yields to supporting it with external percepts and helps in achieving its goals and objectives (Dahya and Travlos, 2000). To measure the CEO duality, a dummy variable was used; more specifically, if the chair of the board position and the CEO position were held by the same person, which is considered as duality, the company was coded 0, and if there is a separation between CEO and chairman roles it was coded 1.

Ownership Structure

The number of shares owned by one individual shareholder shapes the ownership structure of the company (Denis and McConnell, 2003). In this book, two dimensions of ownership structure were included in examining the relationship between corporate governance and IFRS compliance, these are concentrated ownership and institutional ownership. Concentrated ownerships exist if a specific group or individual holds most of the shares of a company, and the opposite is the dispersed ownership, where shares are spread over a large number of shareholders (Haniffa, 1999). Shareholders with high percentage of shares have a higher level of influence over the company's decisions than other shareholders (Haniffa, 1999). For institutional ownership, it was noticed that it plays a major role in shaping corporate governance practices of the firm (Al-Najjar, 2010), as institutional investors eliminate earnings manipulation because of the pressure they practice over managers to achieve long-term profits (Rajgopal et al., 1999). In this book, concentrated ownership was measured by the total percentage of shares owned by major shareholders (shareholders who own more than 5% of the total shares), and institutional ownership was measured by the percentage of shares owned by major institutional shareholders (institutions who own more than 5% of the total shares).

Audit Committee

The existence of board committees improves the effectiveness of the monitoring role of board of directors (Fama and Jensen, 1983). The audit committee plays an important role in advising and assisting the board of directors on main accounting issues, such as the preparation of financial statements and ensuring that they are issued in compliance with accounting rules and regulations (Brennan, 2007), and it is considered as the formal communication channel between board members, internal control, and external auditor (Bradbury et al., 2006). Mixed results were reported regarding the association between the effectiveness of audit committee and the level of disclosure. Allegrini and Greco (2013) asserted that the higher the effectiveness of the audit committee the higher the level of disclosure. Arcay and Vazquez (2005) concluded that the presence of audit committee prevents the company from hiding information. Al-Akra et al. (2010a) and Samaha and Dahawy (2010) reported a positive relationship between audit committee and the level of disclosure. Allegrini and Greco (2013) reported that the number of audit committee meetings has a positive effect on the level of information disclosed by the company. The higher the number of audit committee meetings the lower the financial reporting problems and the lower earnings management level (Xie et al., 2003; Farber, 2005). Koh et al. (2007) demonstrated a negative relationship between audit committee meetings frequency and earnings management. However, Baxter and Cotter (2009) did not find an association between the number of audit committee meetings and earnings management. We measured the quality and effectiveness of audit committee by two aspects; the first one is the committee size, which represents the total number of members in such a committee. The second one is the number of audit committee meetings held during the year. Thus, we have collected the required data related to the number of members of the audit committee and the number of audit committee meetings held during the year from the annual report of each company.

External Auditor

Having an independent external auditor leads to reduce agency cost as it helps in eliminating the conflict between managers' interests and shareholders' interests (Anderson and Daoud 2005; Barako et al., 2006). Such an important role of the external auditor is also essential in eliminating the opportunities for managers to manipulate earnings (Chung et al., 2003), and ensuring the integrity of financial reporting (Hasan et al., 2013). Scholars agreed that the most common measure of the quality of an external auditor is its belonging to one of the big-four audit companies around the world (Brown et al., 2010). Becker et al. (1998) suggested that accounting information is more reliable for big-four audit companies' clients, in comparison with other audit firms. Hence, to measure the quality of the external auditor, a dummy variable was used by coding the company 1 if the external auditor is one of the big-four audit companies around the world, and 0 otherwise.

Firm Characteristics

As discussed previously, firm characteristics were considered one time as independent variables when exploring their effect on the level of compliance with IFRS disclosure requirements, and another time as control variables when exploring the relationship between corporate governance and IFRS compliance. Firm characteristics included in our analysis are firm size, industry type, profitability, leverage, and liquidity. Following is a discussion of each of these characteristics and the measurement that was used as a proxy for each one of them.

Firm Size

Based on the fact that different firms' sizes might need different structure of governance, Booth et al. (2002) concluded that firm size may affect companies' governance practices, additionally, it was reported by previous studies that the size of the firm plays an important role in determining its level of disclosure (see, for example, Singhvi and Desai, 1971; Arcay and Vazquez, 2005). Large companies tend to apply a high level of disclosure (Brown and Martinsson, 2014). In addition, it was argued that big companies can afford the cost of implementing the disclosure requirements of the accounting standards easier than small companies, and hence, they are expected to have a higher level of compliance with IFRS (Alsaqqa and Sawan, 2013; Omar and Simon, 2011). Whilst McNally et al. (1982) concluded that there is no relationship between firm size and the level of disclosure. Thus, to measure firm size and following the previous studies (see, for example, Jaggi et al., 2009; Dimitropoulos and Asterious, 2010), the amount of total assets was collected for each of the targeted companies and then the logarithm of the total assets was calculated as a proxy for firm size. However, the study population includes companies from different countries with different currencies, which creates variations in calculating firm size across these countries, therefore, in order to mitigate the differences in the currency exchange rates and unify the monetary measurement unit for all companies, the total assets of each company was converted into the US dollar before calculating the logarithm, using the US dollar exchange rate for each country as at the end of the year 2016.

Industry Type

Cooke (1991) argued that the type of the industry that the company belongs to is considered one of the factors that affect its implemented level of disclosure. Some studies have reported that the level of disclosure in a specific industry was higher than other types of industries. For example, Cooke (1992) concluded that manufacturing companies experience a higher level of disclosure than other types of companies. Likewise, Al-Janadi et al. (2013) found that financial sector companies disclose more information than services and industrial companies. Omar and Simon (2011) stated that industrial companies disclose more information than services companies. Based on the review of companies' classification in GCC member states, it was noticed that each country has applied its own classification (sectors) for companies, for example, Kuwait identified 10 sectors and Oman has 17 sectors, whilst Bahrain has 4 sectors. Therefore, we have compiled all the existed sectors in these countries, and hence, 5 industry types were included in this book, namely Investment, Industrial, Services, Energy, and Real State. Accordingly, to measure the industry type, a dummy variable is coded 1 if the company belongs to investment sector and 0 otherwise, a dummy variable is coded 1 if the company belongs to the industrial sector and 0 otherwise, a dummy variable is coded 1 if the company belongs to the services sector and 0 otherwise, a dummy variable is coded 1 if the company belongs to the energy sector and 0 otherwise, and a dummy variable is coded 1 if the company belongs to the real state sector and 0 otherwise.

Profitability

Several scholars have reported a positive relationship between profitability and the level of disclosure (see, for example, Apostolou and Nanopoulos, 2009; Al-Akra et al., 2010b). Hasan et al. (2013) stressed that profitability is significantly associated with the level of disclosure. Similarly, Joshi and Al-Mudhahki (2001) found that profitability is one of the main determinants of compliance with international accounting standards. In contrast, Wallace and Naser (1995) stated a negative relationship between profitability and disclosure. Some others did not detect any significant influence of profitability on the level of disclosure (Chau and Gray, 2002; Glaum and Street, 2003; Uyar, 2011). In this book, we measured profitability using the Return on Assets (ROA) ratio, which was calculated by dividing net income over total assets.

Leverage

Leverage is defined as the ability of the company to use its financing resources in improving the return on equity (Ezat and El-Masry, 2008). Mixed results were reported by previous studies regarding the relationship between leverage and the level of disclosure implemented by companies. Robbins and Austin (1986) and Al-Shammari (2005) concluded a positive relationship between the two variables. Whilst Belkaoui et al. (1977) and Hodgdon and Hughes (2016) stated a negative relationship. Some researchers did not detect a significant relationship between leverage and the level of disclosure (see, for example, Ho and Wong, 2001; Haddad et al., 2015). We measured leverage by the total debt to assets ratio by dividing the total liabilities over total assets.

Liquidity

Liquidity refers to the company's ability to meet its short-term debts without selling its long-term assets (Omar, 2007). Liquidity is considered an important indication about the company's ability of the going concern (Omar, 2007). The results of the prior work regarding the relationship between liquidity and the level of disclosure were general. Camfferman and Cooke (2002) asserted a positive relationship between the two variables. Some researchers stated a negative relationship (see, for example, Wallace et al., 1994; Gul and Leung, 2004). Whilst others did not find a significant relationship (Al-Shammari, 2005; Alfaraih, 2009; Aburaya, 2012). In this book, liquidity was measured using the current ratio, which was calculated by dividing current assets over current liabilities.

IFRS Disclosure Index (IFRS Compliance)

To examine the level of compliance with the mandatory disclosure requirements of IFRS, we used a self-built disclosure index which helps in quantifying the degree of companies' adoption of IFRS. Marston and Shrives (1991) illustrated that a well-constructed disclosure index is considered to be a reliable and convenient tool for measuring the degree of companies' compliance with IFRS. Wallace (1988) defined the disclosure index as "the measure by which the level of financial reporting of one company can be compared with another" (p. 355). It can also be used to measure the degree of the disclosure of an item of information by companies within a country and the ratio of actual scores awarded to the company (Wallace, 1988).

Implementing a disclosure index is justified by the following: first, it is the most common tool adopted by prior work to measure the extent of disclosure (see, for example, Haniffa and Cooke, 2002; Abd-Elsalam and Weetman, 2003; Al-Shammari, 2005; Hassaan, 2012). Second, having a disclosure index supports providing a single figure that indicates a summary of the whole content of the annual report of the company, which helps in easily detecting the variations in the disclosure practices among companies (Marston and Shrives, 1991). Third, it helps in quantifying the presence of an information item, which makes it possible to clearly and objectively operationalize the extent of disclosure (Marston and Shrives, 1991; Omar, 2007).

Notably, based on the review of the preceding studies, there is no one common disclosure index that was used by the authors. Disclosure indices previously implemented were built depending on the research purposes, research design, and the relevance and applicability of the disclosure requirements to the research context. Accordingly, we constructed a disclosure index to serve our objectives. The built index addresses the mandatory disclosure requirements in the financial statements prepared under IFRS. These disclosure requirements represent all the disclosure items demanded by IFRS issued by IASB.

Following is a discussion of the criteria used in selecting the IFRS and the disclosure requirements to be included in the disclosure index checklist. Besides a description of the procedures applied in weighting and scoring such a checklist, followed by a demonstration of the method employed in calculating the level of compliance with IFRS for the targeted companies.

Selecting IFRS

Scholars suggested that there is no theory that governs the number and the selection of the standards that should be included in the disclosure index (Barako et al., 2006; Alfaraih, 2009; Hassaan, 2012). The standards' selection process in building the disclosure index usually depends on the focus of the research (Wallace et al., 1994). Therefore, to meet the aims of this book and standing on the fact that all companies operating in GCC member states are legally required to comply with IFRS, our book focuses on all the mandatory disclosure requirements in the financial statements and the notes of these statements of the 42 standards issued by IASB till the end of the year 2016. However, some standards were excluded from the disclosure index as they did not meet one of the following criteria: the applicability of the standard for the fiscal year end December 31, 2016, the relevance of the standard to our focus, and the applicability and the relevance of the standard to the context of GCC member states' financial environment and companies' practices. Following is a demonstration of the standards that were excluded based on each criterion:

1 Applicability of the standard for the fiscal year end December 31, 2016

The usual practice of IASB, when issuing a new standard, is to give companies a time period to prepare for implementing the new standard before making it obligatory. Based on the review of the standards issued by IASB, it was noticed that two standards were issued before or during 2016 but they will be effective after December 31, 2016, therefore, they were excluded. These are IFRS 15 (Revenue from Contracts with Customers), which was issued in 2014 and will be effective on January 1, 2018, and IFRS 16 (Leases), which was issued in 2016 and will be effective on January 1, 2019.

2 The relevance of the standard to book focus

Three standards were excluded according to this criterion as they are out of the focus of this book. Particularly, IFRS 1 (Fist-time Adoption of International Financial Reporting Standards), which is concerned with the requirements and procedures to be followed in adopting IFRS for the first time, was excluded as it technically does not apply to GCC-listed companies since all GCC countries have adopted IFRS before the year 2016. Likewise, the other two standards were excluded because they do not serve the purpose of this book, these are IAS 34 (Interim Financial Reporting); which provides the disclosure requirements of the interim financial statements and our focus is to test the compliance with IFRS disclosure requirements in the annual financial statements only, and IFRS 4 (Insurance Contracts) that is related to insurance companies which are not included in the population.

3 Applicability and relevance to the context of GCC member states' financial environment and companies' practices

The intention of IASB from issuing IFRS is to have global unified high-quality standards to be implemented around the world (Barth et al., 2008). However, some of these standards are irrelevant to the GCC context. To confirm the applicability and relevance of IFRS in GCC countries, and standing on the fact that reporting practices for GCC-listed companies are governed by companies' law and market securities law (Al-Shammari, 2005), the disclosure items of IFRS were checked against these laws and regulations in GCC member states,[1] and hence, IAS 12 (Income Taxes) was excluded as legal authorities in GCC do not impose income tax on their listed companies. IAS 29 (Financial Reporting in Hyperinflationary Economics) was excluded since hyperinflationary economics are defined as economies that suffer more than 100% accumulative rate of inflation in three years (Nobes and Parker, 2008), and none of the GCC member states has such an accumulated rate of inflation. Additionally, oil-listed companies among GCC countries are responsible only for marketing oil not for extracting it, as the latter is done by governmental companies that are not listed in the stock markets, accordingly, IFRS 6 (Exploration for and Evaluation of Mineral Assets) was excluded because it does not apply to any of the targeted companies.

Therefore, based on the assessment demonstrated above, it was concluded that eight standards were not relevant nor applicable, thus, they were excluded. Therefore, the initial disclosure index included 34 standards comprising 473 disclosure items. Furthermore, to ensure the completeness and comprehensiveness of the disclosure index, a further revision of the structured disclosure index was conducted by two academic professors, who are experts in IFRS, and an experienced auditor. This revision helped in confirming the clearance, accuracy, and well-presentation of the disclosure items.

However, during and after the data collection process, it was noticed that few or none of the companies applied some standards, and hence, they were excluded, these are as follows: IAS 8 (Accounting Policies, Change in Accounting Estimates and Errors), IAS 20 (Accounting for Government Grants and Disclosure of Government Assistance), IAS 41 (Agriculture), IFRS 3 (Business Combinations), IFRS 5 (Non-Current Assets Held for Sale and Discontinued Operations), IFRS 13 (Fair Value Measurement), and IFRS 14 (Regulatory Deferral Accounts). Additionally, some disclosure items were excluded, as most or all the companies do not implement these items, especially items that include if condition to be applicable; a specific situation must exist for the item to be applicable.

The final disclosure index included 27 Standards compromising 379 disclosure items divided into 22 sub-indices as each standard is considered a sub-index.[2] The idea of dividing the disclosure index into sub-indices serves the objectives of our book given that it aims to compare the level of compliance with every single standard among GCC member states and among companies operating in these states. Additionally, this structure eases the clear detection of the level of compliance with a group of standards that are related to a certain topic among companies and among GCC countries.

Weighting the Disclosure Items

Despite the fact that using a disclosure index is a common practice in examining the level of compliance with IFRS disclosure requirements, the review of the previous work concluded that the proper weighting process of each disclosure item included in the disclosure checklist is debatable (Chavent et al., 2006; Alfaraih, 2009). In more detail, two methods were previously used in weighting the disclosure items: the weighted approach and the unweighted approach. The weighted approach signifies to assign different weightings to different items in the disclosure index, whilst the unweighted approach means to give equal weights to all of the items in the disclosure index. Scholars suggested that the focus of the research determines which approach to follow; Cooke (1989a) argued that if the research is targeting a particular group of users, the weighted approach is considered as the most appropriate; as this approach enables the researcher to assign higher weights to the items that are considered to be the most important to the targeted users group. Nevertheless, if the research focuses on all users of financial statements, other than one user group, the unweighted approach is considered more appropriate, given that it assumes that all disclosure items are equally important among different groups of users.

We used the unweighted approach. This is justified by the following reasons: first, this book focuses on the level of information delivered to all users of the financial statements not for a particular group, and this is supported by the fact that our constructed disclosure index includes all the mandatory disclosure requirements of IFRS. Thereby, each disclosure item is assumed to have the same importance and equal weight. Second, equal weighting of all disclosure items helps in averting subjectivity in assigning different weights to these items, as there is no clear guidance of how to determine the relative importance of the disclosure items (Singhvi and Desai, 1971; Al-Shammari, 2005). Meanwhile, the relative importance of an item is different among companies, industries, and users, and this relative importance may change from time to time (Abd-Elsalam, 1999; Al-Shammari, 2005; Hassaan, 2012). Third, several previous studies have implemented the unweighted approach (see, for example, Street and Bryant, 2000; Street and

Gray, 2002; Rajhi, 2014). Following is a presentation of the procedures we applied in scoring the disclosure items.

Scoring the Disclosure Items

Scoring the disclosure index was completed in consistent with previous work (see, for example, Haniffa, 1999; Al-Htaybat, 2005; Al-Shammari, 2005; Omar, 2007; Hassaan, 2012), where each disclosure item is coded 1 if the required disclosure was done by the company and 0 if the disclosure item is applicable for the company but was not disclosed. Disclosure items that were not applicable for the company were coded as "NA" (Not Applicable) and they were dropped from the scoring system of the company.

It is not easy, in case if a disclosure item does not exist in the annual report, to determine whether it is not disclosed by the company or it is not applicable, therefore, in order to mitigate the uncertainty in scoring the disclosure index and to avoid penalizing the company for nondisclosing a nonapplicable item, we have implemented the following procedures, first, as suggested by Cooke (1989a) and Cooke (1989b), the entire company's annual report was reviewed carefully before scoring, this enables understanding the nature of the company's operations and helps in determining the applicability of the disclosure items to the company. Thereby, if a disclosure item was not found in the annual report and it was not mentioned in the auditor's annual report it was assumed to be not applicable (Street and Bryant, 2000; Glaum and Street, 2003; Hassaan, 2012). Second, following Al-Shammari (2005) and Alfaraih (2009), a priori assumption was followed in determining the applicability of a disclosure item; in other words, certain disclosure items are applicable for certain types of companies or certain industries; for example, manufacturing companies should have inventory, and hence, these companies must disclose the accounting policy implemented in evaluating inventory (Al-Shammari, 2005; Alfaraih, 2009).

Calculating the Level of Compliance with IFRS

After completing scoring the disclosure index, the level of compliance with IFRS was calculated. As the existing literature suggests, there are two methods that could be applied in calculating the level of compliance with IFRS disclosure requirements, these are dichotomous method and the partial compliance method. The dichotomous method was suggested by Wallace (1988) and Cooke (1992) and was named by Tsalavoutas et al. (2010), Tsalavoutas (2011), and Rajhi (2014) as the Cooke's dichotomous method. Despite the fact that this method has been implemented by several previous studies (see, for example, Street and Bryant, 2000; Abd-Elsalam and Weetman, 2003; Hodgdon et al., 2008), it has been criticized by Al-Shiab (2003) and Tsalavoutas et al. (2010) standing on the idea that it gives, unintentionally, more weight to the standards that include a large number of items to be disclosed (Al-Shiab, 2003). In other words, this method gives equal weight to each disclosure item required by all standards, which ignores the considerable variations in the number of the disclosure items required by each standard; for example, IAS1 (Presentation of Financial Statements) includes 103 items to be disclosed, whilst IAS 23 (Borrowing Cost) includes only 3 disclosure items, and using the previous method will assign more weight to the standard with 103 disclosure items than the standard with 3 disclosure items (Al-Shiab, 2003; Abdullah and Minhat, 2013).

Therefore, the partial compliance method was suggested by scholars to avoid assigning different weights to the standards. In this method, the total level of compliance with IFRS will be calculated by adding the level of compliance of each standard, which gives equal weighting to each standard. In more detail, the total level of compliance of each standard will be separately calculated, and then the results of all the standards will be added together to get the total compliance, thereafter, this total will be divided over the total number of applicable standards for the company. The partial compliance method has been implemented by previous studies (see, for example, Al-Shiab, 2003; Tsalavoutas et al., 2010; Hasan et al., 2013; Rajhi, 2014).

Accordingly, we used the partial compliance method in calculating the level of compliance with IFRS. Thus, the degree of compliance will be expressed as a percentage ranging from 0 if the company did not disclose any item for all the standards to 1 if the company disclosed all items for all of the applicable standards. The calculation of the compliance level (disclosure index) using the partial compliance for each company is as follows:

$$\mathrm{PC} = \frac{\Sigma X}{R}$$

where PC is the total compliance score for a company ($0 \leq \mathrm{PS} \leq 1$); X is the level of compliance of each standard; and R is the number of applicable standards for a company.

Notably, using the partial compliance method avoids penalizing companies of not disclosing an inapplicable item, as the not applicable items are excluded from the calculation of the level of compliance. Specifically, the denominator is calculated by adding only the number of applicable standards.

Research Model

The model that we constructed to test the effect of corporate governance and firm characteristics on the level of compliance with IFRS disclosure requirements is as follows:

$$
\begin{aligned}
COMP_{it} = \alpha_0 &+ \beta_1 INDEP_{it} + \beta_2 BSIZE_{it} + \beta_3 SEPAR_{it} + \beta_4 CONCEN_{it} + \beta_5 INST_{it} \\
&+ \beta_6 ACMEM_{it} + \beta_7 ACMEET_{it} + \beta_8 EXTAUD_{it} + \beta_9 FSIZE_{it} + \beta_{10} PROFT_{it} \\
&+ \beta_{11} LEV_{it} + \beta_{12} LIQ_{it} + \beta_{13} IND\_INV_{it} + \beta_{14} IND\_INDS_{it} + \beta_{15} IND\_SER_{it} \\
&+ \beta_{16} IND\_ENE_{it} + \beta_{17} IND\_RST_{it} + \varepsilon_{it}
\end{aligned}
$$

where

$\boldsymbol{COMP_{it}}$ is the level of compliance with IFRS.

$\boldsymbol{INDEP_{it}}$ is the number of independent outside directors over the total number of board members.

$\boldsymbol{BSIZE_{it}}$ is the number of board members.

$\boldsymbol{SEPAR_{it}}$ is a dummy variable that equals zero if the CEO acts also as the chairman of the board of directors and 1 otherwise.

$\boldsymbol{CONCEN_{it}}$ is the percentage of shares owned by major shareholders.

$\boldsymbol{INST_{it}}$ is the percentage of shares owned by major institutional shareholders.

$\boldsymbol{ACMEM_{it}}$ is the number of audit committee members.

$\boldsymbol{ACMEET_{it}}$ is the number of audit committee meetings held during the year.

$\boldsymbol{EXTAUD_{it}}$ is a dummy variable that equals 1 if the external auditor is one of the BIG-FOUR and 0 otherwise.

$\boldsymbol{FSIZE_{it}}$ is the natural logarithm of the total assets.

$\boldsymbol{PROFT_{it}}$ is the Return on Assets (ROA) ratio.

$\boldsymbol{LEV_{it}}$ is the firm leverage which is calculated by dividing the total debts over the total assets.

$\boldsymbol{LIQ_{it}}$ is the firm's liquidity measured by the current ratio.

$\boldsymbol{IND\_INV_{it}}$ is a dummy variable that equals 1 if the company operates in the investment sector and 0 otherwise.

$\boldsymbol{IND\_INDS_{it}}$ is a dummy variable that equals 1 if the company operates in the industrial sector and 0 otherwise.

$\boldsymbol{IND\_SER_{it}}$ is a dummy variable that equals 1 if the company operates in the services sector and 0 otherwise.

$\boldsymbol{IND\_ENE_{it}}$ is a dummy variable that equals 1 if the company operates in the energy sector and 0 otherwise.

$\boldsymbol{IND\_RST_{it}}$ is a dummy variable that equals 1 if the company operates in the real state sector and 0 otherwise.

Reliability and Validity

Selecting the appropriate methods for measuring variables is very important to conduct proper research; meanwhile, it is also important to ensure the goodness of these methods by confirming that they are actually measuring these variables, which enhances the quality of the research (Sekaran and Bougie, 2010). In this vein, two main concepts that are related to the appropriateness and quality of the research methods should be considered, these are reliability and validity (Sekaran and Bougie, 2010).

Reliability refers to the extent that the findings of the research are consistent (Bryman and Bell, 2015). Sekaran and Bougie (2010) further reported that reliability means the stability of the research results. In addition, reliability could be defined as the credibility of the research findings and the repetition of such findings (Collis and Hussey, 2003). Suwaidan (1997) stated that since the information needed to measure the level of compliance with IFRS for the company are obtained from its annual report, there is no obstacle with repetition. However, the main threat of reliability for this type of research is the treatment of the nondisclosed items (Omar and Simon, 2011). Therefore, to ensure reliability of our results, and following the previous studies that examined the level of disclosure applied by companies (see, for example, Omar and Simon, 2011; Tsalavoutas, 2011; Hassaan, 2012), each company's annual report was comprehensively read before scoring the disclosure index in order to be familiar with the company's activities and the nature of its operations. This helped in deciding whether the disclosure items are applicable or not to the company and avoiding penalizing the company for not disclosing nonapplicable items. Additionally, following Owusu-Ansah (1998), a pilot study was conducted before starting scoring the disclosure index; where a sample of annual reports, from all GCC countries, were randomly selected and scored, thereafter, they were reviewed and rescored by another academic staff who is an expert in IFRS.

Whereas validity refers to the accuracy of the information gathered (Schumacher and McMillan, 1993). It relates to the ability of the research findings to accurately reflect reality (Collis and Hussey, 2003). Additionally, validity is an evidence that the research instrument, procedures, and process that were implemented intending to measure research variables are really measuring these variables (Bryman and Bell, 2015). To ensure the validity, we have constructed a disclosure index to meet our objectives in measuring the level of compliance with IFRS disclosure requirements. As well, to ensure catching all the aspects of such a compliance, the disclosure items included in the disclosure index were taken from the mandatory disclosure requirements of IFRS issued by IASB; these requirements are mandatory for all of the six GCC countries. Moreover, based on the fact that validity is achieved through rating or evaluation by experts of the measurement tool (Hair et al., 2010), and following the practice of the previous studies (see, for example, Cooke, 1992; Al-Shammari, 2005; Tsalavoutas, 2011; Hassaan, 2012), two academics, who are experts in IFRS, and an experienced auditor have reviewed the disclosure index to ensure that it includes all the mandatory disclosure requirements of IFRS.

Population and Sample

Study population is defined as the entire group of units that the researcher seeks to investigate (Bryman and Bell, 2015). Given that we aim to investigate the relationship between corporate governance and IFRS compliance in the GCC region, the population includes all the six GCC member states, namely:

Table 7.1 Listed companies as of December 31, 2016

Country	*No. of listed companies*
Saudi Arabia	116
Kuwait	129
UAE	62
Oman	90
Qatar	31
Bahrain	22
Total	**450**

Saudi Arabia, Kuwait, United Arab Emirates, Oman, Qatar, and Bahrain. The inclusion of all countries in the GCC region stands on the fact that all their listed companies are implementing IFRS in preparing their annual financial statements and they are obliged to follow the corporate governance rules issued by OECD (Boshnak, 2017). Moreover, one of the objectives of this book is to compare the level of compliance with IFRS among companies and among countries, therefore, the containment of all the six countries helps in detecting the impact of state differences on the level of IFRS compliance in the GCC region.

Accordingly, the population comprises all listed companies' annual reports at the fiscal year ending December 31, 2016. However, financial institutions, like Banks and insurance companies were excluded due to their different nature and because their disclosure practices are governed by a different set of instructions and regulations, such as the central banks' requirements and regulations (Abed et al., 2012). Thus, a total of 450 nonfinancial companies were listed in GCC member states as by the end of the year 2016. Table 7.1 presents the number of companies listed in each GCC state as of December 31, 2016.

Sample Selection

The year 2016 was selected as the focus year because, at the time of collecting the data and building the disclosure index, it was the most recent year. We employed the "population-sample design"; more specifically, we considered the entire population rather than selecting a specific sample. Nevertheless, out of the 450 companies, that form the population, 397 companies were included in the analysis, whereas 53 companies were excluded as they do not meet one of the following criteria applied in selecting the targeted companies, these are as follows:

1 The company must have a financial year end as of December 31, 2016.
2 The availability of the data for the year 2016.
3 The company should be listed in the market stock exchange since the begging of 2016.

Table 7.2 Distribution of study sample

	Saudi Arabia	*Kuwait*	*UAE*	*Oman*	*Qatar*	*Bahrain*	*Total*
No. of listed companies	116	129	62	90	31	22	450
Excluded companies under the first criterion	6	4	1	11	2	1	25
Excluded companies under the second criterion	0	10	5	8	1	0	24
Excluded companies under the third criterion	1	0	2	1	0	0	4
Included companies (final Sample)	109	115	54	70	28	21	397

Source: Developed by authors.

Based on the abovementioned criteria, 25 companies were excluded as they do not meet the first criterion, 24 companies were excluded as they do not meet the second criterion, and 4 companies were excluded as they do not meet the third one. Table 7.2 shows the implication of these criteria and the number of included and excluded companies in each country.

Ethical Considerations

Ethical issues are important for all types of research (Sekaran and Bougie, 2010; Bryman and Bell, 2015); researchers should adhere to both general research principles and those are related to the specific type of research in the early stage of the research process. This book is based on the quantitative secondary data; therefore, we took into consideration the ethical aspects of this approach. As stated by Sekaran and Bougie (2010), the ethics of a business research refer to "a code of conduct or expected societal norm of behavior while conducting research" (p. 15). The existence of such codes is essential to ensure that the research is handled in an ethical manner in order to serve the interests of all concerned parties. In quantitative research, ethical codes prevent the falsification and fabrication of data and results; additionally, these codes protect research participants through avoiding harm to them if humans are part of the study. This implies that the final report of the research should not include language or words that are biased, and the findings should not be falsified to meet the researchers' needs (Creswell, 2009). Moreover, the data collected must be adequate and relevant to the objectives of the research, and even if the data is available on the companies' websites, a permission to use it and analyze it is needed (Tripathy, 2013). We are completely aware of the ethical issues associated with the research presented in this book and all issues discussed above were considered.

Summary

This chapter delivered an overview about how the required data to measure corporate governance and firm characteristics variables was collected. Six corporate governance mechanisms and five firm characteristics were included in the analysis. Furthermore, it presented the procedures applied in selecting the accounting standards that should be included in the disclosure index, the procedures implemented in weighting and scoring the disclosure index, and the methods used in calculating the level of compliance with IFRS. The last section delivered an overview about the criteria implemented in selecting the targeted companies.

Notes

1 If an IFRS disclosure requirement contradicts with the requirement of national law, the company must follow the requirement of the national law (Hassaan, 2012).

2 Some standards are qualifying standards; even though they are obligatory for companies to be implemented, they do not include any presentation or disclosure requirements. Specifically, IAS 28 (Investment in Associates and Joint Ventures), IFRS 10 (Consolidated Financial Statements), and IFRS 11 (Joint Arrangements) do not specify any disclosure requirements, instead, the disclosures related to these standards are under IFRS 12 (Disclosure of Interest in Other Entities). Likewise, IAS 32 (Financial Instruments) and IFRS 9 (Financial Instruments) do not state the disclosure requirements of financial instruments as they were moved to IFRS 7 (Financial Instruments: Disclosure).

References

Abd-Elsalam, O.H. (1999). *The introduction and application of international accounting standards to accounting disclosure regulations of a capital market in a developing country: The case of Egypt* (Doctoral dissertation, Heriot-Watt University).

Abd-Elsalam, O.H., & Weetman, P. (2003). Introducing international accounting standards to an emerging capital market: Relative familiarity and language effect in egypt. *Journal of International Accounting, Auditing and Taxation, 12*(1), 63–84.

Abdullah, M., & Minhat, M. (2013). Measuring compliance with IFRS mandatory disclosure requirements: Some evidence from Malaysia. *Australian Journal of Basic and Applied Sciences*, 7(8), 163–169.

Abed, S., Al-Attar, A., & Suwaidan, M. (2012). Corporate governance and earnings management: Jordanian evidence. *International Business Research*, *5*(1), 216–225.

Aburaya, R. (2012). *The relationship between corporate governance and environmental disclosure: UK evidence* (Doctoral dissertation, Durham University).

Al-Akra, M., Eddie, I.A., & Ali, M.J. (2010a). The influence of the introduction of accounting disclosure regulation on mandatory disclosure compliance: Evidence from Jordan. *The British Accounting Review*, *42*(3), 170–186.

Al-Akra, M., Eddie, I.A., & Ali, M.J. (2010b). The association between privatisation and voluntary disclosure: Evidence from Jordan. *Accounting and Business Research*, *40*(1), 55–74.

Alfaraih, M. (2009). *Compliance with international financial reporting standards (IFRS) and the value relevance of accounting information in emerging stock markets: evidence from Kuwait* (Doctoral dissertation, Queensland University of Technology).

Al-Htaybat, K. (2005). *Financial disclosure practices: Theoretical foundation, and an empirical investigation on Jordanian printed and internet formats* (Doctoral dissertation, University of Southampton).

Al-Janadi, Y., Rahman, R.A., & Omar, N.H. (2013). Corporate governance mechanisms and voluntary disclosure in Saudi Arabia. *Corporate Governance*, *4*(4), 25–35.

Allegrini, M., & Greco, G. (2013). Corporate boards, audit committees and voluntary disclosure: Evidence from Italian listed companies. *Journal of Management & Governance*, *17*(1), 187–216.

Al-Najjar, B. (2010). Corporate governance and institutional ownership: Evidence from Jordan. *Corporate Governance: The International Journal of Business in Society*, *10*(2), 176–190.

Alsaqqa, I., & Sawan, N. (2013). The advantages and the challenges of adopting IFRS into UAE stock market. *International Journal of Business and Management*, *8*(19), 1–23.

Al-Shammari, B.A. (2005). *Compliance with international accounting standards by listed companies in the Gulf Co-operation Council member states: An empirical study*. University of Western Australia.

Al-Shiab, M. (2003). *Financial consequences of IAS adoption: The case of Jordan* (Doctoral dissertation, Newcastle University).

Anderson, M., & Daoud, M. (2005). *Corporate governances disclosure by Swedish listed corporations* (Master thesis, Jonkoping International Business School, Jonkoping University, Sweden).

Apostolou, A.K., & Nanopoulos, K.A. (2009). Voluntary accounting disclosure and corporate governance: Evidence from Greek listed firms. *International Journal of Accounting and Finance*, *1*(4), 395–414.

Arcay, M.R.B., & Vazquez, M.F.M. (2005). Corporate characteristics, governance rules and the extent of voluntary disclosure in Spain. *Advances in Accounting*, *21*, 299–331.

Barako, D.G., Hancock, P., & Izan, H.Y. (2006). Factors influencing voluntary corporate disclosure by Kenyan companies. *Corporate Governance: An International Review*, *14*(2), 107–125.

Barth, M.E., Landsman, W.R., & Lang, M.H. (2008). International accounting standards and accounting quality. *Journal of Accounting Research*, *46*(3), 467–498.

Baxter, P., & Cotter, J. (2009). Audit committees and earnings quality. *Accounting & Finance*, *49*(2), 267–290.

Becker, C.L., DeFond, M.L., Jiambalvo, J., & Subramanyam, K.R. (1998). The effect of audit quality on earnings management. *Contemporary Accounting Research*, *15*(1), 1–24.

Beekes, W., Pope, P., & Young, S. (2004). The link between earnings timeliness, earnings conservatism and board composition: Evidence from the UK. *Corporate Governance: An International Review*, *12*(1), 47–59.

Belkaoui, A., Kahl, A., & Peyrard, J. (1977). Information needs of financial analysts: An international comparison. *The International Journal of Accounting Education and Research*, *13*(1), 19–27.

Booth, J.R., Cornett, M.M., & Tehranian, H. (2002). Boards of directors, ownership, and regulation. *Journal of Banking & Finance*, *26*(10), 1973–1996.

Boshnak, H. (2017). *Mandatory and voluntary disclosures in GCC listed firms* (Doctoral dissertation, University of the West of England).

Bradbury, M., Mak, Y.T., & Tan, S.M. (2006). Board characteristics, audit committee characteristics and abnormal accruals. *Pacific Accounting Review, 18*(2), 47–68.

Brennan, N. (2007). *Corporate governance and financial reporting*. London: Sage Publications.

Brown, J.R., Falaschetti, D., & Orlando, M.J. (2010). Auditor Independence and the quality of information in financial disclosures: Evidence for market discipline versus Sarbanes–Oxley proscriptions. *American Law and Economics Review, 12*(1), 39–68.

Brown, J.R., & Martinsson, G. (2014). *Financial* disclosure, corporate transparency, and innovation (Working paper, Iowa State University, January 14).

Bryman, A., & Bell, E. (2015). *Business research methods*. Oxford University Press.

Camfferman, K., & Cooke, T.E. (2002). An analysis of disclosure in the annual reports of UK and Dutch companies. *Journal of International Accounting Research, 1*(1), 3–30.

Chau, G.K., & Gray, S.J. (2002). Ownership structure and corporate voluntary disclosure in Hong Kong and Singapore. *The International Journal of Accounting, 37*(2), 247–265.

Chavent, M., Ding, Y., Fu, L., Stolowy, H., & Wang, H. (2006). Disclosure and determinants studies: An extension using the divisive clustering method (DIV). *European Accounting Review, 15*(2), 181–218.

Chung, R., Firth, M., & Kim, J.B. (2003). Auditor conservatism and reported earnings. *Accounting and Business Research, 33*(1), 19–32.

Coles, J.L., Daniel, N.D., & Naveen, L. (2008). Boards: Does one size fit all? *Journal of Financial Economics, 87*(2), 329–356.

Collis, J., & Hussey, R. (2003). *Business research: A practical guide for undergraduate and postgraduate students* (2nd Edition). Basingstoke: Palgrave Macmillan.

Cooke, T.E. (1989a). Disclosure in the corporate annual reports of Swedish companies. *Accounting and Business Research, 19*(74), 113–124.

Cooke, T.E. (1989b). Voluntary corporate disclosure by Swedish companies. *Journal of International Financial Management & Accounting, 1*(2), 171–195.

Cooke, T.E. (1991). An assessment of voluntary disclosure in the annual reports of Japanese corporations. *The International Journal of Accounting, 26*(3), 174–189.

Cooke, T.E. (1992). The impact of size, stock market listing and industry type on disclosure in the annual reports of Japanese listed corporations. *Accounting and Business Research, 22*(87), 229–237.

Coombes, P., & Wong, S.C. (2004). Chairman and CEO: One job or two? *The Mckinsey Quarterly : A new era in Governance, 2*(1) 43–47.

Creswell, J.W. (2009). *Research design: Qualitative, quantitative, and mixed methods approaches*. Thousand Oaks: Sage publications.

Dahya, J., & Travlos, N. (2000). Does the one man show pay? Theory and evidence on the dual CEO revisited. *European Financial Management, 6*(1), 85–98.

Denis, D.K., & McConnell, J.J. (2003). International corporate governance. *Journal of Financial and Quantitative Analysis, 38*(1), 1–36.

Dharmadasa, P., Gamage, P., & Herath, S.K. (2014). Corporate governance, board characteristics and firm performance: Evidence from Sri Lanka. *South Asian Journal of Management, 21*(1), 7–31.

Dimitropoulos, P.E., & Asteriou, D. (2010). The effect of board composition on the informativeness and quality of annual earnings: Empirical evidence from Greece. *Research in International Business and Finance, 24*(2), 190–205.

Ezat, A., & El-Masry, A. (2008). The impact of corporate governance on the timeliness of corporate internet reporting by Egyptian listed companies. *Managerial Finance, 34*(12), 848–867.

Fama, E.F., & Jensen, M.C. (1983). Separation of ownership and control. *The Journal of Law & Economics, 26*(2), 301–325.

Farber, D.B. (2005). Restoring trust after fraud: Does corporate governance matter? *The Accounting Review, 80*(2), 539–561.

Glaum, M., & Street, D.L. (2003). Compliance with the disclosure requirements of Germany's new market: IAS versus US GAAP. *Journal of International Financial Management & Accounting, 14*(1), 64–100.

Gul, F.A., & Leung, S. (2004). Board leadership, outside directors' expertise and voluntary corporate disclosures. *Journal of Accounting and Public Policy, 23*(5), 351–379.

Haddad, A.E., AlShattarat, W.K., AbuGhazaleh, N.M., & Nobanee, H. (2015). The impact of ownership structure and family board domination on voluntary disclosure for Jordanian listed companies. *Eurasian Business Review, 5*(2), 203–234.

Hair, J.F., Black, W.C., Babin, B.J., & Anderson, R.E. (2010). *Multivariate data analysis: A global perspective* (7th ed.). Upper Saddle River, NJ: Pearson Education.

Haniffa, R.M. (1999). *Culture, corporate governance and disclosure in Malaysian corporations* (Doctoral dissertation, University of Exeter).

Haniffa, R.M., & Cooke, T.E. (2002). Culture, corporate governance and disclosure in Malaysian corporations. *Abacus, 38*(3), 317–349.

Hasan, M.S., Hossain, S.Z., & Swieringa, R.J. (2013). Corporate governance and financial disclosures: Bangladesh perspective. *Research Journal of Finance and Accounting, 4*(1), 109–119.

Hashim, A.H., & Devis, S. (2009). Board characteristics, ownership structure and earning quality Malaysian evidence. *Research in Accounting in Emerging Economies, 8*, 97–123.

Hassaan, M. (2012). *Corporate governance and compliance with International Financial Reporting Standards (IFRSs): Evidence from two MENA stock exchanges* (Doctoral dissertation, Aston University).

Ho, S.S., & Wong, K.S. (2001). A study of the relationship between corporate governance structures and the extent of voluntary disclosure. *Journal of International Accounting, Auditing and Taxation, 10*(2), 139–156.

Hodgdon, C., & Hughes, S.B. (2016). The effect of corporate governance, auditor choice and global activities on EU company disclosures of estimates and judgments. *Journal of International Accounting, Auditing and Taxation, 26* (C), 28–46.

Hodgdon, C., Tondkar, R.H., Harless, D.W., & Adhikari, A. (2008). Compliance with IFRS disclosure requirements and individual analysts' forecast errors. *Journal of International Accounting, Auditing and Taxation, 17*(1), 1–13.

Jaggi, B., Leung, S., & Gul, F. (2009). Family control, board independence and earnings management: Evidence based on Hong Kong firms. *Journal of Accounting and Public Policy, 28*(4), 281–300.

Jensen, M.C. (1993). The modern industrial revolution, exit, and the failure of internal control systems. *The Journal of Finance, 48*(3), 831–880.

Jensen, M.C., & Meckling, W.H. (1976). Theory of the firm: Managerial behavior, agency costs and ownership structure. *Journal of Financial Economics, 3*(4), 305–360.

Joshi, L., & Al-Mudhahki, J. (2001). Empirical study of compliance with international accounting standards (IAS-1) by stock exchange listed companies in Bahrain. *Journal of Financial Management & Analysis, 14*(2), 43.

Joshi, P.L., & Al-Mudhahki, J. (2013). Empirical study of compliance with international accounting standards (IAS-1) by stock exchange listed companies in Bahrain. *Journal of Financial Management & Analysis, 26*(2), 43–54.

Klein, A. (2002). Audit committee, board of director characteristics, and earnings management. *Journal of Accounting and Economics, 33*(3), 375–400.

Koh, P.S., Laplante, S.K., & Tong, Y.H. (2007). Accountability and value enhancement roles of corporate governance. *Accounting & Finance, 47*(2), 305–333.

Laing, D., & Weir, C.M. (1999). Governance structures, size and corporate performance in UK firms. *Management Decision, 37*(5), 457–464.

Lipton, M., & Lorsch, J.W. (1992). A modest proposal for improved corporate governance. *The Business Lawyer, 48* 59–77.

Marston, C.L., & Shrives, P.J. (1991). The use of disclosure indices in accounting research: a review article. *The British Accounting Review, 23*(3), 195–210.

McNally, G.M., Eng, L.H., & Hasseldine, C.R. (1982). Corporate financial reporting in New Zealand: An analysis of user preferences, corporate characteristics and disclosure practices for discretionary information. *Accounting and Business Research, 13*(49), 11–20.

Muth, M., & Donaldson, L. (1998). Stewardship theory and board structure: A contingency approach. *Corporate Governance: An International Review, 6*(1), 5–28.

Nobes, C., & Parker, R.H. (2008). *Comparative international accounting*. Pearson Education.

Noor, M.A.M., & Fadzil, F.H. (2013). Board characteristics and performance from perspective of governance code in Malaysia. *World Review of Business Research, 3*(3), 191–206.

OECD (2015). *Organization for economic cooperation and development. OECD principles of corporate governance*. Ankara: OECD Publications.

Omar, B.F.A. (2007). *Exploring the aggregate, mandatory and voluntary financial disclosure behaviour under a new regulatory environment: The case of Jordan* (Doctoral dissertation, University of Hull).

Omar, B., & Simon, J. (2011). Corporate aggregate disclosure practices in Jordan. *Advances in Accounting, 27*(1), 166–186.

Owusu-Ansah, S. (1998). The impact of corporate attribites on the extent of mandatory disclosure and reporting by listed companies in Zimbabwe. *The International Journal of Accounting, 33*(5), 605–631.

Parum, E. (2005). Does disclosure on corporate governance lead to openness and transparency in how companies are managed? *Corporate Governance: An International Review, 13*(5), 702–709.

Patton, A., & Baker, J.C. (1987). Why won't directors rock the boat. *Harvard Business Review, 65*(6), 10–12.

Rajgopal, S., Venkatachalam, M., & Jiambalvo, J.J. (1999). Is institutional ownership associated with earnings management and the extent to which stock prices reflect future earnings? *Available at SSRN 163433*.

Rajhi, M. (2014). International financial reporting standards and level of compliance with mandatory disclosure requirements. *International Journal of Multidisciplinarity Sciences and Engineering, 5*(5), 1–6.

Robbins, W.A., & Austin, K.R. (1986). Disclosure quality in governmental financial reports: An assessment of the appropriateness of a compound measure. *Journal of Accounting Research, 24*(2) 412–421.

Samaha, K., & Dahawy, K. (2010). An empirical analysis of corporate governance structures and voluntary corporate disclosure in volatile capital markets: The Egyptian experience. *International Journal of Accounting, Auditing and Performance Evaluation,* 7(1-2), 61–93.

Schumacher, S., & McMillan, J. (1993). *Research in education: A conceptual introduction.* New York: Harper Collins.

Sekaran, U., & Bougie, R. (2010). *Research method for business: A skill building approach.* Chichester, UK: John Wiley & Sons.

Shamser, M., & Annuar, M.N. (1993). Management versus shareholders' interest: Board composition, market risk and shareholder returns of Malaysian listed firms'. *Malaysian Management Review, 29*, 44–52.

Singhvi, S.S., & Desai, H.B. (1971). An empirical analysis of the quality of corporate financial disclosure. *The Accounting Review, 46*(1), 129–138.

Street, D.L., & Bryant, S.M. (2000). Disclosure level and compliance with IASs: A comparison of companies with and without US listings and filings. *The International Journal of Accounting, 35*(3), 305–329.

Street, D.L., & Gray, S.J. (2002). Factors influencing the extent of corporate compliance with International Accounting Standards: Summary of a research monograph. *Journal of International Accounting, Auditing and Taxation, 11*(1), 51–76.

Suwaidan, M.S. (1997). *Voluntary disclosure of accounting information: The case of Jordan* (Doctoral dissertation, University of Aberdeen).

Tripathy, J.P. (2013). Secondary data analysis: Ethical issues and challenges. *Iranian Journal of Public Health, 42*(12), 1478–1479.

Tsalavoutas, I. (2011). Transition to IFRS and compliance with mandatory disclosure requirements: What is the signal? *Advances in Accounting, 27*(2), 390–405.

Tsalavoutas, I., Evans, L., & Smith, M. (2010). Comparison of two methods for measuring compliance with IFRS mandatory disclosure requirements. *Journal of Applied Accounting Research, 11*(3), 213–228.

Uyar, A. (2011). Firm characteristics and voluntary disclosure of graphs in annual reports of Turkish listed companies. *African Journal of Business Management, 5*(17), 7651–7657.

Wallace, R.O., & Naser, K. (1995). Firm-specific determinants of the comprehensiveness of mandatory disclosure in the corporate annual reports of firms listed on the stock exchange of Hong Kong. *Journal of Accounting and Public policy, 14*(4), 311–368.

Wallace, R.O., Naser, K., & Mora, A. (1994). The relationship between the comprehensiveness of corporate annual reports and firm characteristics in Spain. *Accounting and Business Research, 25*(97), 41–53.

Wallace, R.S.O. (1988). Corporate financial reporting in Nigeria. *Accounting and Business Research, 18*(72), 352–362.

Xie, B., Davidson III, W.N., & DaDalt, P.J. (2003). Earnings management and corporate governance: The role of the board and the audit committee. *Journal of Corporate Finance, 9*(3), 295–316.

Yermack, D. (1996). Higher market valuation of companies with a small board of directors. *Journal of Financial Economics, 40*(2), 185–211.

8 Empirical Results

Introduction

The overall aim of this book is to explore the relationship between corporate governance and the level of compliance with International Financial Reporting Standards (IFRS) in the Gulf Cooperation Council (GCC) countries. As presented in Chapter 7, we have used a self-built disclosure index to measure the level of compliance with IFRS disclosure requirements. The built index includes all the mandatory disclosure requirements of IFRS as for the year ended December 31, 2016; it comprises 379 disclosure items divided into 22 sub-disclosure indices, as each standard represents a sub-index.[1] Regarding corporate governance, eight variables were included, these are board independence, board size, CEO duality, concentrated ownership, institutional ownership, audit committee size, audit committee meetings, and external auditor quality. Finally, firm characteristics included firm size, profitability, liquidity, leverage, and industry type. Following is a discussion of the descriptive analysis of the level of compliance with all standards and the level of compliance with each standard for the listed companies in GCC member states.

Descriptive Statistics of IFRS Compliance for the GCC-Listed Companies

This section presents the descriptive statistics of the level of compliance with IFRS disclosure requirements for all of the GCC countries together and for each country. Then it highlights the descriptive statistics of the level of compliance with each standard of IFRS.

Descriptive Statistics of the Total IFRS Disclosure Index Score

The total level of compliance with IFRS disclosure requirements was calculated using the partial compliance method by adding together the level of compliance with each standard for each company to get a total compliance; thereafter, this total compliance was divided over the number of

DOI: 10.4324/9781003211556-8

Table 8.1 Descriptive statistics of IFRS compliance (all standards)

Country	*Minimum*	*Maximum*	*Mean*	*Standard Deviation*
All GCC countries	.535	.896	.741	.065
Saudi Arabia	.543	.827	.713	.065
Kuwait	.535	.872	.726	.062
Oman	.576	.896	.770	.056
UAE	.693	.875	.793	.042
Qatar	.568	.813	.743	.061
Bahrain	.635	.837	.741	.052

Source: Authors' data.

applicable standards for each company. This method produces a ratio that indicates the company's compliance score, this ratio ranges from 0 (if the company did not disclose any applicable disclosure item) to 1 (if the company disclosed all of the applicable disclosure items). Table 8.1 presents the descriptive statistics of the total level of compliance with IFRS disclosure requirements for all GCC countries and for each country.

As indicated in Table 8.1, across the six GCC countries, the average level of compliance with IFRS did not exceed 80%. This result is consistent with previous work as the majority of it had reported an average level of compliance with IFRS between 70% and 80%. Moreover, the table shows that the average level of compliance varies across countries; specifically, the highest average level of compliance was for the UAE at 79.3% followed by Oman at 77%, Qatar at 74.3%, Bahrain at 74.1%, Kuwait at 72.6%, and the lowest was for Saudi Arabia at 71.3%. Additionally, the minimum and maximum values of the level of compliance with IFRS were different across countries. In more detail, the lowest value of the minimum score of compliance was found in Kuwait at 53.5% and the highest was for the UAE at 69.3%. Whilst regarding the maximum value of the level of compliance, the highest value was detected in Oman at 89.6%, and the lowest was for Qatar at 81.3%. As well, the lowest value of standard deviation was noted in the UAE at 4.2%, which implies that the variations in the level of compliance with IFRS among the UAE's listed companies is the lowest in comparison with other GCC countries. Furthermore, our results show that among all the six GCC countries, none of the targeted companies had fully complied with all of the IFRS disclosure requirements; as the maximum total score of the level of compliance was 89.6%.

Descriptive Statistics for Sub-indices (All Countries)

As previously mentioned, the disclosure index was divided into 22 sub-indices, as each standard is considered a sub-index. Table 8.2 presents the descriptive statistics for each standard for all of the GCC countries by presenting the minimum and maximum compliance scores, the average

Table 8.2 Descriptive statistics of sub-indices compliance (all countries)

Standard	*Minimum*	*Maximum*	*Mean*	*Standard Deviation*	*Applicability*
IAS 1	.824	.988	.931	.029	390
IAS 2	.166	1.000	.869	.174	311
IAS 7	.428	1.000	.920	.114	390
IAS 10	.000	1.000	.761	.422	345
IAS 11	.000	1.000	.614	.368	65
IAS 16	.000	1.000	.932	.195	384
IAS 17	.000	1.000	.576	.323	98
IAS 18	.666	1.000	.994	.039	390
IAS 19	.000	1.000	.197	.105	390
IAS 21	.000	1.000	.785	.365	251
IAS 23	.000	1.000	.439	.314	347
IAS 24	.076	1.000	.595	.197	388
IAS 26	.000	.782	.077	.078	390
IAS 33	.000	1.000	.987	.069	390
IAS 36	.000	1.000	.754	.315	142
IAS 37	.000	1.000	.917	.217	341
IAS 38	.000	1.000	.784	.276	185
IAS 40	.000	1.000	.814	.164	155
IFRS 2	.250	1.000	.720	.340	17
IFRS 7	.360	1.000	.858	.155	390
IFRS 8	.000	1.000	.734	.332	384
IFRS 12	.333	1.000	.997	.038	299

Source: Authors' data.

level of compliance, the standard deviation, and the number of companies for which the standard was applicable. As indicated in the table, there are huge variations in the level of compliance with IFRS disclosure requirements for each standard (sub-index). Explicitly, the average level of compliance with these standards ranged from 7.7% for IAS 26 (Accounting and Reporting by Retirement Benefit Plans) to 99.7% for IFRS 12 (Disclosure of Interest in Other Entities). The highest level of compliance (more than 90%) was for IAS 1 (Presentation of Financial Statements), IAS 7 (Statement of Cash Flows), IAS 16 (Property, Plant and Equipment), IAS 18 (Revenue), IAS 33 (Earnings Per Share), IAS 37 (Provisions, Contingent Liabilities, and Contingent Assets), and IFRS 12 (Disclosure of Interest in Other Entities). Whilst the lowest (less than 50%) was for IAS 23 (Borrowing Costs), IAS 19 (Employees Benefits), and IAS 26 (Accounting and Reporting by Retirement Benefit Plans).

The high level of compliance with the previously mentioned standards could be related to the nature of the information included in these standards. In more detail, some of these standards include proprietary information related to the evaluation of managers' performance. Dye (1985) defined proprietary information as the information that is potentially disclosed to affect managers' compensation. Such information is important to the company and managers to signal their good performance. In other words, the information under these standards affects the company's financial position and competitive advantages, such as cash flows, revenues, and Earnings per Share, and hence, companies are more motivated to comply with this type of disclosure items. Another explanation is related to their relative ease of application in comparison to other standards. For example, IAS 1 (Presentation of Financial Statements) includes disclosure items that are linked with low cost and do not require a high level of financial expertise. The majority of the items under this standard are straightforward and are related to general information about the company that must be disclosed in the body of the financial statements, such as the name of the company, the currency of the numbers presented in these statements, and the classification of assets; it is assumed that companies are sufficiently experienced in applying these items. Other examples are IFRS 12 (Disclosure of Interest in Other Entities) and IAS 33 (Earnings per Share); these standards have a small number of items to be disclosed; four items and three items, respectively, which makes the application of these standards easier for companies.

However, although Table 8.2 shows that some companies have fully complied with all of the disclosure items of IAS 19 (Employees Benefits) and IAS 26 (Accounting and Reporting by Retirement Benefit Plans), these standards had the lowest average level of compliance. The latter implies that these standards were not properly applied in GCC countries. Further, this low average of compliance with these two standards may be explained based on the fact that they require a very complicated and controversial accounting treatment, making their adoption harder than other standards. Moreover, another justification may be related to the lack of expertise in the area of employees' benefits and retirement plans, which may lead to misunderstanding and difficulties in interpreting such standards, and hence, more training is needed for accountants in the field to achieve the appropriate application of these standards. This supports the cost-benefit analysis regarding the applicability of some standards in the Middle Eastern context.

Moreover, Table 8.2 shows the applicability of each standard among the targeted companies; this figure is related to the number of companies for which the standard was applicable. Results show that there are huge variations in the number of companies that are supposed to comply with each standard, for example, only seven standards out of the 27 standards were applicable for all companies, whilst only 17 companies were applying IFRS 2 (Shares Based Payments); this implies that only 17 companies had shares based payments plans in their financial statements, which indicates that they are not common in GCC member states. The variations in the applicability of the standards are related to the procedures we implemented in scoring the disclosure index. In other words, as previously mentioned, to avoid penalizing the company for not disclosing a nonapplicable item when scoring its disclosure index, such an item was coded as "NA" (Not Applicable), which resulted in some entire standards not being applicable for some companies.

Descriptive Statistics for Sub-indices (Each Country)

After discussing the variations in the score of compliance for each standard among all GCC member states together, the next step is to discuss the variations in the level of compliance for each standard in each country. Accordingly, Table 8.3 presents the compliance scores with each standard for each of the six GCC member states. As indicated in the table, some standards have a relative similarity in their compliance scores in all of the six countries; meanwhile, some variations were detected for other standards. For example, the compliance score for IAS 1 (Presentation of Financial Statements) ranged from 92.1 % to 94.3, and for IAS 19 (Employees Benefits), it ranged from 18.1% to 22.9%. Additionally, in all GCC member states, the lowest average level of compliance was for IAS 26 (Accounting and Reporting by Retirement Benefit Plans); the level of compliance with such a standard lies between 4.1% in Kuwait and 11.3% in Bahrain, which implies that, on average, companies disclose almost only 3 out of the 23 disclosure items required under this standard, at most. This supports the idea that there are difficulties related to adopting this standard in GCC countries. Furthermore, the table shows that the highest average level of compliance was for IFRS 12 (Disclosure of Interest in Other Entities) in all GCC countries; it was further noted that the average level of compliance for this standard was 100% in five

Table 8.3 Descriptive statistics of sub-indices compliance (each country)

	Saudi Arabia	*Kuwait*	*Oman*	*UAE*	*Qatar*	*Bahrain*
IAS 1	.921	.934	.943	.923	.941	.940
IAS 2	.841	.797	.969	.898	.915	.791
IAS 7	.872	.921	.939	.949	.967	.961
IAS 10	.750	.567	.914	.976	.607	.650
IAS 11	.767	.543	.938	.930	.697	.277
IAS 16	.99	.792	.978	.995	.956	.978
IAS 17	.584	.527	.800	.779	.625	.166
IAS 18	.986	.994	1.000	1.000	1.000	1.000
IAS 19	.201	.181	.188	.229	.195	.213
IAS 21	.565	.891	.933	.730	.690	.888
IAS 23	.404	.412	.469	.519	.531	.380
IAS 24	.540	.644	.575	.598	.674	.576
IAS 26	.087	.041	.088	.104	.078	.113
IAS 33	.967	.991	1.000	.995	1.000	1.000
IAS 36	.884	.704	.883	.923	.569	1.000
IAS 37	.952	.809	.973	.988	.932	.909
IAS 38	.801	.661	.864	.920	.864	.656
IAS 40	.745	.856	.688	.807	.822	.769
IFRS 2	1.000	.531	.750	1.000	.500	.750
IFRS 7	.652	.964	.866	.930	.979	.973
IFRS 8	.658	.875	.674	.718	.598	.731
IFRS 12	1.000	.993	1.000	1.000	1.000	1.000

Source: Authors' data.

out of the six GCC countries, which signifies that all companies for which the standard was applicable had fully complied with all of its disclosure items. This indicates the easiness of implementing the disclosure requirements of such a standard.

Nevertheless, a wide variation across GCC countries was found in the average level of compliance with some standards, such as IAS 10 (Events After Reporting Period), which has the lowest level of compliance in Kuwait at 56.7%, and the highest was for the UAE at 97.6%. Similarly, for IAS 17 (Leases), the highest level of compliance was found in Oman and the lowest was in Bahrain, at 80% and 16.6% respectively. Moreover, for IAS 21 (The Effects of Change in Foreign Currency Rates), the lowest level of compliance was for Saudi Arabia at 56.6%, and the highest was for Oman at 93.3%. Likewise, IFRS 7 (Financial Instruments: Disclosure), where the lowest was for Saudi Arabia at 65.2% and the highest for Qatar at 97.9%. These differences in the average level of compliance for some standards relate to the capacity in enforcing the application of the requirements of these standards in each country.

Descriptive Statistics for Independent Variables

As mentioned in Chapter 7, the number of companies included in the sample was 397. However, some companies were further excluded due to the unavailability of corporate governance data; accordingly, the number of companies was reduced to 314. In other words, the implemented tests regarding the descriptive analysis of the level of compliance and the tests employed in examining the existence of significant statistical differences in the level of compliance with IFRS across GCC countries were run for all the included companies. Nevertheless, the descriptive analysis for independent variables and the regression analysis was run for 314 companies. Having two different numbers of observations is justified by the intention of avoiding losing more observations in analyzing the level of compliance with IFRS, which enhances the generalizability of the results. Accordingly, the following analysis is based on 314 companies as the targeted companies.

Board Independence

Board independence was measured by calculating the percentage of independent directors to the total number of directors on the board. As indicated in Table 8.4, the ratio of board independence ranged from 0% to 100%, and the average of independent directors for all of the targeted companies was 49.6%. This means that, among all GCC countries, nearly half of the board members were independent directors. The analysis shows that the minimum value of this variable is 0, which indicates that there were companies that did not have any independent members on their boards. At the country level, the highest board independence was for the UAE at

Table 8.4 Descriptive statistics of independent variables

	N	*Minimum*	*Maximum*	*Mean*	*Standard Deviation*
Board independence	314	.000	1.000	.496	.270
Board size	314	5.000	12.000	7.697	1.650
CEO duality	314	.000	1.000	.978	.147
Institutional ownership	314	.000	.991	.354	.275
Concentrated ownership	314	.000	.991	.429	.272
Audit committee size	314	2.000	8.000	3.395	.712
Audit committee meetings	314	.000	13.000	5.096	1.832
External auditor quality	314	.000	1.000	.669	.471
Firm size	314	5.947	11.031	8.606	.791
Profitability (ROA)	314	-.353	.284	.040	.073
Liquidity	314	.050	15.025	2.370	2.273
Leverage	314	.010	1.361	.393	.235
Investment	314	.000	1.000	.121	.326
Industrial	314	.000	1.000	.427	.495
Services	314	.000	1.000	.248	.432
Energy	314	.000	1.000	.076	.266
Real estate	314	.000	1.000	.127	.333
Valid *N* (listwise)	314				

Source: Authors' Data.

71.7%, followed by Oman at 59.7%, Saudi Arabia at 52.2%, Bahrain at 49.8%, and the lowest was for Kuwait at 22.8%, and Qatar at 20.6%. This implies that board independence is more recognized in the UAE, Saudi Arabia, and Oman, than in other GCC countries.

Board Size

Board size represents the number of directors on the board. Table 8.4 shows that board size ranged from 5 to 12 members, with an average of 7.69 members. This variation in the minimum and the maximum number of members on the board stands on the absence of a clear determination of the appropriate number of board members among GCC countries' corporate governance codes. At the country level, the highest board size was for Oman at 12 members, followed by Saudi Arabia, Qatar, and Bahrain at 11 members, whilst in the UAE and Kuwait, the maximum number of members was 10. Additionally, the minimum number of members for all GCC countries was 5, except for Bahrain, where it was 6. This implies that board size does not considerably vary in these states, as the average board size ranged from 6.46 in Kuwait to 8.53 in Bahrain.

CEO Duality

CEO duality appears if the chairman of the board also holds the same position as the CEO; this variable was coded 1 if there was a separation between these two positions, and 0 otherwise. As Table 8.4 shows, the average of CEO duality was 97.8%, which means that 97.8% of the targeted companies separated those two positions. This is justified by the fact that, in all GCC countries, the corporate governance codes require the separation between the two positions. At the country level, the analysis shows that all of the targeted listed companies in the UAE and Bahrain have better applied the recommendations of OECD regarding the separation of CEO and chairman of the board; the mean of this variable was 100% in these countries. Regarding the other four countries, three of them shared almost the same mean; specifically, 99.1% for Saudi Arabia, 98% for Kuwait, and 98.6% for Oman, whilst Qatar had the lowest average at 84.6%.

Institutional Ownership

Institutional ownership was measured by the percentage of shares owned by major institutional shareholders to the total number of shares. As shown in Table 8.4, for all of the targeted companies, the lowest institutional ownership was 0% and the highest was 99.1%, with an average of 35.4%. This implies that 35.4% of the shares of all companies are owned by institutional investors. At the country level, the highest level of institutional ownership was detected in Oman with an average of 56.6%, and a relatively low average was found for the other five countries; it was 39% for the UAE, 34.2% for Bahrain, 36% for Qatar, 28.1% for Saudi Arabia, and 18.2% for Kuwait. This means that the percentage of shares owned by institutional investors varied among GCC countries, and it was least dominant in Kuwait.

Concentrated Ownership

Concentrated ownership was calculated by dividing the number of shares owned by major individual shareholders over the total number of shares in the company. As shown in Table 8.4, concentrated ownership ranged from 0% to 99.1%, with an average of 42.9%. This implies that 42.9% of the shares of all companies were owned by major shareholders, which is higher than the average percentage of institutional ownership. This indicates that major shareholders were presented by individuals more than by institutions. At the country level, the highest average of concentrated ownership was for Oman at 65%, followed by the UAE at 49.9%. In Bahrain, it was 42.8%, in Qatar it was 38.8%, in Saudi Arabia it was 35.3%, and in Kuwait, it was 23.8%. This implies that concentrated ownership was more dominant in Oman than in other GCC countries.

Audit Committee Size

The audit committee size represents the number of members of the audit committee in the company. Table 8.4 presents the number of audit committee members for all of the targeted companies, which ranged from 2 members to 8 members, with an average of 3.39. In all GCC countries, the corporate governance codes state that the minimum number of members in the audit committee should be 3. However, the descriptive statistics show that some companies were not applying these codes, as the minimum number of audit committee members was 2 for some companies. At the country level, all GCC member states had 3 members as the lowest number of members in such a committee, except for Saudi Arabia where it was 2. As well, the average of audit committee size ranged from 3.16 to 3.56 for all GCC countries. This implies that no wide difference exists in the size of the audit committee among GCC countries.

Audit Committee Meetings

Audit committee meetings represent the number of meetings held by the committee during the year. Table 8.4 shows that the lowest number of meetings was 0 and the highest was 13, with an average of 5.09. The minimum number of meetings of 0 indicates that audit committee diligence is not achieved in some companies. At the country level, the highest average of the number of meetings was for Saudi Arabia and Qatar at 5.87 and 5.03, respectively. This was followed by Oman at 4.91, the UAE at 4.79, Bahrain at 4.38, and Kuwait at 4.16. This indicates that, in all GCC countries, the audit committee, on average, meets at least four times a year.

External Auditor

If the external auditor of the company was one of the big-four audit companies around the world the company was coded 1, and 0 otherwise. As indicated in Table 8.4, the minimum of this variable was 0 and the maximum was 1, with an average of 66.9%. This implies that 66.9% of the targeted companies were being audited by one of the big-four audit companies for the year 2016. At the country level, the highest average of these variables was for the UAE and Qatar at 85.7% and 84.6%, respectively. For Bahrain and Oman, it was 76.9% and 73.9%, respectively. In Kuwait, it was 71.4%, and the lowest was for Saudi Arabia at 46.3%. Hence, it could be concluded that the majority of the GCC-listed companies are being audited by one of the big-four audit companies.

Firm Size

Firm size was measured by calculating the natural logarithm of the total assets for each company. Yet, as the amount of total assets was reported in different currencies, the amount of total assets was converted into the US dollar using the exchange rates as at the end of 2016. Table 8.4 highlights that firm size ranged from 5.94 to 11.03, with an average of 8.60. This indicates a wide variation in the size of the targeted companies. At the country level, the highest average of firm size was in Qatar at 9.11, followed by the UAE at 8.85, Saudi Arabia at 8.82, Kuwait at 8.60, Bahrain at 8.30, and Oman at 7.96. This implies that the largest targeted companies are listed in Qatar in comparison to other GCC countries.

Profitability

Profitability was measured by the ROA ratio by dividing the net income over the total assets. As indicated in Table 8.4, the lowest ROA was −0.353; as some companies had a net loss for the year 2016, and the highest was 0.284, with an average of 0.040. This signifies that the targeted companies, on average, have a return on assets of 4%. At the country level, the highest mean of ROA was for Bahrain at 6.8%, followed by Qatar at 5.4%, Oman at 4.2%, Saudi Arabia at 4.2%, Kuwait at 2.7%, and the UAE at 3.1%. This indicates that Bahrain's listed companies are the highest profitable companies across GCC countries.

Liquidity

Liquidity was measured by the current ratio by dividing the amount of current assets over the amount of current liabilities. Table 8.4 shows that liquidity ranged from 0.05 to 15.02, with an average of 2.37. This implies that some of the targeted companies have critical liquidity problems. At the country level, Bahrain's listed companies were found to have the highest average of liquidity at 3.06, followed by Qatar at 2.73, Kuwait at 2.47, the UAE at 2.39, Saudi Arabia at 2.33, and Oman at 2.05. This signifies that listed companies in Bahrain and Qatar have the highest ability to meet their short-term obligations in comparison to other GCC countries.

Leverage

Leverage was calculated by dividing the total liabilities over the total assets. Table 8.4 highlights that leverage ranged from 0.01 to 1.36, with an average of 0.393, which implies that some companies have a high level of debt. At the country level, the highest average of leverage was found in Oman at 45.1%, then in Qatar at 39.6%, in Saudi Arabia at 39.5%, in the UAE at 38.9%, in Kuwait at 35.7%, and in Bahrain at 20.5%. This indicates that listed companies in Oman depend more on debts as a major source of finance than other countries within the book context.

Industry Type

As previously noted in chapter seven, the targeted companies were distributed over five different sectors in order to be able to detect the effect of the type of the industry in which the company operates on the level of compliance with IFRS. These sectors are investment, industrial, services, energy, and real estate. The descriptive statistics in Table 8.4 state that out of the targeted companies, 12.1% (almost 38 companies) are operating under the investment sector, 42.7% (almost 134 companies) are under the industrial sector, 24.8% (almost 78 companies) are services companies, 7.6% (almost 24 companies) are energy companies, and 12.7% (almost 40 companies) are real estate companies. This implies that most of the companies under interest are operating under the industrial sector, as it has the highest mean.

Propositions Testing

This section presents the empirical results of the *t*-test and the multiple regression analysis implemented using SPSS as the most suitable methods for testing our propositions. In this book, 12 propositions were developed; the first one was related to the differences in the level of compliance between GCC member states, which was tested using the *t*-test. The other propositions were related to examining the effect of a number of firm characteristics and corporate governance mechanisms on the level of IFRS compliance, which were tested using the multiple regression analysis.

Differences among GCC Countries in the Level of Compliance with IFRS

Proposition 1 was related to exploring the existence of significant statistical differences regarding the level of compliance with IFRS across GCC countries; the *t*-test was implemented to test this proposition. As indicated in Table 8.5, the results show that there are statistically significant differences ($p < .001$) in the level of compliance with IFRS among GCC countries. The existence of these differences supports the results that were presented in Table 8.1 regarding the average level of compliance with IFRS

Table 8.5 *t*-Test results

	Sum of Squares	*df*	*Mean Square*	*F*	*Sig.*
Between groups	.309	5	.062	17.459	.000***
Within groups	1.357	384	.004		
Total	1.666	389			

Source: Authors' data,
* $p < .05$,
** $p < .01$,
*** $p < .001$.

in GCC countries. In other words, it was concluded that the ranking of the GCC countries, according to their level of compliance with IFRS, is as follows: the UAE has the highest level of compliance with an average of 79.3%, followed by Oman with an average of 77%, then Qatar at 74.3%, Bahrain at 74.1%, Kuwait at 72.6%, and the lowest average compliance was detected for Saudi Arabia at 71.3%.

Multiple Regression Analysis

Multiple regression analysis is used to examine the effect of a number of corporate governance mechanisms and firm characteristics on the level of compliance with IFRS; Table 8.6 presents the results of the multiple regression analysis of the model used to examine these relationships in the form of the 11 propositions as stated below. The model fitness statistics are first presented and then the propositions testing results.

The model summary and fitness statistics are recorded in Table 8.6. The value of R^2 of IFRS compliance is ($R^2 = .17$, $p < .001$), which means that 17% of the IFRS compliance is explained by corporate governance mechanisms and firm characteristics. Additionally, the *F*-ratio is considered an indication of the goodness of the model in predicting the outcomes (Field, 2018). Given the fact that the *F*-ratio is highly significant ($p < .001$), it is concluded that the model is able to explain the changes in the dependent variable. Additionally, comparing the values of R^2 and adjusted R^2 helps in determining the generalizability of the model (Field, 2018). The current results show that the value of R^2 is close to the value of the adjusted R^2; which supports the generalizability of the results of the current model. In other words, the reduction in the value of R^2 is an indication of the variance in the level of compliance with IFRS if the model was derived from the population of which the sample was taken. The difference between the two numbers is not significant (.17 − .125 = .045); which implies that if the model was run for the entire population, it would be resulted for about 4.5% less variance in IFRS compliance.

Field (2018) suggested that when using dummy variables in representing groups, the number of variables should be one less than the number of groups under analysis. In other words, one of the groups should be dropped, the

Table 8.6 Model summary and fitness

R	R^2	*Adjusted* R^2	*Standard Error*	*F*	*Sig.*	*Durbin Watson*
.412	.170	.125	.139	3.789	.000***	2.067

Source: Authors' data,
* $p < .05$,
** $p < .01$,
*** $p < .001$.

justification of such a practice is to avoid having a linear dependence in the data, which is called perfect collinearity (Gujarati, 2003). In this book, the industry type was determined in five groups as a classification of the type of companies' operations, these are investment, industrial, services, energy, and real estate, which resulted to have five dummy variables. Accordingly, one of the dummy variables must be excluded from the regression analysis. The exclusion of one dummy variable does not mean losing data, as each one of them represents a unique group. As a matter of fact, Field (2018) stated that the excluded dummy variable will be treated as the baseline group, which is treated as the reference group and as the control group. The group that should be dropped is the group that represents the majority of the sample, which allows comparing the other groups against the majority (Field, 2018). Therefore, in this book, the industrial sector was excluded when running the multiple regression analysis, as it represents the majority (42.7%, see Table 8.4 for more details).

Table 8.7 presents the results of the multiple regression analysis for all variables and their relationship with IFRS compliance. The results of the regression analysis in the table show that only four of the independent variables have a significant effect on the level of compliance with IFRS, these are board independence, concentrated ownership, external auditor quality, and leverage. Regarding the other independent variables, the results are not indicative of significant contributions in terms of their

Table 8.7 Regression analysis for independent variables and IFRS compliance

Variable	β	*t*	*Sig.*
Board independence	**.119**	**2.108**	**.036***
Board size	−.074	−1.189	.235
CEO duality	.044	.812	.417
Institutional ownership	−.067	−.570	.569
Concentrated ownership	**.240**	**2.031**	**.043***
Audit committee size	.069	1.186	.237
Audit committee meetings	−.006	.−.107	.915
External auditor quality	**.181**	**2.901**	**.004****
Firm size	.057	.836	.404
Profitability	−.004	.071	.943
Liquidity	.033	.526	.599
Leverage	**.207**	**2.979**	**.003****
Investment	.072	1.199	.232
Services	.063	1.013	.312
Energy	−.112	−1.866	.063
Real state	0.54	.900	.369

Source: Authors' data, Note: $N = 314$. Industrial sector is the omitted benchmark sector.
* $p < .05$,
** $p < .01$,
*** $p < .001$.

relationship with IFRS compliance. The next chapter critically discusses these results.

Proposition 1. There are significant statistical differences between GCC member states in their levels of compliance with the overall mandatory disclosure requirements of IFRS. In the results, statistically significant differences were detected in the level of compliance across GCC member states ($p < .001$). Therefore, the findings support Proposition 1.

Proposition 2. There is a significant relationship between firm size and the extent of compliance with IFRS disclosure requirements in GCC member states. In the results, a statistically nonsignificant relationship between firm size and IFRS compliance was detected ($\beta = .057$; $t = .836$, $p > .05$). Hence, the findings did not support Proposition 2.

Proposition 3. There is a significant relationship between industry type and the extent of compliance with IFRS disclosure requirements in GCC member states. The results showed a not significant relationship between industry type and IFRS compliance; investment sector ($\beta = .072$; $t = 1.199$, $p > .05$), services sector ($\beta = .063$; $t = 1.013$, $p > .05$), energy sector ($\beta = -.112$; $t =.-1.866$, $p > .05$), and real estate sector ($\beta = .054$; t = .900, $p > .05$).Thus, the findings did not support Proposition 3.

Proposition 4. There is a significant relationship between profitability and the extent of compliance with IFRS disclosure requirements in GCC member states. Our findings did not detect asignificant relationship between profitability, and the level of compliance with IFRS ($\beta = -.004$; $t = -.071$, $p > .05$), and hence, Proposition 4 was not supported.

Proposition 5. There is a significant relationship between between leverage and the extent of compliance with IFRS disclosure requirements in GCC member states. In the current results, a significant and positive relationship was found between leverage and the level of compliance with IFRS ($\beta = .207$; $t = 2.979$, $p <. 01$). Accordingly, the findings support Proposition 5.

Proposition 6. There is a significant relationship between liquidity and the extent of compliance with IFRS disclosure requirements in GCC member states. A nonsignificant relationship was detected between liquidity and IFRS compliance ($\beta = .033$; $t = .526$, $p > .05$). Therefore, the results did not support Proposition 6.

Proposition 7. There is a significant relationship between board independence and the extent of compliance with IFRS disclosure requirements in GCC member states. A significant and positive relationship was determined in the results regardingthe relationship between board independence and IFRS compliance (β = .119, t = 2.108, p < .05). Thus, the findings support Proposition 7.

Proposition 8. There is a significant relationship between board size and the extent of compliance with IFRS disclosure requirements in GCC member states. A nonsignificant path was determined in the results regarding the relationship between board size and IFRS compliance (β = −.074, t = 1.189, p > .05). Thus, the findings did not support Proposition 8.

Proposition 9. There is a significant relationship between CEO duality and the extent ofcompliance with IFRS disclosure requirements in GCC member states. In the current results, a statistically not significant relationship was detected between CEO duality and IFRS compliance (β = .044, t = .812, p > .05). Thus, the results did not support Proposition 9.

Proposition 10. There is a significant relationship between ownership structure and the extent of compliance with IFRS disclosure requirements in GCC member states. This proposition is divided into two sub-propositions. The results indicated that this proposition is partially supported as follows.

Proposition 10a. There is a significant relationship between concentrated ownership and the extent of compliance with IFRS disclosure requirements in GCC member states. In the current results, a significant positive relationship was detected between the concentrated ownership and the level of compliance with IFRS (β = .240, t = 2.031, p < .05). Therefore, the results support Proposition 10a.

Proposition 10b. There is a significant relationship between institutional ownership and the extent of compliance with IFRS disclosure requirements in GCC member states. A nonsignificant relationship between institutional ownership percentage and the level of compliance with IFRS disclosure requirements (β = −.067, t = .570, p > .05). Thus, the results did not support Proposition 10b.

Proposition 11. There is a significant relationship between the effectiveness ofaudit committee and the extent of compliance with IFRS disclosure requirements in GCC member states. This proposition is divided into two sub-propositions. The results indicated that this proposition is not supported as follows.

Proposition 11a. There is a significant relationship between the number ofaudit committee members and the extent of compliance with IFRS disclosure requirements in GCC member states.The results indicate a nonsignificant relationship between number of members of audit committee and the level of compliance with IFRS ($\beta = .069$, $t = 1.186$, $p > .05$). Hence, the findings did not support Proposition 11a.

Proposition 11b. There is a significant relationship between the number of audit committee meetings held during the yearand the extent of compliance with IFRS disclosure requirements in GCC member states. In the current results, a statistically not significant relationship was detected between the number of audit committee meetings held during the yearand the level ofIFRS compliance ($\beta = -.006$, $t = -.107$, $p > .05$). Accordingly, the results did not support Proposition 11b.

Proposition 12. There are significant statistical differences between the quality of external auditor and the extent of compliance with IFRS disclosure requirements in GCC member states. A positive and significant relationship was found between the quality of the external auditor measured by the belonging to one of the big-four audit companies around the world and the level of compliance with IFRS ($\beta = .181$, $t = 2.901$, $p < .01$). Therefore, the results support Proposition 12.

Summary

This chapter highlighted the empirical results of the model that was developed in this book to examine the proposed relationships between the variables under interest. The chapter started with a demonstration of the descriptive statistics of the level of compliance with IFRS across all GCC countries and at the country level as well. This was followed by the description of the descriptive analysis of the independent variables among all GCC countries. Thereafter, the procedures implemented in performing the multivariate analysis were highlighted. These results showed the existence of significant statistical differences in the level of compliance with IFRS across GCC countries. Additionally, the regression analysis concluded that board independence, concentrated ownership, external auditor quality, and leverage have significant positive effects on the level of compliance with IFRS disclosure requirements. Whilst nonsignificant effects were detected for board size, CEO duality, institutional ownership, audit committee size, audit committee meetings, firm size, industry type, profitability, and liquidity on the level of compliance with IFRS.

Note

1 Some standards are qualifying standards; even that they are obligatory for companies to be implemented, they do not include any presentation or disclosure requirements. Specifically, IAS 28 (Investment in Associates and Joint Ventures), IFRS 10 (Consolidated Financial Statements), and IFRS 11 (Joint Arrangements) do not specify any disclosure requirements, instead, the disclosures related to these standards are under

IFRS 12 (Disclosure of Interest in Other Entities). Likewise, IAS 32 (Financial Instruments) and IFRS 9 (Financial Instruments) do not state the disclosure requirements of financial instruments as they were moved to IFRS 7 (Financial Instruments: Disclosure). Accordingly, the discussion of IFRS 12 includes IAS 28, IFRS 10, and IFRS 11. As well as, the discussion of IFRS 7 consists of IAS 32 and IFRS 9.

References

Dye, R. (1985). Disclosure of nonproprietary information. *Journal of Accounting Research*, *23*(1), 123–145.

Field, A. (2018). *Discovering statistics using IBM SPSS statistics*. Sage, London.

Gujarati, D.N. (2003). *Basic Econometrics* (4th edition). McGraw-Hill, London.

9 Discussion of Central Prepositions

Introduction

Having presented the data analysis in the previous chapter, below is the discussion of our findings based on the stated propositions. The discussion of each proposition will start with a comparison between our findings and the findings of the prior studies to show the consistency and inconsistency with the existing literature. This is followed by a presentation of the existing theories that support the discussion of the current results.

The Level of Compliance with IFRS in the GCC Member States

The first proposition examined the existence of significant statistical differences in the level of compliance with international financial reporting standards (IFRS) among Gulf Cooperation Council (GCC) countries. The results in chapter 8 revealed that the level of compliance with IFRS significantly varies across GCC countries. From the analysis, it was shown that the UAE's listed companies had the highest level of compliance with IFRS, while companies listed in Saudi Arabia had the lowest level of compliance with IFRS.

Our findings indicate the presence of significant statistical differences in the level of compliance with IFRS between GCC countries. These findings may be explained based on a number of environmental and institutional factors. Institutional theory concerns with the existed values and beliefs of social and organizational life (Scott, 2001; Irvine, 2008). In addition, the main interest of the institutional theory is the influence of the institutional environment in shaping the social beliefs and practices of various actors within the society (Mallin 2013). Organizational practices are influenced by the rules and structure of their wider environment (Paauwe and Boselie, 2003; Haak-Saheem et al., 2017). Accordingly, the discussion of the current results will be referred to the national culture which lies under the umbrella of the institutional theory.

From the perspective of the institutional theory, aspects of national culture are considered the main determinants of the level of IFRS adoption

DOI: 10.4324/9781003211556-9

(Abdelqader et al., 2021) as the cultural backgrounds of financial statements preparers and users determine their awareness about the importance of financial disclosure and their level of knowledge and education about the international accounting standards, which were proved to have an effect on the level of the adoption of IFRS (Cooke and Wallace, 1990; Saudagaran and Meek, 1997; Alsaqqa and Sawan, 2013).

The disclosure style implemented by countries can be clarified based on their national culture (Shehata, 2013). Herath and Alsulmi (2017) stated that national culture has a significant impact on the interpretation and implementation of accounting standards across countries. Emerging markets are expected to be relatively more secretive and conservative in comparison to other developed countries, hence, it is expected that these markets will have lower level of disclosure (Haddad et al., 2015). It is also suggested that the tendency of secrecy affects the extent of disclosure in the accounting reports (see Perera, 1989; Hassaan, 2012). Based on Hofstede's (1980) cultural dimensions model and Gray's (1988) accounting subcultural model, Abd-Elsalam (1999) and Al-Htaybat (2005) stated that one of the cultural values that affects the level of compliance with IFRS is the secrecy versus transparency; this implies that companies, in general, tend to keep confidential information restricted only for the users who are closely involved in managing and financing the company.

Furthermore, the variations in the extent of the enforcement procedures across countries is a proof of the role of culture and environment in affecting the level of compliance with IFRS. In other words, the formulation and enforcement of the laws and regulations settled by authorities are resulted from the national culture and environment. Hence, although accounting standards are the same, the enforcement mechanisms and monitoring procedures over the compliance with these standards vary according to the national culture and values (Nobes, 2006). This stands on the fact that culture, in terms of values and norms, affects the enforcement procedures of monitoring companies' implementation of IFRS disclosure requirements; it was concluded that national culture is responsible for forming the laws and regulations that shape the enforcement mechanisms of monitoring IFRS adoption, and the lack of appropriate enforcement procedures leads to variations in the level of compliance with IFRS across countries (Rahman, 1999; Rajhi, 2014).

From a legitimacy theory point of view, the level of compliance with IFRS is an indication of the extent of the rules and regulations that govern and control such a compliance, which affects companies' tendency to implement these standards. In emerging markets, it was evidenced that the cost of non-compliance, in terms of penalties, is lower than the cost of compliance with IFRS (Al-Htaybat, 2005; Dahawy and Conover, 2007), which explains the fact that none of the targeted companies had fully complied with IFRS disclosure requirements. The previous discussion implies that the predictions of both the institutional theory and legitimacy theory, regarding explaining the differences in the level of compliance among countries, are to some extent relevant within GCC context.

The fact that the UAE's listed companies had the highest level of compliance with IFRS is attributed to the nature of these companies and the environment in the UAE. In other words, since most of the listed companies in the UAE are international companies, it was expected that they will have a high level of compliance with IFRS. This stands on the notion that the existence of international companies increases the motivation and realization of the importance of adopting the international accounting standards. In addition, the openness of the UAE capital markets motivates companies to comply with the disclosure requirements of IFRS in order to meet the needs of the users of financial statements and decrease the level of information asymmetry as these companies lie under the eyes of not only the local investors but also the external ones (Irvine and Lucas, 2006). As well, the existence of such a type of companies facilitates to them acquiring the required level of knowledge and experience of implementing IFRS and provides them with the needed financial experts to ease the implementation of these standards. Moreover, the advanced technology and the diversification of the listed companies in the UAE are other factors that played significant roles in enhancing the effectiveness of the enforcement mechanisms and regulations that are related to monitoring the adoption of IFRS in these companies.

Furthermore, Oman's listed companies had the second highest level of compliance with IFRS. This may be justified based on the fact that Oman is considered the first GCC country that has adopted IFRS (since 1986). Hence, it was expected that the early adopters of IFRS will have a high level of compliance as they have more experience in implementing these standards and enforcing their listed companies to adopt IFRS disclosure requirements. Additionally, the previous justifications were supported by the results presented in chapter 8 regarding the level of compliance with each standard in each country. Notably, there were huge variations in the level of compliance with some standards across GCC countries and the comparison of these levels of compliance concludes that the highest levels of compliance with most of these standards were recorded in the UAE and Oman. For example, IAS 10 and IAS 11 were found to have the highest levels of compliance in both the UAE and Oman (above 90%), where they were below 76% in the other countries.

Saudi listed companies had the lowest level of compliance with IFRS. This is may be attributed to the particular nature of the Saudi Arabia context. Herath and Alsulmi (2017) stated that the implementation of the international accounting standards was faced by many challenges in Saudi Arabia due to several environmental factors, such as culture, Sharia law, and accounting educational and professional preparation. They further suggested that in order to achieve the best practices of IFRS implementation in Saudi Arabia, the need of an accounting system that takes into consideration the use of accounting as a tool that serves its Sharia law is essential.

Firm Size and the Level of IFRS Compliance in the GCC Member States

The second proposition examined the effect of firm size on the level of compliance with IFRS. The results in chapter 8 revealed that firm size was not linked to the level of the adoption of IFRS disclosure requirements. From the analysis, it was shown that firm size had no significant impact on IFRS compliance.

These findings indicate the presence of a non-significant relationship between firm size and the level of compliance with IFRS. In other words, the size of the firm does not affect its level of IFRS adoption. These results are in contradiction with the prior work conducted by (Arcay and Vazquez, 2005; Alsaqqa and Sawan, 2013; Ballas et al., 2018). The previous mentioned research found significant variations in the level of disclosure of companies with different sizes. Firm size was reported as one of the main factors that explain the variations in the level of disclosure in the Jordanian context, as investment decisions motivate large companies to disclose information more than smaller firms as the former need to attract more capital (Al-Shiab, 2003; Omar and Simon, 2011; Alhazaimeh et al., 2014). In Kuwait, Al-Shammari (2005) and Alfaraih (2009) found that there is a significant relationship between company's size and the level of compliance with IFRS. Boshnak (2017) suggested that firm size affects the level of compliance with IFRS in the GCC context. However, our results are similar to the findings of the previous studies that concluded the absence of a significant relationship between firm size and the level of disclosure (see Street and Gray, 2002; Samaha and Dahawy, 2010; Al-Moataz and Hussainey, 2012). As well, using a sample of Italian listed firms, Pichler et al. (2018) stated that the size of the firm is not an influential determinant of the adoption of IFRS.

The expected impact of the size of the firm on its level of compliance with IFRS was based on the cost-benefit analysis; complying with the disclosure requirements of IFRS requires high costs, and it was anticipated that large firms can easily afford these costs (Omar and Simon, 2011); hence, they were expected to have a higher level of compliance with IFRS. Additionally, agency theory assumes that big firms are expected to have a higher level of compliance as large companies lie under the eyes of investors and they are subject to greater regulations (Donnelly and Mulcahy, 2008; Kent and Stewart, 2008; Boshnak, 2017). To enhance their image in the investors' minds and facilitate the collection of the needed capital in case of issuing new shares, signaling theory presumes that large firms will have a higher level of compliance with IFRS. However, such results indicate to the limited contributions of the agency theory and the signaling theory within the GCC context.

As the institutional theory reminds us, companies' disclosure tendency in developing countries is significantly affected by their national cultural and their unique environmental features (Gray, 1988; Chau and Gray, 2002). Hence, the rationale of the current findings may be related to the tendency of the listed companies in GCC toward secrecy over transparency in their financial statements. In other words, companies in emerging markets tend to keep information restricted only for the users who are involved in managing these companies (Hassaan, 2012; Haddad et al., 2015), which makes managers selective in their disclosure practices aiming to avoid competition and protect the company's reputation, hence, they do not fully comply with the disclosure requirements of IFRS (Shehata, 2013).

Moreover, the extent of the enforcement mechanisms affects the level of compliance with IFRS (see Nobes, 2006; Rajhi, 2014); thus, standing on the idea that the enforcement mechanisms in emerging markets are not appropriate in monitoring the adoption of IFRS, the cost of non-compliance with IFRS became lower than the cost of compliance. In more details, due to the low cost of non-compliance and the high costs that are linked with the compliance with IFRS (Al-Htaybat, 2005; Dahawy and Conover, 2007), the size of the company is no longer a factor that plays a significant role in determining the level of compliance with IFRS as companies are not fully applying IFRS disclosure requirements in the GCC context. This also may be supported by the existence of some problematic standards that require high costs and a high level of financial expertise to implement, which creates difficulties in their implementation by all of the targeted companies despite of their size. The high cost associated with the compliance with these problematic standards and the low cost of non-compliance had drove companies not to comply with such standards. This was proved by the results presented in chapter 8 regarding the level of compliance with each standard of IFRS. More specifically, IAS 19 and IAS 26 are considered the most complicated standards among all of the other standards, and it was shown that they had the lowest level of compliance for all of the targeted companies, regardless of their size. Additionally, the existence of other factors that may affect the relationship between firm size and the level of IFRS compliance may be another justification, such as listing status (being listed in more than one country) or listing time (for how long the company was listed) as multi-listed companies and companies being listed for several years may have a higher level of compliance (Shehata, 2013).

Industry Type and the Level of IFRS Compliance in the GCC Member States

The third proposition examined the effect of the industry type on the level of compliance with IFRS. The results in chapter 8 revealed that industry type was not linked to the level of the adoption of IFRS disclosure requirements. From the analysis, it was shown that sectoral analysis had no significant impact on IFRS compliance.

These findings, which indicate the presence of a non-significant relationship, implies that no dependency relationship exists between these two variables. In other words, the type of the company's operations does not affect its level of IFRS adoption. These results are consistent with prior work (e.g. Wallace et al., 1994; Glaum and Street, 2003; Anderson and Daoud, 2005), where they all found no evidence of an association between industry type and the level of disclosure. Using a sample of US companies, Street and Bryant (2000) reported that industry type does not influence companies' level of compliance with IFRS. However, they contradict with Street and Gray (2002) and Al-Shammari (2005), as they reported the existence of significant differences in the level of disclosure among different types of industries. Alfaraih (2009) and Al Mutawaa and Hewaidy (2010) encountered significant differences in the level of compliance with IFRS across industry categories in Kuwait. Moreover, Boshnak (2017) found that companies operating in the energy sector in GCC countries have a higher level of compliance with IFRS than other sectors.

Based on the signaling theory, it was expected that the type of the company's industry will have an impact on its level of compliance with IFRS. This is due to the idea that the existence of dominant companies with high level of compliance with IFRS in a specific industry affects and leads the compliance practices of all other companies operating within the same industry (Omar and Simon, 2011). This implies that the propositions of the signaling theory, regarding the relationship between industry type and the level of IFRS compliance, are not necessarily relevant within the GCC context.

The current findings may also be justified in light of the exiting institutional realties and national cultures and their potential impacts within different contexts. For instance, it is argued that national culture is responsible for determining the level of the awareness regarding the importance and benefits of implementing IFRS (Cooke and Wallace, 1990; Alsaqqa and Sawan, 2013). Our results show that companies across different sectors have the same tendency toward the implementation of IFRS as none of the targeted companies had fully applied all of the IFRS disclosure requirements, and as the five industries had almost the same average level of compliance with IFRS. This implies that companies across the five sectors have the same level of attentiveness regarding the benefits of implementing IFRS, which means that the understanding of the importance of implementing IFRS must be enhanced in GCC countries. Additionally, the absence of dominant companies in the industry sectors (none of the targeted companies had fully complied with IFRS) emphasizes the idea of the institutional theory that each company imitates other companies' practices regarding the implementation of IFRS, which was proved by the fact that all of the five sectors are sharing almost the same average.

Furthermore, such findings may be attributed to the distribution of the targeted companies. In more details, the inclusion of the six GCC countries and all of the industry types in these countries may mitigate the differences in the level of compliance with IFRS among these industry types. It was noticed that most of the industrial companies, which shape the majority of the targeted companies, are listed in Saudi Arabia and Kuwait (which were reported to have the lowest level of compliance with IFRS) and the majority of the other companies in the other sectors were listed in the UAE and Oman (which had the highest level of compliance with IFRS). This has created a balance in the level of compliance across the different sectors, which is consistent with the descriptive statistics that show that the average level of compliance among these types of industries is almost the same. Accordingly, there were no statistical differences in the level of compliance with IFRS across the five industry sectors.

Profitability and the Level of IFRS Compliance in the GCC Member States

The fourth proposition examined the effect of profitability on the level of compliance with IFRS. The results in chapter 8 revealed that profitability was not linked to the level of the adoption of IFRS disclosure requirements. From the analysis, it was shown that profitability had no significant impact on IFRS compliance.

Despite the relationship was positive, it was not significant, which indicates that the level of profitability that the company has does not affect its level of the adoption of IFRS. These findings are similar to what argued by Chau and Gray (2002), Barako et al. (2006) and Uyar (2011), who stated that the level of profitability does not have an impact on companies' disclosure practices. Al Mutawaa and Hewaidy (2010) and Demir and Bahadir (2014) did not find a significant relationship between profitability and IFRS compliance in Kuwait and Turkey, respectively. Ballas et al. (2018) also concluded that the level of the company's profitability does not explain its level of compliance with IFRS in Greece. However, Al-Janadi et al. (2013) and Hasan et al. (2013) reported a positive relationship between profitability and the level of disclosure.

This result is counter-intuitive to the predictions of agency theory, where profitability is one of the determinants of the company's level of disclosure standing on the fact that profitability is one of the significant indicators of managers' performance that affects their benefits and compensations. Managers of high profitable organizations are expected to disclose more information to justify their compensations, enhance shareholders' confidence, and reassure their managerial positions (Singhvi and Desai, 1971; Omar and Simon, 2011). Additionally, companies with high profitability were anticipated to disclose more information to signal their good performance and differentiate themselves from other companies in order to be well-known by investors (Wallace and Naser, 1995; Boshnak, 2017).

The lack of a significant relationship between profitability and the level of compliance with IFRS may be explained based on the propositions of the institutional theory. In more details, companies operating in emerging markets may be seen in a safe position where they do not need to prove their financial position in the market (Shehata, 2013). Therefore, they favor to apply the same IFRS compliance practices irrespective to their level of profitability, especially in the presence of the fact that the non-compliance cost became lower than the compliance cost due to the inappropriate enforcement mechanisms in these countries. Additionally, developing countries have secretive culture, which is associated with the uncertainty avoidance that may lead to restrict information disclosure in order to avoid competition and preserve security (Gray, 1988; Hassaan, 2012). This implies that companies in these countries prefer secrecy over transparency and as a confidentiality act, managers tend to be selective in deciding which disclosure items to comply with, regardless of their companies' profitability level.

Leverage and the Level of IFRS Compliance in the GCC Member States

The fifth proposition examined the effect of leverage on the level of compliance with IFRS. The results in chapter 8 revealed that leverage was linked to the level of the adoption of IFRS disclosure requirements. As the results show, it was indicated that leverage had a significant impact on IFRS compliance.

Such findings indicate the presence of a significant positive relationship between leverage and the level of compliance with IFRS. This implies that companies with high leverage have higher levels of compliance with IFRS. These results align with the previous research results, which suggest that companies with high leverage ratio have higher levels of disclosure (see Alfaraih, 2009; Haji and Ghazali, 2013; Anis, 2016). Al-Shammari (2005) concluded that leverage has a positive impact on the level of compliance with IFRS in the GCC context. Similarly, Al-Akra et al. (2010) suggested that Jordanian listed companies with high leverage have more preference to prepare their financial statements in accordance with IFRS. Yet, they contradict with Hodgdon and Hughes (2016) who reported a negative relationship between leverage and disclosure using a sample of 147 companies from 24 EU countries. They also contradict with Hassaan (2012) and Haddad et al. (2015) who did not detect a significant relationship between leverage and the level of disclosure of the Jordanian listed companies.

Looking closely at the agency theory, it was expected that companies with higher leverage will disclose more information in order to prove for shareholders their debts' repayment ability (Ahmed and Courtis, 1999). Lopes and Rodrigues (2007), Hassan (2009), and Franzen and Weißenberger (2018) stated that having a high level of leverage increases agency cost, therefore, companies with high amount of debts tend to disclose more information to mitigate such a cost. Companies with high leverage ratio are expected to comply more with IFRS in order to reduce agency cost and prove that the interests of debt holders are protected (Al-Shammari, 2005). From a signaling theory point of view, companies with high leverage prefer to prove for creditors that they are capable to pay their debts (Ezat and El-Masry, 2008; Pichler et al., 2018). When the company's level of debts increased, owners and creditors need more information to assess the ability of the company to meet its obligations (Wallace et al., 1994; Boshnak, 2017). Hence, it could be argued that such theoretical articulations discussed above would have relevance in emerging markets, particularly the GCC region as evidenced in this book.

Another explanation of the current findings may be based on the institutional theory and legitimacy theory, where both suggest that companies always attempt to avoid legislation risks by disclosing more information (Watts and Zimmerman, 1986). Demir and Bahadir (2014) stated that companies with high leverage ratio are expected to disclose more information to improve their chances of receiving funds from financial institutions. In GCC countries, banks are considered the main source of borrowings, which usually apply restrictive contracts with their clients that require more detailed information to be disclosed in their financial statements. Such contracts help these banks in assessing the company's ability of meeting its obligation and to evaluate the company's future risks in settling its debts commitments, complying with IFRS and disclosing more information are assumed to satisfy the requirements of these banks and ensure the company's commitment with these contracts.

Liquidity and the Level of IFRS Compliance in the GCC Member States

The sixth proposition examined the effect of liquidity on the level of compliance with IFRS. The results in chapter eight revealed that liquidity was not linked to the level of the adoption of IFRS disclosure requirements. As the analysis shows, it was noticed that liquidity had no significant impact on IFRS compliance.

These findings indicate the presence of a non-significant relationship between liquidity and the level of compliance with IFRS. In whatever way this relationship is positive, while at the same time not significant, means that there does not exist any relationship of dependency amongst these two variables. In other words, liquidity does not affect the level of IFRS adoption. The current results are consistent with some other previously conducted studies in the Middle Eastern context, which concluded a non-significant relationship between liquidity and the level of disclosure of the company (see Barako et al., 2006; Aburaya, 2012; Haddad et al., 2015). Likewise, Al-Shammari (2005) and Boshnak (2017) did not find a significant relationship between the company's liquidity and the level of compliance with IFRS in GCC countries. However, they contradict with the findings of (Wallace et al., 1994; Gul and Leung, 2004; Hassaan, 2012).

The signaling theory suggests that companies with high level of liquidity will disclose more information to signal themselves from other companies with lower liquidity (Abd-Elsalam, 1999; Barako et al., 2006). Companies with high liquidity disclose more information that will be perceived as a signal for their good performance (Anis, 2016). However, agency theory states that companies with low liquidity will have a higher level of disclosure to meet shareholders' and lenders' needs for more affirmations about the ability of the company to pay its short term debts (Wallace and Naser, 1995). Additionally, companies with low liquidity disclose more information to minimize the conflict of interests between owners and managers (Abd-Elsalam, 1999). However, the current results tell us that the presumptions of both the signaling theory and the agency theory seem not to be relevant to the GCC context.

This is perhaps explained by the fact that companies in emerging markets are not motivated to improve their financial position in the market comparing to their rivals as they are assumed to be in a safe position (Shehata, 2013). Thus, they tend to have the same IFRS compliance practices regardless of their liquidity, particularly with the low non-compliance costs resulted from the inappropriate enforcement procedures regarding monitoring the implementation of IFRS in these countries. Moreover, the current findings may be attributed to the idea that national cultural and social environment affect the disclosure practices of the companies operating in developing countries (Chau and Gray, 2002). This implies that managers in these countries have the tendency to be secretive and conservative in comparison with other developed countries through keeping information inside the firm instead of disclosing such information to external parties, which results lower level of disclosure and lower level of compliance with IFRS (Haddad et al., 2015).

Board Independence and the Level of IFRS Compliance in the GCC Member States

The seventh proposition examined the effect of board independence on the level of compliance with IFRS. The results in chapter 8 revealed that board independence was linked to the level of the adoption of IFRS disclosure requirements. As the analysis show, it was noticed that board independence had a significant positive impact on IFRS compliance; this implies that as the percentage of the independent directors in the board increases the level of compliance with IFRS increases.

These results support the idea that outside directors are seen as an effective tool in monitoring the flow of the disclosed information (Biondi et al., 2009). Such findings are similar to other results which were reported by Al-Janadi et al. (2013), Verriest et al. (2013), and Agyei-Mensah (2017) that the existence of independent members in the board enhances companies' level of disclosure. Additionally, Boshnak (2017) found a weak positive relationship between board independence and the mandatory disclosure requirements of IFRS in the GCC context (it was accepted at a significant level of 10%). In France, Hlel and Nafti (2019) stated that independent members in the board play a significant role in enhancing the transparency of the company. Mnif and Znazen (2020) concluded that board interdependence has a positive effect on the level of compliance with IFRS in Canada. Nevertheless, these results are in contradiction with some prior research where some of them had concluded a negative or non-significant relationship between board independence and the level of disclosure (see, for example, Hasan et al., 2013; Alhazaimeh et al., 2014). As well, Hassaan (2012) did not detect a significant relationship between board independence and the level of compliance with IFRS within the Jordanian and Egyptian contexts.

These findings indicate that independent members in the board are effective in enhancing the level of compliance with IFRS. The agency theory stated that the existence of independent members in the board improves the effectiveness of its controlling function and efficiently enhances its performance (Volonté, 2015). Independent members help in mitigating the conflict of interests between managers and shareholders (Singh et al., 2018), which assists in improving the board's supervision over the activities of opportunistic managers and detecting the expropriation of the company's resources. Biondi et al. (2009) pointed out that the existence of independent members reduces the level of information asymmetry between managers and shareholders as they monitor the flow of the disclosed information. Moreover, since the independent members may be working outside the company in different industries, the resource dependency theory supports the fact that those directors serve the company in getting its needed resources because they have more relations, knowledge, and experience (Barako et al., 2006). Additionally, it looks to the outside directors as a channel to link the company with the outside environment.

Furthermore, the current results could be supported by the fact that most of the listed companies in GCC countries are applying the requirements of corporate governance codes regarding the required percentage of independent members in their boards. In more details, the corporate governance codes in all GCC countries recommend companies to have at least one-third of the total number of board members as independent members, and as it was shown in chapter 8, the average of the percentage of independent members in the board is almost half of the board members, which proves the effectiveness of those members in improving the compliance with IFRS in these countries. The positive impact of board independence on the level of compliance with IFRS concludes that independent members in the GCC listed companies are effective in handling their responsibilities regarding properly monitoring and controlling managers' disclosure actions. In other words, they are not facing any pressure in relation to disclosing the needed information that serve the benefits of financial statements users. As well, the results indicate that independent members have the required level of financial experience of confirming the implementation of the disclosure requirements of IFRS by their companies.

Board Size and the Level of IFRS Compliance in the GCC Member States

The eighth proposition examined the effect of board size on the level of compliance with IFRS. The results in chapter 8 revealed that board size was not linked to the level of the adoption of IFRS disclosure requirements. From the analysis, it was shown that board size had a non-significant impact on IFRS compliance.

This implies that no dependency relationship exists between these two variables. In other words, the number of members in the board does not affect the level of compliance with IFRS. These findings point out the same outcomes as what Arcay and Vazquez (2005), Samaha et al. (2012), Hasan et al. (2013), and Bouchareb et al. (2014) reported. Additionally, these results are consistent with prior research who did not find a significant relationship between board size and the level of compliance with IFRS (see Hassaan, 2012). Likewise, Juhmani (2017) reported a non-significant relationship between board size and the level of compliance with IFRS in Bahrain. However, some scholars reported the existence of a positive relationship between board size and the level of disclosure (Allegrini and Greco, 2013; Hlel and Nafti, 2019). While Ahmed et al. (2006) in New Zealand, and Bradbury et al. (2006) in Singapore and Kuala Lumpur, concluded a negative relationship between the two variables.

The anticipated relationship between board size and the level of compliance with IFRS was built based on the proposition of the agency theory, which states that as the number of board members increases its effectiveness in monitoring function and making strategic decisions increases (Singh et al., 2018). It further suggested that in case of having a large number of members in the board, the possibility of having dominant managers will decrease, which affects the level of compliance with IFRS disclosure requirements (Samaha et al., 2012). Additionally, resource dependency theory looks at large boards as a tool to provide the company with more experience and knowledge, which is considered an enhancement in its monitoring and controlling functions (Haniffa and Cooke, 2002; Klein, 2002).

However, the current findings indicate that board members, regardless of their number, are not playing any significant role in enhancing the level of compliance with IFRS. This signifies that they are not effective in monitoring and controlling managers' behaviors. These results may be justified based on the idea that in emerging markets, board members may lack the motivation toward improving the level of compliance with IFRS as the advantages of implementing such standards are not part of their national culture (Hassaan, 2012). In other words, they are not aware enough about the important role of increasing the level of disclosure in improving the transparency of financial statements and serving the benefits of the users of these statements. Building on this, it is argued that there are other factors related to the secretive culture of developing countries that influence the level of IFRS adoption (Chau and Gray, 2002). In comparison with developed countries, companies operating in developing countries are less encouraged to disclose more information; instead they tend to maintain such information exclusively to the insiders of the company (Haddad et al., 2015).

Moreover, the absence of a significant relationship between board size and IFRS compliance means that the former does not contribute to the explanation of the variations in the level of compliance with IFRS. This may be due to the nationalities of the board members, their age, their experience, the industries in which they previously worked to earn their experience, and their educational backgrounds. In other words, the lack of financial expertise that board members have may limit their influence and their monitoring efficiency in tracking the company's IFRS compliance practices. Another explanation could be referred to the absence of specific and clear requirements of the optimum size of the board within the GCC region; as indicated in chapter 2, only two countries out of the six GCC countries have determined the number of members that should be in the board in their corporate governance codes.

CEO Duality and the Level of IFRS Compliance in the GCC Member States

The ninth proposition examined the effect of CEO duality on the level of compliance with IFRS. The results in chapter 8 revealed that CEO duality was not linked to the level of the adoption of IFRS disclosure requirements. From the analysis, it was shown that CEO duality had a not significant impact of IFRS compliance.

These findings indicate the presence of a non-significant relationship between CEO duality and the level of compliance with IFRS. Despite the relation was positive it was not significant, which implies that the separation between the chair position and the CEO position is not necessarily influential in enhancing the level of compliance with IFRS. The present results are in parallel with prior studies (see, for example, Ahmed et al., 2006; Petra, 2007; Mnif and Znazen, 2020). Moreover, Ezat and El-Masry (2008) and Al-Shammari and Al-Sultan (2010) did not find a significant relationship between CEO duality and the level of disclosure in Egypt and Kuwait, respectively. As well, Hassaan (2012) showed that the separation between CEO and chairman of the board does not necessarily enhance the level of compliance with IFRS disclosure requirements in both Jordan and Egypt. Nevertheless, some other scholars had reported the existence of a negative relationship between CEO duality and the level of disclosure (see Beekes et al., 2004; Firth et al., 2007; Al-Janadi et al., 2013). While Samaha et al. (2012) reported a positive relationship between CEO duality and the level of disclosure in Egypt.

Despite the fact that agency theory had suggested that the separation between the CEO position and the chair of the board position enhances the latter's ability to effectively monitor and control management activities (Al-Janadi et al., 2013), and the fact that most of the targeted companies have separated these two positions (see chapter 8), the current results indicate that having two different persons in these two positions does not improve the level of compliance with IFRS. Based on the resource dependency theory, it was expected that having an outside CEO will link the company with the needed resources from the external environment and will bring external prospects to the company (Dahya and Travlos, 2000).

Despite the above mentioned perspectives and the fact that most of the targeted companies had separated the CEO position and the chairman of the board position, there was a lack of a significant impact of such a separation on the level of compliance with IFRS. This lends weight to the institutional theory that the awareness about the importance of separating these two positions in improving the independence of the chairman is relatively absent in emerging markets' setting. Therefore, the separation between these two positions seems not achieving its desired benefits in enhancing the board's monitoring and controlling functions over managers' behaviors. This may be attributed to the idea that companies segregate the two positions only to gain legitimacy and show that they are applying the rules of corporate governance but without an effective activation of this important feature. Consequently, the separation between the CEO and the chairman of the board positions does not improve the level of compliance with IFRS because of the lack of the chair of the board's independence and the lack of the CEO role effectiveness. Moreover, the current results may be referred to some other factors, such as the CEO's nationality (being local or foreigner, which affects the level of influence that can be exerted over financial disclosure decisions), the CEO's educational backgrounds (which affects the level of financial knowledge about IFRS disclosure requirements), the CEO's age, and the CEO's previous experience (which affects the level of managerial skills).

Ownership Structure and the Level of IFRS Compliance in the GCC Member States

The tenth proposition examined the effect of ownership structure on the level of compliance with IFRS. However, two aspects of ownership structure were included in this book, these are concentrated ownership and institutional ownership. Therefore, this proposition was divided into two sub-propositions as follows.

Concentrated Ownership and the Level of IFRS Compliance in the GCC Member States

The first sub-proposition of the tenth proposition examined the effect of the concentrated ownership on the level of compliance with IFRS. The results in chapter 8 revealed that concentrated ownership was associated with the level of the adoption of IFRS disclosure requirements. From the analysis, it was shown that concentrated ownership had a significant positive impact on IFRS compliance. This indicates that as the percentage of concentrated ownership increases the level of compliance with IFRS increases.

These results are similar to what reported by Patelli and Prencipe (2007), Baek et al. (2009), and Al-Janadi et al. (2016) that there is a positive impact of the concentrated ownership on the level of disclosure. As well, Abad et al. (2018) reported a negative relationship between concentrated ownership and the level of information asymmetry in Spain. However, some other scholars found a negative effect of the level of ownership concentration on companies' disclosure practices (see Alves et al., 2012; Samaha et al., 2012). Likewise, Ezat and El-Masry (2008) stated that companies with diffused ownership are more motivated to disclose information in Egypt. While Anis (2016) concluded a non-significant relationship between concentrated ownership and the disclosure quality using 232 non-financial listed firms in the United Kingdom.

In this book, concentrated ownership was measured as the percentage of shares owned by major individual shareholders, thus, it has been anticipated that the existence of shareholders with high ownership percentage improves the level of compliance with IFRS. However, the agency theory suggests that companies with dispersed ownership will have a higher level of compliance with IFRS as these companies are lying under the public eyes (Samaha et al., 2012). Therefore, they were expected to disclose more information in order to show that they are serving the benefits of their owners (Barako et al., 2006; Anis, 2016). Hence, such findings indicate that the above mentioned articulations are not relevant to the GCC context.

The current results could be attributed to the fact that the high level of concentration of ownership increases the monitoring power of shareholders over managerial decisions. This is based on the fact that shareholders with high percentage of shares are motivated to track their company's performance and its strategic decisions more than other shareholders with lower percentage of shares (Brennan, 2007; Verriest et al., 2013). Additionally, major shareholders have more powerful influence over managers' decisions, as the latter usually take into consideration the desires and needs of large shareholders (O'Sullivan et al., 2008). Maher and Andersson (2000) and Lee and Yeh (2004) suggested that the probability that managers utilize the company's resources into their own benefits is higher in companies with dispersed ownership. Moreover, based on the coercive isomorphism introduced by the institutional theory, companies' disclosure practices are affected by their major stakeholders due to the pressure that the latter put over managers' decisions.

Institutional Ownership and the Level of IFRS Compliance in the GCC Member States

The second sub-proposition of the tenth proposition examined the effect of institutional ownership on the level of compliance with IFRS. The results in chapter 8 revealed that institutional ownership was not linked to the level of the adoption of IFRS disclosure requirements. As the analysis show, it was noted that institutional ownership had a non-significant impact on IFRS compliance, which implies that the percentage of shares owned by institutional shareholders does not affect the company's level of compliance with IFRS.

These results are similar to prior work (e.g. Haniffa and Cooke, 2002; Donnelly and Mulcahy, 2008; Mallin and Ow-Yong, 2009). All of these studies had reported that there is a not significant relationship between institutional ownership and the level of disclosure. Likewise, Shehata (2013) stated that institutional investors in the GCC context are not effective in monitoring the performance of companies that they invest in and they do not exert any pressure to influence the disclosure practices implemented by these companies. However, they contradict with some prior researchers who reported the existence of a positive relationship between institutional ownership and the level of disclosure (e.g. Gao and Kling, 2012; Rouf and Harun, 2011). While Boshnak (2017) reported a negative relationship between the percentage of institutional ownership and the level of compliance with IFRS in the GCC context.

Conventional predictions of the agency theory would expect that the existence of institutional shareholders will enhance the level of compliance with IFRS as their presence mitigates the agency problem through pushing companies to disclose more information in order to reduce the level of the information asymmetry (Jensen and Meckling, 1976; Donnelly and Mulcahy, 2008). Nevertheless, the lack of a significant relationship between institutional ownership and the level of compliance with IFRS implies that the presence of institutional shareholders does not affect the level of the adoption of IFRS.

The relative inapplicability of the agency theory within the GCC member states may be justified based on the idea that institutional investors in these countries do not monitor the performance of their companies and do not perform any pressure to influence their disclosure practices and their compliance with IFRS as what they are supposed to do (Bos and Donker, 2004). Shehata (2013) concluded that the lack of the effect of institutional ownership on the level of disclosure in GCC countries may be related to the identity of institutional investor (being local or international). Another explanation may be related to the ability of institutional owners to access their companies' information. Institutional owners may have more efficient and timely ways to obtain value relevant information (Donnelly and Mulcahy, 2008). In other words, they can obtain information from sources other than the financial statements. Such information, which could not be included in the financial statements, may be extracted through the formal meetings with management. Donnelly and Mulcahy (2008) stated that there is a crucial difference between the information released in the annual reports and the information released in the formal meetings. Accordingly, the existence of these shareholders does not affect the level of compliance with IFRS as it does not affect their abilities of getting their needed information about the company.

Audit Committee and the Level of IFRS Compliance in the GCC Member States

The eleventh proposition examined the effect of the effectiveness of the audit committee on the level of compliance with IFRS. However, two aspects of the effectiveness of the audit committee were included in this book, these are the number of audit committee members and the number of audit committee meetings held during the year. Therefore, this proposition was divided into two sub-propositions as follows.

Number of Audit Committee Members and the Level of IFRS Compliance in the GCC Member States

The first sub-proposition of the eleventh proposition examined the effect of the number of audit committee members on the level of compliance with IFRS. The results in chapter 8 revealed that audit committee size was not linked to the level of the adoption of IFRS disclosure requirements. As the analysis show, it was noted that audit committee size had no significant impact on IFRS compliance.

Such findings indicate that audit committee, despite of its size, does not significantly affect the company's disclosure practices and its level of compliance with IFRS disclosure requirements. These results tally with the results reported by Ho and Wong (2001), Nasir and Abdullah (2004), and Al-Janadi et al. (2013) that the number of members of the audit committee does not affect companies' disclosure practices. Similarly, Othman et al. (2014) stated that even the size of the audit committee is small or large, it does not affect the level of disclosure in Malaysia. Sellami and Fendri (2017) did not find a significant relationship between the number of members in the audit committee and the level IFRS compliance in South Africa. In Canada, Mnif and Znazen (2020) reported a non-significant relationship between audit committee size and the level of compliance with IFRS. Nevertheless, Verriest et al. (2013) and Bouchareb et al. (2014) found a significant relationship between audit committee size and the company's level of disclosure.

Based on the predictions of the agency theory, audit committee is considered a monitoring tool over management's activities (Fama and Jensen, 1983; Allegrini and Greco, 2013). Meanwhile, the existence of such a committee will improve the quality of the information flow between managers and owners (Bradbury, 1990; Alanezi and Albuloushi, 2011). This was based on the role of such a committee in advising and supporting the board of directors in the major accounting issues, preparing the financial statements, and ensuring that these statements were prepared in accordance with the accounting rules and regulations (Brennan, 2007). However, the current results reveal that such predictions are not relevant to the GCC context.

The rationale of the absence of a significant relationship between the number of members in the audit committee and the level of compliance with IFRS may be related to the idea that audit committee is not playing an effective role in ensuring the quality of financial information due to the shortage of the needed experience that audit committee members should have. This may lead to produce an inadequate quality of financial disclosure and make the committee more reliance on the external auditor's opinion (Al-Janadi et al., 2013). Furthermore, as shown in the descriptive analysis in chapter 8, the average number of members in such a committee among GCC countries is three, accordingly, the relatively small number of members may be one of the reasons that caused the absence of a significant relationship. In other words, increasing the committee's number of members may increase the level of compliance with IFRS.

The Number of Audit Committee Meetings Held During the Year and the Level of IFRS Compliance in the GCC Member States

The second sub-proposition of the eleventh proposition examined the relationship between the number of audit committee meetings held during the year and the level of compliance with IFRS. The results in chapter 8 revealed that the number of audit committee meetings was not linked to the level of the adoption of IFRS disclosure requirements. As the analysis show, it was indicated that the number of audit committee meetings had no significant impact on IFRS compliance.

These findings indicate the presence of a non-significant relationship between audit committee meetings frequency and IFRS compliance, which implies that the number of meetings held by such a committee does not affect the level of the adoption of IFRS. These findings are supporting to the results of the previous studies (see, for example, Pucheta-Martínez and De Fuentes, 2007; Sellami and Fendri, 2017). Madi et al. (2014) and Othman et al. (2014) concluded that audit committee meetings do not enhance its monitoring role over companies' disclosure practices in Malaysia. Menon and Williams (1994) also reported that the number of audit committee meetings does not indicate the accomplishment of work. Mnif and Znazen (2020) stated that the frequency of audit committee meetings is not significantly related to the level of compliance with IFRS in Canada. Nevertheless, they are in contradiction with what reported by Allegrini and Greco (2013) that the number of audit committee meetings is significantly associated with the level of disclosure.

The number of meetings held by the audit committee is considered an indication of its diligence (Kelton and Yang, 2008). It was suggested by the agency theory that the existence of the audit committee plays an important role in enhancing the quality of financial reporting (Bradbury, 1990; Alanezi and Albuloushi, 2011). However, our findings indicate that audit committee is not rigor in governing the company's disclosure practices and the transparency of its financial statements.

The current results may be attributed to the idea that audit committee is not effective in monitoring the level of compliance with IFRS as it was proved by the results of the previous proposition. In other words, audit committee in the emerging markets is not acting in line with the intended benefits and desires of its existence. Therefore, the rational of the current results may be related to the inefficiency of the audit committee meetings, this means that the diligence of the audit committee should be enhanced toward monitoring and controlling the best IFRS compliance practices as the higher the effectiveness of audit committee the higher the level of disclosure (Allegrini and Greco, 2013). Another explanation may be based on the frequency of the audit committee meetings, this means that increasing the number of its meetings during the year may lead to enhance its effectiveness in supervising managers' disclosure practices and improve its capacity in applying the best IFRS compliance practices. As well, it is expected that the increase in the number of audit committee meetings will increase its ability in spotting and resolving the divergences in accounting and financial issues between management and the external auditor, and hence, the level of compliance will be higher and the probability of non-compliance will be lower (Pucheta-Martínez and De Fuentes, 2007).

The Quality of the External Auditor and the Level of IFRS Compliance in the GCC Member States

The twelfth proposition examined the relationship between the quality of the external auditor and the level of compliance with IFRS. The results in chapter 8 revealed that the quality of the external auditor was linked to the level of the adoption of IFRS disclosure requirements. From the analysis, it was shown that the quality of the external auditor had a significant positive impact on the level of IFRS compliance, this signifies that big-four audit firms enhance the level of compliance with IFRS of their clients.

Several studies had reported the existence of a positive relationship between the quality of the external auditor and the level of disclosure (see, for example, Hassaan, 2012; Demir and Bahadir, 2014; Ballas et al., 2018). In Saudi Arabia, Al-Janadi et al. (2013) concluded that big-four audit companies have more independence than other audit companies, and hence, companies that were audited by one of the big-four audit companies have a higher level of disclosure. Riccardi (2019) stated that reporting quality of big-four audit companies' clients is higher than not big-four audit companies' clients. However, Hassaan (2012) reported a not significant relationship between the quality of the external auditor and the level of compliance with IFRS in Egypt. In addition, other scholars found a non-significant relationship between the type of the external auditor and the level of disclosure (see Al-Shammari, 2005; Barako et al., 2006).

The quality of the external auditor was evaluated as its belonging to one of the big-four audit companies around the world (Brown et al., 2010). Agency theory presumes that the independence of the external auditor helps in monitoring managers' actions in order to ensure the integrity of financial reporting (Chung et al., 2003; Hasan et al., 2013). Moreover, the quality of the external auditor plays an important role in determining the level of disclosure and providing a reasonable assurance to shareholders that financial statements were prepared in accordance with accounting rules and regulations (Brennan, 2007).

The size of the external auditor's firm influences the disclosure practices implemented by companies, the latter contributed to the idea that big audit firms have more resources and experience that are needed to encourage their clients to have higher levels of compliance with IFRS in comparison with small audit firms (Omar and Simon, 2011; Demir and Bahadir, 2014). In addition, the significant positive association between external auditor quality and IFRS compliance supports the fact that large audit firms care about their reputation more than small audit firms (Wang et al., 2008). Large audit firms have more clients, therefore, they are less dependent on them in comparison with small audit firms, which gives the former more chance to exert pressure to force their clients to disclose more information (Owusu-Ansah, 1998; Shehata, 2013). Furthermore, companies that are being audited by one of the big-four audit companies are lying under the public eyes, accordingly, they should have a higher quality financial reporting, and hence, a higher level of compliance with IFRS.

Summary

This chapter has discussed our findings that have resulted from the empirical testing of our propositions. This chapter showed the consistency and inconsistency of the current findings with the prior studies and discussed the main theories that are related to the relationship between the variables. This book aims to explore the existence of significant differences in the level of compliance with IFRS among GCC countries and examine the impact of a number of firm characteristics and corporate governance mechanisms on the level of compliance with IFRS disclosure requirements. The main findings of this book indicate that the level of compliance with IFRS significantly varies among GCC countries. Additionally, the findings show that three of the corporate governance mechanisms and one of the firm characteristics have an effect on the level of the adoption of IFRS within the GCC member states.

References

Abad, D., Cutillas-Gomariz, M.F., Sánchez-Ballesta, J.P., & Yagüe, J. (2018). Does IFRS mandatory adoption affect information asymmetry in the stock market? *Australian Accounting Review, 28*(1), 61–78.

Abdelqader, M., Nimer, K., & Darwish, T.K. (2021). IFRS compliance in GCC countries: Do corporate governance mechanisms make a difference? *International Journal of Disclosure and Governance, 18*(4), 411–425.

Abd-Elsalam, O.H. (1999). *The introduction and application of international accounting standards to accounting disclosure regulations of a capital market in a developing country: The case of Egypt* (Doctoral dissertation, Heriot-Watt University).

Aburaya, R. (2012). *The relationship between corporate governance and environmental disclosure: UK evidence* (Doctoral dissertation, Durham University).

Agyei-Mensah, B.K. (2017). The relationship between corporate governance mechanisms and IFRS 7 compliance: Evidence from an emerging market. *Corporate Governance: The International Journal of Business in Society, 17*(3), 446–465.

Ahmed, K., & Courtis, J.K. (1999). Associations between corporate characteristics and disclosure levels in annual reports: A meta-analysis. *The British Accounting Review, 31*(1), 35–61.

Ahmed, K., Hossain, M., & Adams, M.B. (2006). The effects of board composition and board size on the informativeness of annual accounting earnings. *Corporate Governance: An International Review, 14*(5), 418–431.

Al Mutawaa, A., & Hewaidy, A.M. (2010). Disclosure level and compliance with IFRSs: An empirical investigation of Kuwaiti companies. *The International Business & Economics Research Journal, 9*(5), 33–50.

Al-Akra, M., Eddie, I.A., & Ali, M.J. (2010). The influence of the introduction of accounting disclosure regulation on mandatory disclosure compliance: Evidence from Jordan. *The British Accounting Review, 42*(3), 170–186.

Alanezi, F.S., & Albuloushi, S.S. (2011). Does the existence of voluntary audit committees really affect IFRS-required disclosure? The Kuwaiti evidence. *International Journal of Disclosure and Governance, 8*(2), 148–173.

Alfaraih, M. (2009). *Compliance with international financial reporting standards (IFRS) and the value relevance of accounting information in emerging stock markets: Evidence from Kuwait* (Doctoral dissertation, Queensland University of Technology).

Alhazaimeh, A., Palaniappan, R., & Almsafir, M. (2014). The impact of corporate governance and ownership structure on voluntary disclosure in annual reports among listed Jordanian companies. *Procedia-Social and Behavioral Sciences, 129*, 341–348.

Al-Htaybat, K. (2005). *Financial disclosure practices: Theoretical foundation, and an empirical investigation on Jordanian printed and internet formats* (Doctoral dissertation, University of Southampton).

Al-Janadi, Y., Rahman, R.A., & Alazzani, A. (2016). Does government ownership affect corporate governance and corporate disclosure? Evidence from Saudi Arabia. *Managerial Auditing Journal, 31*(8/9), 871–890.

Al-Janadi, Y., Rahman, R.A., & Omar, N.H. (2013). Corporate governance mechanisms and voluntary disclosure in Saudi Arabia. *Corporate Governance, 4*(4), 25–35.

Allegrini, M., & Greco, G. (2013). Corporate boards, audit committees and voluntary disclosure: Evidence from Italian listed companies. *Journal of Management & Governance, 17*(1), 187–216.

Al-Moataz, E., & Hussainey, K. (2012). Determinants of corporate governance disclosure in Saudi companies. *Journal of Economics and Management, 5*(1), 52–84.

Alsaqqa, I., & Sawan, N. (2013). The advantages and the challenges of adopting IFRS into UAE stock market. *International Journal of Business and Management, 8*(19), 1–23.

Al-Shammari, B., & Al-Sultan, W. (2010). Corporate governance and voluntary disclosure in Kuwait. *International Journal of Disclosure and Governance,* 7(3), 262–280.

Al-Shammari, B.A. (2005). *Compliance with international accounting standards by listed companies in the Gulf Co-operation Council member states: An empirical study* (Doctoral dissertation, University of Western Australia).

Al-Shiab, M. (2003). *Financial consequences of IAS adoption: The case of Jordan* (Doctoral dissertation, Newcastle University).

Alves, H.R.A.M., Rodrigues, A.M., & Canadas, N. (2012). Factors influencing the different categories of voluntary disclosure in annual reports: An analysis for Iberian Peninsula listed companies. *Tékhne, 10*(1), 15–26.

Anderson, M., & Daoud, M. (2005). *Corporate governances disclosure by Swedish listed corporations* (Master thesis, Jonkoping International Business School, Jonkoping University, Sweden).

Anis, R.M.M. (2016). *Disclosure quality, corporate governance mechanisms and firm value* (Doctoral dissertation, University of Stirling).

Arcay, M.R.B., & Vazquez, M.F.M. (2005). Corporate characteristics, governance rules and the extent of voluntary disclosure in Spain. *Advances in Accounting, 21*, 299–331.

Baek, H.Y., Johnson, D.R., & Kim, J.W. (2009). Managerial ownership, corporate governance, and voluntary disclosure. *Journal of Business and Economic Studies, 15*(2), 44–61.

Ballas, A., Sykianakis, N., Tzovas, C., & Vassilakopoulos, C. (2018). Measuring compliance with IFRS mandatory disclosure requirements: Some evidence from greece. In *Perspectives, Trends, and Applications in Corporate Finance and Accounting* (pp. 273–300). IGI Global.

Barako, D.G., Hancock, P., & Izan, H.Y. (2006). Factors influencing voluntary corporate disclosure by Kenyan companies. *Corporate Governance: An International Review, 14*(2), 107–125.

Beekes, W., Pope, P., & Young, S. (2004). The link between earnings timeliness, earnings conservatism and board composition: Evidence from the UK. *Corporate Governance: An International Review, 12*(1), 47–59.

Biondi, Y., Giannoccolo, P., & Reberioux, A. (2009, October). Financial disclosure and the board: Is independence of directors always effecient? *Forum de La Regulation.* Paris.

Bos, A.D., & Donker, H. (2004). Monitoring accounting changes: Empirical evidence from the Netherlands. *Corporate Governance: An International Review, 12*(1), 60–73.

Boshnak, H. (2017). *Mandatory and voluntary disclosures in GCC listed firms* (Doctoral dissertation, University of the West of England).

Bouchareb, M., Ajina, A., & Souid, S. (2014). Does the adoption of IAS/IFRS with a strong governance mechanism can deter earnings management?. *International Journal of Academic Research in Economics and Management Sciences, 3*(1), 264–282.

Bradbury, M., Mak, Y.T., & Tan, S.M. (2006). Board characteristics, audit committee characteristics and abnormal accruals. *Pacific Accounting Review, 18*(2), 47–68.

Bradbury, M.E. (1990). The incentives for voluntary audit committee formation. *Journal of Accounting and public policy, 9*(1), 19–36.

Brennan, N. (2007). *Corporate governance and financial reporting*. SAGE Publications.

Brown, J.R., Falaschetti, D., & Orlando, M.J. (2010). Auditor independence and earnings quality: Evidence for market discipline vs. Sarbanes-Oxley proscriptions. *American Law and Economics Review, 12*(1), 39–68.

Chau, G.K., & Gray, S.J. (2002). Ownership structure and corporate voluntary disclosure in Hong Kong and Singapore. *The International Journal of Accounting, 37*(2), 247–265.

Chung, R., Firth, M., & Kim, J.B. (2003). Auditor conservatism and reported earnings. *Accounting and Business Research, 33*(1), 19–32.

Cooke, T.E., & Wallace, R.O. (1990). Financial disclosure regulation and its environment: A review and further analysis. *Journal of Accounting and Public Policy, 9*(2), 79–110.

Dahawy, K., & Conover, T. (2007). Accounting disclosure in companies listed on the Egyptian stock exchange. *Middle Eastern Finance and Economics, 1*(1), 5–20.

Dahya, J., & Travlos, N. (2000). Does the one man show pay? Theory and evidence on the dual CEO revisited. *European Financial Management, 6*(1), 85–98.

Demir, V., & Bahadir, O. (2014). An investigation of compliance with international financial reporting standards by listed companies in Turkey. *Accounting and Management Information Systems, 13*(1), 4–34.

Donnelly, R., & Mulcahy, M. (2008). Board structure, ownership, and voluntary disclosure in Ireland. *Corporate Governance: An International Review, 16*(5), 416–429.

Ezat, A., & El-Masry, A. (2008). The impact of corporate governance on the timeliness of corporate internet reporting by Egyptian listed companies. *Managerial Finance, 34*(12), 848–867.

Fama, E.F., & Jensen, M.C. (1983). Separation of ownership and control. *The Journal of Law & Economics, 26*(2), 301–325.

Firth, M., Fung, P.M., & Rui, O.M. (2007). Ownership, two-tier board structure, and the informativeness of earnings – Evidence from China. *Journal of Accounting and Public Policy, 26*(4), 463–496.

Franzen, N., & Weißenberger, B.E. (2018). Capital market effects of mandatory IFRS 8 adoption: An empirical analysis of German firms. *Journal of International Accounting, Auditing and Taxation, 31*(*C*), 1–19.

Gao, L., & Kling, G. (2012). The impact of corporate governance and external audit on compliance to mandatory disclosure requirements in China. *Journal of International Accounting, Auditing and Taxation, 21*(1), 17–31.

Glaum, M., & Street, D.L. (2003). Compliance with the disclosure requirements of Germany's new market: IAS versus US GAAP. *Journal of International Financial Management & Accounting, 14*(1), 64–100.

Gray, S.J. (1988). Towards a theory of cultural influence on the development of accounting systems internationally. *Abacus, 24*(1), 1–15.

Gul, F.A., & Leung, S. (2004). Board leadership, outside directors' expertise and voluntary corporate disclosures. *Journal of Accounting and Public Policy, 23*(5), 351–379.

Haak-Saheem, W., Festing, M., & Darwish, T.K. (2017). International human resource management in the Arab Gulf States – an institutional perspective. *The International Journal of Human Resource Management, 28*(18), 2684–2712.

Haddad, A.E., AlShattarat, W.K., AbuGhazaleh, N.M., & Nobanee, H. (2015). The impact of ownership structure and family board domination on voluntary disclosure for Jordanian listed companies. *Eurasian Business Review, 5*(2), 203–234.

Haji, A.A., & Ghazali, N.A.M. (2013). The quality and determinants of voluntary disclosures in annual reports of Shari'ah compliant companies in Malaysia. *Humanomics, 29*(1), 24–42.

Haniffa, R.M., & Cooke, T.E. (2002). Culture, corporate governance and disclosure in Malaysian corporations. *Abacus, 38*(3), 317–349.

Hasan, M.S., Hossain, S.Z., & Swieringa, R.J. (2013). Corporate governance and financial disclosures: Bangladesh perspective. *Research Journal of Finance and Accounting, 4*(1), 109–119.

Hassaan, M. (2012). *Corporate governance and compliance with International Financial Reporting Standards (IFRSs): Evidence from two MENA stock exchanges* (Doctoral dissertation, Aston University).

Hassan, M. (2009). UAE corporations-specific characteristics and level of risk disclosure. *Managerial Auditing Journal, 24*(7), 668–687.

Herath, S.K., & Alsulmi, F.H. (2017). International financial reporting standards (IFRS): The benefits, obstacles, and opportunities for implementation in Saudi Arabia. *International Journal of Social Science and Business, 2*(1), 1–18.

Hlel, K., & Nafti, I.K. (2019). Board characteristics, IFRS adoption and voluntary disclosure: Evidence from management forecasts accuracy in France. *International Journal of Management and Enterprise Development, 18*(1/2), 41–62.

Ho, S.S., & Wong, K.S. (2001). A study of the relationship between corporate governance structures and the extent of voluntary disclosure. *Journal of International Accounting, Auditing and Taxation, 10*(2), 139–156.

Hodgdon, C., & Hughes, S.B. (2016). The effect of corporate governance, auditor choice and global activities on EU company disclosures of estimates and judgments. *Journal of International Accounting, Auditing and Taxation, 26* (*C*), 28–46.

Hofstede, G. (1980). *Culture's consequences: International differences in work-related values.* Newbury Park, CA: SAGE Publications.

Irvine, H. (2008). The global institutionalization of financial reporting: The case of the United Arab Emirates. *Accounting Forum, 32*(2), 125–142.

Irvine, H.J., & Lucas, N. (2006). *The rationale and impact of the adoption of International Financial Reporting Standards: The case of the United Arab Emirates.* (University of Wollonglon Australia).

Jensen, M.C., & Meckling, W.H. (1976). Theory of the firm: Managerial behavior, agency costs and ownership structure. *Journal of Financial Economics, 3*(4), 305–360.

Juhmani, O. (2017). Corporate governance and the level of Bahraini corporate compliance with IFRS disclosure. *Journal of Applied Accounting Research, 18*(1), 22–41.

Kelton, A.S., & Yang, Y.W. (2008). The impact of corporate governance on Internet financial reporting. *Journal of Accounting and Public Policy, 27*(1), 62–87.

Kent, P., & Stewart, J. (2008). Corporate governance and disclosures on the transition to international financial reporting standards. *Accounting & Finance, 48*(4), 649–671.

Klein, A. (2002). Audit committee, board of director characteristics, and earnings management. *Journal of Accounting and Economics, 33*(3), 375–400.

Lee, T.S., & Yeh, Y.H. (2004). Corporate governance and financial distress: Evidence from Taiwan. *Corporate Governance: An International Review, 12*(3), 378–388.

Lopes, P.T., & Rodrigues, L.L. (2007). Accounting for financial instruments: An analysis of the determinants of disclosure in the Portuguese stock exchange. *The International Journal of Accounting*, *42*(1), 25–56.

Madi, H., Ishak, Z., & Manaf, N.A.A. (2014). The impact of audit committee characteristics on corporate voluntary disclosure. *Procedia-Social and Behavioral Sciences*, *164*, 486–492.

Maher, M., & Andersson, T. (2000). Corporate governance: Effects on firm performance and economic growth. *OECD Working Papers. Available at SSRN 218490.*

Mallin, C., & Ow-Yong, K. (2009). Corporate governance in alternative investment market (AIM) companies: Determinants of corporate governance disclosure. *Third Singapore International Conference on Finance 2009, Available at SSRN 1326627.*

Mallin, C.A. (2013). *Corporate governance* (4th ed.). New York: Oxford University Press.

Menon, K., & Williams, J.D. (1994). The use of audit committees for monitoring. *Journal of Accounting and Public Policy*, *13*(2), 121–139.

Mnif, Y., & Znazen, O. (2020). Corporate governance and compliance with IFRS 7: The case of financial institutions listed in Canada. *Managerial Auditing Journal*, *35*(3), 448–474.

Nasir, M.N., & Abdullah, S.N. (2004). Accrual management and the roles of boards of directors and audit committees among Malaysian listed companies: Evidence during the Asian financial crisis. *IIUM Journal of Management and Economics*, *12*(1), 48–80.

Nobes, C. (2006). The survival of international differences under IFRS: Towards a research agenda. *Accounting and Business Research*, *36*(3), 233–245.

O'Sullivan, M., Percy, M., & Stewart, J. (2008). Australian evidence on corporate governance attributes and their association with forward-looking information in the annual report. *Journal of Management & Governance*, *12*(1), 5–35.

Omar, B., & Simon, J. (2011). Corporate aggregate disclosure practices in Jordan. *Advances in Accounting*, *27*(1), 166–186.

Othman, R., Ishak, I.F., Arif, S.M.M., & Aris, N.A. (2014). Influence of audit committee characteristics on voluntary ethics disclosure. *Procedia-Social and Behavioral Sciences*, *145*, 330–342.

Owusu-Ansah, S. (1998). The impact of corporate attributes on the extent of mandatory disclosure and reporting by listed companies in Zimbabwe. *The International Journal of Accounting*, *33*(5), 605–631.

Paauwe, J., & Boselie, P. (2003). Challenging 'strategic HRM' and the relevance of the institutional setting. *Human Resource Management Journal*, *13*(3), 56–70.

Patelli, L., & Prencipe, A. (2007). The relationship between voluntary disclosure and independent directors in the presence of a dominant shareholder. *European Accounting Review*, *16*(1), 5–33.

Perera, M.H.B. (1989). Towards a framework to analyze the impact of culture on accounting. *The International Journal of Accounting*, *24*(1), 42–56.

Petra, S.T. (2007). The effects of corporate governance on the informativeness of earnings. *Economics of Governance*, *8*(2), 129–152.

Pichler, S., Cordazzo, M., & Rossi, P. (2018). An analysis of the firms-specific determinants influencing the voluntary IFRS adoption: Evidence from Italian private firms. *International Journal of Accounting, Auditing and Performance Evaluation*, *14*(1), 85–104.

Pucheta-Martínez, M.C., & De Fuentes, C. (2007). The impact of audit committee characteristics on the enhancement of the quality of financial reporting: An empirical study in the Spanish context. *Corporate Governance: An International Review*, *15*(6), 1394–1412.

Rahman, M.Z. (1999). *The role of accounting disclosure in the East Asian financial crisis: Lessons learned?* United Nations Conference on Trade and Development, Geneva.

Rajhi, M. (2014). International financial reporting standards and level of compliance with mandatory disclosure requirements. *International Journal of Multidisciplinarity Sciences and Engineering*, *5*(5), 1–6.

Riccardi, W.N. (2019). Do audit firm tenure and size moderate changes in financial reporting quality due to mandatory IFRS Adoption? *Auditing: A Journal of Practice & Theory*, *38*(4), 201–224.

Rouf, A., & Harun, A.A. (2011). Ownership structure and voluntary disclosure in annual reports of Bangladesh. *Pakistan Journal of Commerce & Social Sciences*, *5*(1), 129–139.

Samaha, K., & Dahawy, K. (2010). An empirical analysis of corporate governance structures and voluntary corporate disclosure in volatile capital markets: The Egyptian experience. *International Journal of Accounting, Auditing and Performance Evaluation*, 7(1-2), 61–93.

Samaha, K., Dahawy, K., Hussainey, K., & Stapleton, P. (2012). The extent of corporate governance disclosure and its determinants in a developing market: The case of Egypt. *Advances in Accounting*, *28*(1), 168–178.

Saudagaran, S.M., & Meek, G.K. (1997). A review of research on the relationship between international capital markets and financial reporting by multinational firms. *Journal of Accounting Literature*, *16*, 127–159.

Scott, W.R., (2001). *Institutions and organizations* (2nd ed.). Thousand Oaks, CA, SAGE Publications.

Sellami, Y.M., & Fendri, H.B. (2017). The effect of audit committee characteristics on compliance with IFRS for related party disclosures: Evidence from South Africa. *Managerial Auditing Journal*, *32*(6), 603–626.

Shehata, N. (2013). *Corporate governance disclosure in the Gulf countries* (Doctoral dissertation, Aston University).

Singh, S., Tabassum, N., Darwish, T.K., & Batsakis, G. (2018). Corporate governance and Tobin's Q as a measure of organizational performance. *British Journal of Management*, *29*(1), 171–190.

Singhvi, S.S., & Desai, H.B. (1971). An empirical analysis of the quality of corporate financial disclosure. *The Accounting Review*, *46*(1), 129–138.

Street, D.L., & Bryant, S.M. (2000). Disclosure level and compliance with IASs: A comparison of companies with and without US listings and filings. *The International Journal of Accounting*, *35*(3), 305–329.

Street, D.L., & Gray, S.J. (2002). Factors influencing the extent of corporate compliance with international accounting standards: Summary of a research monograph. *Journal of International Accounting, Auditing and Taxation*, *11*(1), 51–76.

Uyar, A. (2011). Firm characteristics and voluntary disclosure of graphs in annual reports of Turkish listed companies. *African Journal of Business Management*, *5*(17), 7651–7657.

Verriest, A., Gaeremynck, A., & Thornton, D.B. (2013). The impact of corporate governance on IFRS adoption choices. *European Accounting Review*, *22*(1), 39–77.

Volonté, C. (2015). Boards: Independent and committed directors? *International Review of Law and Economics*, *41*, 25–37.

Wallace, R.O., & Naser, K. (1995). Firm-specific determinants of the comprehensiveness of mandatory disclosure in the corporate annual reports of firms listed on the stock exchange of Hong Kong. *Journal of Accounting and Public Policy*, *14*(4), 311–368.

Wallace, R.O., Naser, K., & Mora, A. (1994). The relationship between the comprehensiveness of corporate annual reports and firm characteristics in Spain. *Accounting and Business Research, 25*(97), 41–53.

Wang, K., Sewon, O., & Claiborne, M.C. (2008). Determinants and consequences of voluntary disclosure in an emerging market: Evidence from China. *Journal of International Accounting, Auditing and Taxation, 17*(1), 14–30.

Watts, R.L., & Zimmerman, J.L. (1986). *Positive accounting theory*. Prentice-Hall.

10 Synthesis and Conclusions

Introduction

Based on the discussion of the central propositions and research main findings presented earlier in this book, this chapter aims to present the main conclusions and contributions to the accounting literature. In addition, it aims to draw out the wider implications for theory, practice, and methodology. The chapter then presents a number of important future directions in relation to corporate governance and IFRS.

Conclusions

This book aimed to explore the effect of a number of corporate governance mechanisms and firm characteristics on the level of compliance with IFRS mandatory disclosure requirements within the listed companies in the GCC member states, namely Saudi Arabia, Kuwait, UAE, Oman, Bahrain, and Qatar. The extensive review of the existing literature regarding the effect of corporate governance and firm characteristics on companies' disclosure practices had produced 12 propositions. The first proposition was related to the differences in the level of compliance with international financial reporting standards (IFRS) practices across Gulf Cooperation Council (GCC) countries. Eight propositions examined the relationship between corporate governance mechanisms (board independence, board size, CEO duality, institutional ownership, concentrated ownership, audit committee size, audit committee meetings, and the quality of the external auditor) and the level of compliance with IFRS. The other five propositions examined the relationship between firm characteristics (firm size, industry type, profitability, leverage, and liquidity) and the level of compliance with IFRS.

Using a self-built disclosure index derived from the IFRS mandatory disclosure requirements as at the end of 2016, we firstly examined the existence of significant differences in the level of compliance with IFRS among GCC countries, the results were supportive to the first proposition. The findings concluded that there are significant statistical differences in the compliance practices with the mandatory disclosure requirements of IFRS

DOI: 10.4324/9781003211556-10

across the listed companies within the GCC countries. Companies listed in the UAE were reported to have the highest level of compliance with IFRS, while Saudi Arabia's listed companies had the lowest level of compliance with IFRS across the six GCC countries.

Overall, the findings supported the existence of positive effects of corporate governance mechanisms on the level of compliance with IFRS disclosure requirements in GCC member states. Particularly, three corporate governance mechanisms were significantly linked to the level of compliance with IFRS, these are board independence, concentrated ownership, and the quality of the external auditor. However, for the other corporate governance mechanisms (board size, CEO duality, institutional ownership, audit committee size, and audit committee meetings), the findings of this book did not detect any significant impact related to their relationships with IFRS compliance.

Regarding the effect of firm characteristics on the level of compliance with IFRS disclosure requirements, the results indicated the presence of only one positive significant distinctive contribution that has an impact on the level of IFRS compliance. This positive interaction was detected between leverage and the level of the adoption of IFRS. Nevertheless, the findings were not supportive to the proposed propositions of the other four firm characteristics (profitability, liquidity, firm size, and industry type).

Accordingly, it could be concluded that companies in GCC countries with high level of compliance with IFRS are more likely to have more independent members in their boards, a high level of concentrated ownership, being audited by one of the big-four audit companies, and are highly leveraged. Following is a discussion of the book contributions and the theoretical, practical, and methodological implications of the current findings.

Contributions

This book contributes to our overall understanding regarding the impact of corporate governance and firm characteristics on IFRS compliance as follows:

Firstly, we aimed to enrich the existing accounting literature that discussed the disclosure practices of companies and provide insights about the compliance level of the listed companies within GCC countries with IFRS disclosure requirements. The capital markets under analysis are early adopters of IFRS, which implies that they have a high level of experience in complying with the disclosure requirements of IFRS. Accordingly, examining the level of compliance with IFRS in these countries enables providing a better explanation of the factors that affect the level of the implementation of the mandatory disclosure requirements of these standards. Additionally, this book contributes to the existing literature by extending the international accounting compliance studies in developing countries as most of the previously conducted studies in these countries have examined the compliance with voluntary disclosure requirements or they examined the level of compliance with only some selected standards.

Secondly, there is a shortage in the number of studies that examined the relationship between corporate governance and IFRS compliance in emerging markets in general and the GCC context in particular. In addition, based on the review of the previous studies, it was noticed that none of the previous studies has comprehensively examined the level of compliance with IFRS at the Gulf region level. Therefore, this book takes a further step by examining the relationship between corporate governance and IFRS compliance on all listed companies in GCC member states in order to ensure the generalizability of the results and detect the country's effect on the extent of IFRS compliance and on the association between corporate governance and IFRS compliance.

Thirdly, this book contributes to the existing literature by adopting multiple theoretical frameworks to interpret our empirical findings and understand IFRS compliance practices in depth. Most of the previous studies that examined the relationship between corporate governance and IFRS compliance have mainly relied on the agency theory. Nevertheless, this book has adopted a number of relevant theories that were used in empirical governance and disclosure studies to enhance the understanding of corporate governance behaviors and IFRS compliance practices. This helps in providing evidence on the theoretical foundation of the financial disclosure practices within GCC countries. The employment of other theories in the book is justified standing on the fact that it aims to improve the integration between the empirical findings and the theoretical foundations and to provide evidence on the relative applicability of Western developed theories on developing capital markets. Additionally, implementing such theories helps in gaining a better understanding of the compliance behaviors and the factors affecting the level of compliance with IFRS. This allows using these theories in explaining companies' disclosure practices, especially, in developing countries context where culture influence is dominant.

Fourthly, this book supports the existing literature through providing a recent evidence regarding the relationship between corporate governance and IFRS compliance in GCC member states' listed companies as there is a scarcity in the studies that used recent data to examine the level of compliance with IFRS mandatory disclosure requirements in the Middles East, in general, and in the GCC region, in particular. However, the IFRS' environment is highly dynamic and changeable as several standards were amended or new standards were issued, such as IAS 1 (Presentation of Financial Statements), IAS 16 (Property, Plant and Equipment), IAS 19 (Employees Benefits), IAS 38 (Intangible Assets), IFRS 7 (Financial Instruments: Disclosure), and IFRS 9 (Financial Instruments). Hence, a further examination of the level of compliance with these standards is needed as they were not tested before among GCC countries.

Fifthly, some important standards, namely IAS 19 (Employees Benefits) and IAS 26 (Accounting and Reporting by Retirement Benefits Plans), which are related to employees' benefits and end of service benefits, were intentionally ignored and excluded from almost all the prior studies as for reasons related to the nature of the country's labor laws. In other words, studies have justified the exclusion of these standards standing on the idea that the country's labor laws determine the amount and the calculation of employees' benefits and retirements. However, the way of determining how employees should be paid is not the concern of these specific standards. These standards, like all other standards, show how to calculate the amounts that must be paid to employees, the accounting treatment for these amounts, and how to report and disclose them in the financial statements. The latter implies that when it comes to how much the company should pay for the employees, the labor law will be the reference, but when it comes to how to record these benefits in the books of the company, the company must follow the accounting standards. Therefore, excluding these standards based on the previous justification is invalid, except for some research contexts, such as Jordan and Egypt. In more details, IAS 19 and IAS 26 show the accounting treatment for two types of employees' benefits, the first one, is the short-term benefits, such as employees' salaries, annual leave, and sick leave. The second type is the post-employment benefits, which are divided into contribution benefit plans and defined benefit plans. Contribution benefit plans are related to post-employment benefits that paid by a third party (most likely a by a mutual fund or a social security). For this type of benefit plans, the responsibility of the company is limited only to the monthly amount that it pays to that third party who is responsible to account and pay such benefits. This type of employees' benefits is being applied in some countries such as Jordan and Egypt, which makes the excuse of excluding these standards for the studies that examined the level of IFRS compliance in these countries valid. The second form of post-employment benefits is the defined benefit plans, which has a very complicated and controversial accounting treatment. Within this regard, the company itself is responsible for the post-employment benefits through setting a plan of payment that is determined either by the internal policy of the company or by the country's company law. Hence, the standards are not related to the way of determining these amounts; they are rather more concerned with how to calculate and how to report and disclose the plan's liabilities, assets, actuarial losses and gains, and the current and previous cost. Consequently, after the extensive review of these two standards and the labor laws in GCC member states, it was concluded that each company in the Gulf region is concerned with both plans (contribution benefit plans for employees who are the citizens of the country and defined benefit plans for the expats), which makes the exclusion of these standards according to the previous fact invalid in the GCC context, and hence, these two standards are considered applicable in GCC context and were included in our analysis.

Sixthly, there are two methods were used by previous studies to calculate the compliance score with IFRS for each company, these are the dichotomous method and the partial compliance method. Several prior studies had implemented the dichotomous method, however, we used the partial compliance method in calculating the level of compliance with IFRS disclosure requirement. This is justified standing on the argument provided by (Al-Shiab, 2003; Tsalavoutas, 2011) that dichotomous method has an important limitation as it gives different weights to the standards. In more details, the number of disclosure items under each standard considerably varies across the standards, therefore, using the dichotomous method treats the standards with more items as more important than other standards with lower number of items. Accordingly, to avoid assigning different weights to the standards and following the recommendations of (Al-Shiab, 2003; Tsalavoutas et al., 2010; Tsalavoutas, 2011) the partial compliance method was implemented in this book in calculating the compliance score with IFRS.

Seventhly, this book provides a guidance for all of the parties involved in the financial disclosure practices in the GCC countries regarding the barriers of the full compliance with IFRS. This was achieved through identifying the effect of a number of corporate governance mechanisms on the level of compliance with IFRS aiming to enhance their knowledge and understanding about the importance of implementing better corporate governance practices in GCC countries.

Finally, the effect of a number of corporate governance mechanisms on the level of compliance with IFRS were not tested before in the GCC context, such as the concentrated ownership and audit committee effectiveness (in terms of both the number of its members and the number of its meetings that were held during the year). Therefore, this book has included such mechanisms in exploring the relationship between corporate governance and the level of the adoption of IFRS disclosure requirements.

Implications for Theory

This book enhances our overall understanding and provides a recent evidence to the IFRS compliance literature in general and in developing countries in particular through analyzing and assessing the possibility of implying Western developed theories in the context of the Middle East. Following is a presentation of a number of implications for theory.

Firstly, the findings of this book confirm the relative applicability of some of the institutional theory's propositions within the GCC context. The existence of significant differences in the level of compliance with IFRS across GCC countries and the absence of significant effects of a number of corporate governance mechanisms and firm characteristics on the level of compliance with IFRS are associated with the articulations provided by the institutional theory. In more details, the institutional theory stated that culture at the national level is responsible for forming the level of compliance with IFRS from two perspectives. Firstly, the cultural backgrounds of the financial statements preparers and users are responsible for determining the level of the awareness and understanding of the importance of implementing the disclosure requirements of IFRS in improving the transparency of financial statements (Saudagaran and Meek, 1997). Secondly, the national cultural aspects form the country's laws and regulations, which shapes the extent of the enforcement mechanisms that are related to monitor IFRS adoption over its listed companies. The lack of appropriate enforcement actions may lead to variations in the level of compliance with IFRS across countries, which was proved by the current results as the level of IFRS compliance was significantly different across GCC countries. In other words, the differences in the cultural backgrounds of financial statements users and preparers in these countries have resulted in the differences in the awareness of implementing these standards and created variations in their enforcement mechanisms' extent. Additionally, the lack of significant impacts of a number of firm characteristics and corporate governance mechanisms on IFRS compliance supports the cultural dimensional model provided by (Gray, 1988), which states that companies, in developing counties, prefer secrecy over transparency of their financial statements and they tend to keep information only for internal users.

Secondly, the arguments of the legitimacy theory that companies follow rules and regulations to avoid penalties and maintain their legitimacy are supported by the current findings. The level of compliance with IFRS is the result of the extent of the enforcement procedures implemented in monitoring companies' disclosure practices as the effectiveness of these procedures influences the level of compliance with the disclosure requirements of IFRS. However, in emerging markets settings, it was evidenced that the cost of non-compliance, in terms of penalties, is lower than the cost of compliance with IFRS (Al-Htaybat, 2005; Dahawy and Conover, 2007). Accordingly, due to the high costs that are linked with the compliance with IFRS and the low non-compliance costs, companies turned to be less motivated to comply with IFRS, which is proved by the current findings as none of the targeted companies had fully complied with the disclosure requirements of IFRS. In addition, the existence of a significant positive relationship between leverage and the level of compliance with IFRS confirms the suggestions of the legitimacy theory, which assumes that companies with high leverage have a higher level of compliance with IFRS due to the restrictions enforced by banks over their clients regarding disclosing the required information to confirm their abilities to meet their debts.

Thirdly, according to the signaling theory, it was expected that companies with high level of profitability and high level of liquidity will have a higher level of compliance with IFRS as they are motivated to confirm their financial position to all stakeholders. However, the lack of significant relationships between these firm characteristics and the level of compliance with IFRS signifies that the predictions of the signaling theory are relatively not applicable within the GCC context. This is due to the tendency of companies based in developing countries toward secrecy over transparency. As well, companies in developing countries are seen in a safe position, which resulted in managers of these companies to keep information restricted only for internal users in order to avoid competition and to protect their companies.

Finally, with regard to the agency theory, the separation between ownership and control in developing countries needs to be more recognized by their listed companies, as well, the effectiveness of the monitoring function of the board of directors over managers' actions still need to be enhanced. This was proved by the absence of significant effects of board size and audit committee effectiveness on the level of compliance with IFRS. Additionally, despite the fact that most of the targeted companies had separated between the CEO position and chairman of the board position, there is a lack in the awareness of the importance of such a practice, which was evidenced by the lack of a significant relationship between CEO duality and the level of IFRS compliance.

Implication for Practice

Firstly, this book provides a better understanding for policy makers and regulatory agencies about the relationship between corporate governance and IFRS compliance in the non-financial listed companies in the GCC member states. The findings indicate the need that regulatory bodies in GCC countries to carry out additional corporate governance reforms to enhance companies' disclosure practices and their level of compliance with IFRS. In other words, policy makers and regulatory agencies could improve their corporate governance codes to improve the level of disclosure and transparency of financial statements of their listed companies.

Secondly, our findings confirmed that none of the targeted companies had fully complied with all of the disclosure requirements of IFRS. This was justified by the lack of an adequate regulatory framework enforcement mechanisms, which has resulted that the non-compliance costs to become lower than the compliance costs. Accordingly, policy makers and stock exchange markets authorities are suggested to increase the degree of compliance with IFRS through strengthening their monitoring and enforcement actions.

Thirdly, according to the present findings, board independence had a significant positive impact on IFRS compliance. This result suggests that the existence of the independent members in the board has a significant role in improving the level of compliance with IFRS disclosure requirements. Therefore, this provides a recommendation for policy makers and regulators in GCC countries to increase the proportion of independent members in the board of their listed companies to be the majority of the board rather than, as it is currently, only one-third.

Fourthly, it is also recommended, based on the current findings, to increase the number of audit committee meetings that must be held during the year, which is expected to enhance the diligence of such a committee and help its members to track the disclosure practices and the implementation of IFRS disclosure requirements by their companies more effectively. Additionally, increasing the number of the members in the audit committee helps the latter in improving their monitoring role, enhancing their ability to oversee companies' financial reporting practices, and working as a linking channel between managers and the external auditor.

Fifthly, regarding the size of the board in the GCC listed companies, the current findings recommend the issuance of a clearer guidance regarding the number of the members in the board. As it was presented in chapter two, corporate governance codes in most of the GCC countries do not specify the minimum and maximum number of members in the board. In addition, it is recommended to specify the minimum number of board members who should have a financial background in order to improve the board's effectiveness in tracking the disclosure behaviors of the company.

Sixthly, the IFRS disclosure requirements were originated in developed countries, hence, more attention could be given to the application of these requirements in developing countries. It is essential to emphasize the awareness of the importance of complying with IFRS among all parties who are in charge of enforcing such a compliance. This could be achieved through conducting workshops and training programs by professional institutions in these countries in order to familiarize the compliance monitoring staff with the updates of IFRS and their best application practices. Similarly, the same could be done for accounting professionals who are working in their listed companies to enhance their understanding about the compliance with IFRS and the importance of implementing all their required disclosure items.

Seventhly, the findings of this book indicate that some companies did not comply with the best practices of corporate governance, which also refers to the inappropriate enforcement mechanisms or the lack of awareness regarding the implication of the corporate governance codes issued by OECD. Therefore, it is recommended that professional agencies, such as OECD may update their strategies to increase the recognition of corporate governance practices in developing countries. This can be done by conducting more training programs to capital market staff and companies' managers aiming to ensure that listed companies in developing countries are applying corporate governance best practices and to enhance the public awareness about the importance of corporate governance in improving companies' disclosure practices.

Eighthly, to improve the level of disclosure and the level of compliance with IFRS, professional accounting bodies around the GCC and other comparable contexts could improve the accounting professional education through compiling a checklist that incorporate all of the disclosure requirements that are applicable in these countries. Such a checklist could be periodically updated according to the amendments made by IASB and the issuance of new standards.

Ninthly, the significant positive relationship between concentrated ownership and the level of compliance raises the need to increase the awareness of small investors about their companies' procedures that had been implemented in disclosing financial information. As well as, recognizing their rights in asking management to comply with the disclosure requirements of IFRS to improve the transparency of financial statements.

Tenthly, the highly significant relationship between the quality of the external auditor (being one of the big-four audit companies around the world) and the level of compliance with IFRS could be a motivation for regulatory agencies within the GCC countries to mandate all their listed companies to be audited by one of the big-four audit companies as it was proved to be a significant variable in explaining the differences in the level of compliance with IFRS.

Eleventh, it was recorded in the current findings that companies being listed in the UAE had the highest level of implementation of most of corporate governance mechanism under interest, this may be due to the fact that only the UAE's corporate governance code was issued on comply/penalize basis. Hence, it is recommended that corporate governance codes for other countries could be issued on comply/penalize basis rather than as they are currently on comply/explain basis.

Lastly, to properly score the built disclosure index that was used in this book and to avoid penalizing the company of not disclosing a non-applicable item, the company's full annual report was reviewed in order to get a comprehensive understanding about the nature of the company's operations. Likewise, corporate governance information was obtained from the disclosed information in the annual reports. However, the unavailability of the annual reports for some companies has made collecting the required data not possible, therefore, these companies were excluded. Accordingly, it is recommended that stock markets authorities could track the availability of companies' full annual reports either on their official websites or on the company's website to avoid losing observations and to enable testing such a relationship using a larger number of companies, which may enhance the generalizability of the results.

Methodological Implications

Firstly, as noted earlier, two methods are available to calculate the compliance score with IFRS for each company, these are the dichotomous method and the partial compliance method. However, the dichotomous method has been criticized by some scholars (e.g. Al-Shiab, 2003; Tsalavoutas et al., 2010; Rajhi, 2014) as it ignores the considerable variations in the number of the disclosure items included under each standard. Therefore, to avoid assigning more weights to the standards that include a high number of disclosure items and avoid having misleading results, the partial compliance method was implemented in this book. This method provides equal weights to each standard despite of its required number of disclosure items.

Secondly, to provide more reliable results and better achieve our stated objectives, this book has implemented the 'population-sample design', this implies that we have considered the whole population rather than selecting a specific sample. In other words, all of the listed companies in the GCC member states were included in examining the relationship between corporate governance and IFRS compliance. This enhances the generalizability of the current findings.

Finally, the framework and the findings of this book may be considered a reference for future work in relation to corporate governance and its effect on the level of compliance with IFRS in the GCC context and other comparable contexts.

Future Directions

The IFRS environment is highly dynamic and changeable as the disclosure requirements under these standards are periodically amended and new standards may be issued in the future. Companies should keep updated with these amendments and the new issued standards in order to achieve the desired level of compliance with these standards' disclosure requirements. Prior studies have reported several factors that have effects of the level of compliance with such requirements, nevertheless, future work will benefit from exploring other factors that may have an impact of the level of compliance with IFRS. Accordingly, the recommendations of opportunities for future work are as follows.

Firstly, the variations and changes in the level of compliance among countries and among companies operating in these countries should be explained and interpreted by future work. Hence, the longitudinal design could be implemented in the future work in order to conclusively replicate the current findings and examine the existence of improvements in the level of compliance with IFRS overtime by comparing to the current findings.

Secondly, future work could address the level of compliance with IFRS in financial institutions, such as banks and insurance companies, which allows the comparison of the level of compliance between financial and non-financial companies as the former follow different rules and regulations.

Thirdly, there is a lack of studies that examined the relationship between corporate governance and the level of compliance with IFRS in developing countries, therefore, future work should continue testing the level of the adoption of IFRS disclosure requirements and how such a level is affected by corporate governance practices and firm characteristics.

Fourthly, it would be interesting to reveal more information regarding the differences in the level of compliance with IFRS between developed and developing countries, as well as, to examine to what extent the institutional factors affect the level of compliance among these countries. Future work could conduct comparative studies by including a larger number of countries from the Middle East and North Africa (MENA) region in order to determine if they are following the same procedures in implementing IFRS and to introduce an investigation about the existence of statistical significant differences in the level of compliance across these countries.

Finally, future work could also examine other mechanisms of corporate governance on the level of compliance with IFRS within GCC countries, such as governmental ownership, the educational background of the board members, the level of financial experience of the audit committee members, and the independence of the audit committee members.

References

Al-Htaybat, K. (2005). *Financial disclosure practices: theoretical foundation, and an empirical investigation on Jordanian printed and internet formats* (Doctoral dissertation, University of Southampton).

Al-Shiab, M. (2003). *Financial consequences of IAS adoption: The case of Jordan* (Doctoral dissertation, Newcastle University).

Dahawy, K., & Conover, T. (2007). Accounting disclosure in companies listed on the Egyptian stock exchange. *Middle Eastern Finance and Economics, 1*(1), 5–20.

Gray, S.J. (1988). Towards a theory of cultural influence on the development of accounting systems internationally. *Abacus, 24*(1), 1–15.

Rajhi, M. (2014). International financial reporting standards and level of compliance with mandatory disclosure requirements. *International Journal of Multidisciplinarity Sciences and Engineering, 5*(5), 1–6.

Saudagaran, S.M., & Meek, G.K. (1997). A review of research on the relationship between international capital markets and financial reporting by multinational firms. *Journal of Accounting Literature, 16*, 127–159.

Tsalavoutas, I. (2011). Transition to IFRS and compliance with mandatory disclosure requirements: What is the signal? *Advances in Accounting, 27*(2), 390–405.

Tsalavoutas, I., Evans, L., & Smith, M. (2010). Comparison of two methods for measuring compliance with IFRS mandatory disclosure requirements. *Journal of Applied Accounting Research, 11*(3), 213–228.

Index

Page numbers in **bold** type refer to tables.
Page numbers in *italics* refer to figures.